Start and Run a Money-Making Bar

2nd edition

Bruce Fier

TAB Books
Division of McGraw-Hill

New York San Francisco Washington, D.C. Auckland Bogotá
Caracas Lisbon London Madrid Mexico City Milan
Montreal New Delhi San Juan Singapore
Sydney Tokyo Toronto

© 1993 by **Bruce Fier**.
TAB Books is a division of McGraw-Hill, Inc.

pbk   7 8 9 10 DOC/DOC 0 9 8 7 6 5 4 3 2 1 0

Library of Congress Cataloging-in-Publication Data

Fier, Bruce.
    [Starting and running a money-making bar]
    Start and run a money making bar / by Bruce Fier.—[2nd ed.,
  rev. and enl.]
        p.   cm.
    First ed. published in 1986 under title: Starting and running a
  money-making bar.
    Includes index.
    ISBN 0-8306-4247-1   ISBN 0-8306-4246-3 (pbk.):
    1. Bartending. I. Title.
  TX950.7.F54   1993
  647.95—dc20   93-18893
                                                     CIP

Acquisitions editor: Kimberly Tabor
Managing editor: Lori Flaherty
Editor: Carol J. Amato
Book design: Jaclyn J. Boone
Associate designer: Brian K. Allison
Cover design: Holberg Design, York, Pa.
Cover photo: Kincaids Bay House, Burlingame, Ca.

Contents

Acknowledgments

Four individuals spent many hours reading, editing the manuscript, and suggesting ideas for this book. I owe them endless thanks and appreciation: Linda Reed, my loving companion and wife, who is no longer with us and who, besides doing all of this, painstakingly did the pasteup for all the forms), Judy Buckner, Florence Feiler (my agent), and Rick Lombardo.

The following people lent their expertise and assisted in making this book as up-to-date as possible: Don Miller, Fred Pourfarzib, and Robert Voskanian of Fantasia (American Discotheque Corp.); Ray Farlisi (The Candy Canyon); Ed King (Video Music Systems); Andrew Lee (Sound Chamber); Stephen Moore (restaurant and bar design consultant); Ann Rosenthal, Thomas McGee (The Perlick Company); Dale Seiden (DSR Mfg. Co.); Ron Lincoln (Libbey Glass); Sol Blumenfeld (city planner); Rick Perkal, John Hawck (W.R. Grace Restaurants); J.R. Vallance (T.J. Applebee's); Ken Detwiler (Lounge Concept Director, Ramada Inns); Star Restaurant Supply Co. (Van Nuys, California); the staffs at the National Restaurant Association, DISCUS, and Anheuser-Busch, Inc. (Van Nuys, California); all the members of my family, Tom Fier, John Fier, Leonard Fier, and Vivian Fier Walker; and all the equipment manufacturers who kindly supplied photographs of their products.

For the second edition, I want to thank all who purchased the first edition and who spoke with me at national conventions or by phone. Your questions guided me to the topics where additional information was needed.

A special thanks to my beautiful five-year-old son, Zack Reed-Fier, for his patience at watching Dad typing at his computer instead of running around the yard playing games.

And many thanks to Kim Tabor, my acquisitions editor, for extending my deadline too many times I'm sure, and the entire editorial and production staff at TAB books for their patience and understanding during all phases of this project.

Introduction

Starting and Running a Money-Making Bar is a comprehensive manual for entrepreneurs, potential and current owners, investors, managers, and employees who want to see their dream of owning, starting, managing, and promoting a bar come true. Its purpose is to save you from making hundreds of thousands of dollars in mistakes and to teach you in an easy-to-follow, step-by-step manner how to make money and stay in a successful and profitable business.

Money-Making Bar discusses the fundamental characteristics about the business and how to perform the essential marketing research to decide on the type of bar, the location, clientele, concept development, and bar design. You'll learn how to:

- Write a comprehensive business plan.
- Secure a loan.
- Scout locations.
- Buy and stock fixtures and inventory.
- Price and merchandise drinks and other items.
- Promote and advertise.
- Handle transactions.
- Manage employees.
- Keep track of inventory and bookkeeping methods.

The duties and responsibilities of the owner, manager, bartender, cocktail server, and other employees are detailed and include interviewing and training techniques and sources of finding employees.

Running a bar is an exciting enterprise. The rewards are substantial, yet it takes an acute awareness of the dynamics of the business to be successful year after year. *Money-Making Bar* can assist you in all aspects of starting and running your own bar—from cost controls to choice of ice cubes and glassware and, of course, how to make money!

Helpful advice about the liquor trade, entertainment, and food service businesses is included, including how to keep abreast of new trends. By following the advice in this book, your experience as owner or employee of a small pub or a large nightclub will prove prosperous.

Each chapter can be read separately in the order of your needs or from beginning to end. If you are interested in being an owner or investor, read every word. If you are interested in being a manager, you, too, should read every word. If you are interested in being an employee, read chapter 13 first, then read chapter 15 on management. This will teach you how to be successful at your job. It will also show you how all the jobs interrelate. Then read the rest of the book to gain an understanding about other areas of the business. The more you know, the more valuable you'll be to your employer.

If you are currently employed in or own a bar, let this book stimulate you to improve, expand, and gain knowledge about the business. Check out chapter 11, which contains more than 100 promotions. Keep a copy of *Money-Making Bar* in your office as a reference for yourself and your employees. The information that does not seem to apply to your business right now might be useful at a later date. No matter why you bought this book, the bar business is a business, and the more knowledgeable you are about it, the more successful you will be.

Since this book was first published in 1986, thousands have purchased and profited from its contents. Many have called to tell me how much this book has meant to them. It has helped people open their first place and helped those already in business stay in business. Read it and reap your rewards.

With this second edition, I have updated, expanded, and added new material based on my consulting work with you and the changing nature of the bar business. The changes in this edition were added to make the information in this book, and there is lots of it, even more helpful.

When searching for a bar or a location, I have added information on how to conduct a focus group as part of your marketing research. Focus groups allow you to interview your potential customers to find out what they want. Many ideas for bars are fantastic but fail because the owner's needs were met and not the clientele's. The needs of the community where you will operate also require attention, so I have broadened the discussion on social responsibilities to encompass a global, as well as a local, social, and environmental concerns.

You'll learn new and creative ways to merchandise, garnish, and promote drinks. I have significantly expanded chapter 11, which has been renamed "Successful Promotions." You'll now find a step-by-step guide on how to design and plan a promotion, including how to analyze your needs, appeal to your customers, cross-promote with other businesses, set up a timetable, and reach your goals. A case study brings it all together. This is followed by more than "100 Successful Promotions, " organized by month and topic.

In several places throughout the book, I have added short sections with tips and ideas on such topics as construction, word-of-mouth advertising, and tips for successful managing on the floor. In other sections, I've provided real-life solutions for the daily problems you'll encounter running your bar.

Chapter 15 contains an all new management troubleshooting section and alcohol awareness training information, including sample situations, exercises, and solutions. New information on improving sales and up-selling and on motivational techniques for your staff is also included.

The Entertainment chapter has been updated and expanded to include material on coin-operated games and promoting more play. You'll read about how to hire and work with a DJ and about the latest entertainment trends. Finally, the book ends with a chapter on food service, with a special emphasis on raw bars.

Throughout the Second Edition, I have tried to heighten your awareness of all the areas where you can save money and time in the pursuit of being more profitable. Better training and more knowledge should make your job of making money easier.

I have worked for more than 20 years in the restaurant and bar business, walked the planks behind many bars pouring drinks, worked for many owners, owned a restaurant and bar myself, consulted on restaurant and bar designs and operations, written and produced advertising for bars and restaurants, written employee manuals, conducted training sessions, and developed drink manuals. I have witnessed failures and successes. Many people dream about owning their own bar. I want this book to help you make your dreams come true. I welcome your comments and suggestions for future editions. My address and phone number are:

7450 Beckford Avenue,
Reseda, CA 91335,
(818) 344-5527.

Cheers!

1

The bar business

Your eyes, adjusting to the dim light at first, gradually bring the bar into view. You see lots of tilted heads engaged in animated conversation. Ice cubes clink together, a fire crackles, and the murmur of voices bring warmth and glowing comfort, a welcome relief from the world you left outside.

This could be your own bar or one in your neighborhood. Let's examine the trends of the alcoholic beverage industry, then we'll look at some of the reasons why people will come to your place and spend their money.

In the past few years, beer and particularly wine consumption have almost doubled. Consumption of whiter beverages such as vodka, gin, rum, and tequila have increased, and white wine is fast becoming the number one "cocktail" asked for in bars. Liqueurs, with their lower alcoholic content, have also shown a tremendous rise in sales. Why? People are concerned about their health. They are pursuing a healthier lifestyle. Consumers today want a lighter beverage, and as a result, browner liquors such as whiskeys and scotches have declined in popularity.

How can you use this information? Of course, local tastes and sales vary, but if you are a bar owner or are considering opening a bar, you might consider stocking more wine and beer. You could probably sell premium wines by the glass at higher prices than your liquor drinks. With beer, you can advertise and promote your selections.

Opening or owning a bar is a good business. There is a place for you. It might surprise you that bars do not just sell drinks. Their popularity stems from the few simple needs we all desire to fulfill: companionship, meeting other people, sharing our views, and engaging in social play. Bars provide just this atmosphere. People feel comfortable in groups. People want to be where people are.

Reading this book will provide you with the basics you need for understanding what makes the bar business work. The best way to discover if you enjoy the business is to frequent many different bars and observe what makes them successful. Try working in one. It is an ideal business for people to enter at any stage of their life, as a bartender, cocktail server, manager, owner, or investor. Age is no barrier. The skills of the business can be easily explained and taught. You don't need a lot of training to make it work. As an employee, it costs very little to enter the business, perhaps only the cost of a uniform.

For an owner or investor, the return on investment can be substantial. Typically, a new bar owner is in the black within three to six months of opening, and the return on initial investment paid back within three to five years or less. In addition, it is possible to earn a good living during this period. The bar business is a cash business, and at the end of every day, you know exactly what you've made.

Before we get too far ahead of ourselves, however, let's step back in time and look at the history of alcohol and bars first so you'll have a better understanding of how it all began.

A brief history of alcohol

People have had a love affair with alcohol for a long time. Clay tablets with cuneiform writing dating back to 2000 B.C. tell stories of beer and wine being used for sacramental purposes as well as for pleasure. The most readily available local material—dates, almonds, grapes, palms, pineapples, corn, rye, barley, roses, pears, and apples—were fermented to produce these early drinks. Fruit juices became wines, grains turned into beers, and fermented honey into mead. Later, both fruits and grains became distilled spirits, liquor, and liqueurs. Finally, herbs were often added and this enticing liquid was used as medicine. During the Middle Ages, European monks perfected these herbal libations, keeping their recipes a secret for centuries.

In most parts of the world, early fermented beverages were more nutritional and safer than drinking the local waters. Liquor survived long sea journeys in barrels. The first immigrants to America carried this mistrust of water with them. Drinking alcohol was commonplace and the familiar English pub was transformed into the American tavern. Not only did taverns serve as a way station for travelers, but local meeting places as well, including holding religious services.

The homey atmosphere of the tavern was the source of all of the local news and gossip. In fact, taverns were required by law in most of the Colonies. Land grants and tax exemptions were granted to tavern owners, and the local tavern owner usually received the only newspaper in Colonial towns. Taverns were as bars are today, centers of cultural and intellectual discoveries.

Many famous Americans owned drinking establishments: Ethan Allen, John Adams, William Penn, Andrew Jackson, even Lincoln had a license for a tavern. Shakespeare, Dickens, Francis Scott Key, Thomas Jefferson, Jack London, and countless others penned their prose while in a tavern. At any time during our history, bars and saloons have played a part.

In the 1950s, people gathered at bars to watch a new invention called television. In the 1970s, they came to see large-screen TVs, and in the 1980s, TV programs from around the world, obtained direct from satellites. Today, taverns and local neighborhood bars have continued in popularity for individuals in all walks of life.

As our society has become more complex and diversified, so has the concept of the local tavern and neighborhood pub. Although they continue to be places for people to exchange ideas, larger drinking establishments offering a variety of atmospheres and clientele have evolved.

Bars also provide us with entertainment for listening or dancing. To attract and keep a certain clientele, some bar owners offer total entertainment centers featuring the latest technological advances in audio and visual sensations. Obviously, this type of bar costs millions of dollars a year to operate.

The type of operation you desire should reflect your image and personality. Only your imagination limits what you can do with your bar. And whatever you choose, rest assured you will be in good company, as the history of taverns and bars clearly shows.

Alcohol has been a part of man's diet for several thousand years. The earliest written records date back to almost 2000 B.C. Today's bars are sophisticated entertainment centers offering customers hundreds of choices of alcoholic beverages, a far cry from the fermented grapes stored in goats' stomachs and unfired clay vessels of yesteryear.

An eye towards the future

The sale of alcoholic beverages in eating and drinking establishments in the United States is more than $20 billion annually, or about 40 percent of all alcohol sales. Total consumption averages two drinks per day for every adult. Over the years, per capita consumption rises and falls. Since 1980, consumption of distilled spirits has decreased while wine and beer consumption has increased.

As the drinking age population continues to increase and affect drinking patterns, new trends, such as the recent shift from drinking hard liquor to lighter liqueurs and wines, will continue. The taxes derived from the sale of alcohol ($5.5 billion) rank it third among major sources of federal revenues. Only personal and corporate income taxes come before it. By comparison, the taxes on all petroleum products lag far behind with $4.7 billion.

Liquor, beer, and wine companies spend more than $1 billion annually to advertise their products. Advertising expenditures have increased sixfold in the last 15 years and mil-

lions of dollars more are pumped into the economy every day. Their advertising only stands to help bars.

The total number of licenses nationwide for selling distilled spirits in restaurants and bars exceeds 225,000. Beer and wine licenses more than double that figure. There are 400,000 bartenders employed, with one out of every ten owning his own place. An additional 2 million food servers and 600,000 managers work in the industry.

As the population and two-income families continue to grow, the demand for restaurants and bars will increase. New licenses are issued based on population growth by county. More people, more leisure time, and more vacations, combined with higher disposable incomes, will lead to more money spent outside the home on food and beverages. This service-oriented industry is expected to increase its employment by 20 percent in the 1990s.

Nationally, the alcohol industry is big business. Locally, it can also be big business, even for a small operation. Those who want to own or manage a bar can make a good living and, in time, make a fortune. It takes a knowledgeable, competent individual to succeed in today's marketplace. In California alone, which accounts for 10 percent of all liquor sales in the United States, one out of every three licenses changes hands every year. The three major reasons cited for this turnover in ownership are: the owner's and management's lack of knowledge of the business; necessary marketing research was not done; and undercapitalization. All of which is addressed in the following chapters.

2

Types of ownership

Who owns this place, anyway? The legal form a business can take is sole proprietorship, partnership, corporation, or franchise. What is best for you depends on several things: your commitment in time and money (how involved do you want to be?); your experience and whether it needs to be supplemented; your desire to assume full control and authority or share the responsibilities and liabilities; the continuity of the business (what happens if you can't work or die); and your particular tax considerations. You might need to obtain a lawyer to advise you, especially if you are just starting out. An attorney can save you from making costly mistakes.

Sole proprietorship

The owner as *sole proprietor* is by far the most popular way of owning a bar. Everyone loves to be recognized by the owner of his or her favorite place. As the owner, you are your own boss. You work for yourself and others work for you. Your personality and special talents create the atmosphere and tone of your business. You define the policy and concepts, and set the morale of the place. You hire, fire, oversee, and train your employees. Every decision you make

affects your business. You may have a philosophy or a particular statement to make or a need to fulfill. You see the results immediately waiting for you at the end of each day—in the cash register—as the money you'll take daily to the bank for your efforts.

In terms of taxes, the business profit will be treated and taxed as if it is your own personal income. Many sole owners build their bar business up for a few years and then sell the whole operation. This affords them an income during those years, and later they can often double and triple their original investment upon the sale. Many owners then reinvest in a larger operation. By repeating this every few years, they quickly pyramid their money.

Remember, owning a bar is a business. For survival, you will need to know how to manage people, how to manage money, and how to manage the records of your business. The finer points of these areas are discussed in later chapters.

As in any business, the sole owner faces some disadvantages. Because you are the sole owner of your business, you will have to face all problems head-on. You will deal with employees, competitors, and customers. The higher the financial return, the higher the risk. If these problems are facing you, there are solutions. You may wish to have someone share the work responsibilities. You can hire individuals, such as managers or accountants, to help you, or you can bring in a partner.

Partnership

A *partnership* is a great way to share the responsibilities of the business. It is also one way to invest in a business with an individual who might have the total knowledge to run the business. Your partner or partners can complement your strengths and weaknesses. The sum of the partners will be greater than the individuals standing alone.

There are two types of partnerships: *general* and *limited*. In a *general partnership*, all individuals are equal, and there is no limit to the number of general partners. Everyone works in the business. All partners share in the unlimited liabilities.

In *limited partnership*, there is no limit to the number of limited partners. At least one person must be the general partner, who has unlimited liability. The limited partners have limited liability and are not required to take an active role in the business. Not being an active partner is known as a *silent partner*. This silent partner makes no decisions about the business. Although not legally required, it is a good idea to have a partnership *agreement* signed by all parties. In case of disputes or the adding of additional partners, the original arrangements will be clearly defined. Make sure your agreement outlines what will happen if a partner dies, wants to sell his or her share, or withdraws.

The biggest advantage of a partnership is the pooling of resources and talent, assets, and credit. Sharing the responsibilities is the major factor in acquiring partners. You'll share in the profits as arranged in your original agreement, and you'll be taxed only on that profit as personal income. In some states, partnerships must register with local and state agencies. Contact your county clerk or local elected representative for this information.

Partnerships can be a tremendous boost for all concerned. Problems do occur, and in partnerships, you have the benefit of discussing the solutions. Be prepared, and know your partners well before you begin anything. Partners are only necessary if they have the finances available and can offer advice and assistance.

If you are a sole owner and contemplating taking in partners, limited or unlimited (general), be sure your interests are taken care of in any formal written agreements. In small operations, partnerships are highly recommended. However, as you expand, a *corporation* is probably the right course to follow. It offers numerous tax and nontax advantages.

Corporation

A corporation is a legal entity separate from its owners or stockholders and pays taxes as a separate taxpayer. Three or more persons obtain a state charter and elect a Board of Directors who run the corporation. Each person's investment is secured by shares of stock in the corporation. Profits per share or dividends are distributed to the shareholders. Salary or dividends are taxed as personal income. Additional funds for the corporation can be raised by issuing or selling more stock.

A big advantage of a corporation is the nonliability of the individual. Because the corporation is a "legal person," all liability shifts from the investors to the corporation. Numerous tax advantages exist in the form of deductions and employee benefits.

Federal and state taxes can be quite heavy for a corporation. Many small corporations of 35 or less stockholders form a *Subchapter "S" corporation*. This avoids the federal corporate taxes and treats the business as a partnership. Thus, income or dividends received by each shareholder is reported as personal income. Some states however, do not recognize this type of corporation for taxation purposes. Consult your State and Federal Internal Revenue Services for their differences.

Franchise

What about franchises? *Franchise* is a term with a variety of meanings. It can mean a license to sell or service an idea or product in a certain territory for a small fee. It can also mean acquiring a business, setup and ready-to-operate, with a continuing relationship to the parent company. Buying a franchise involves a larger on-going fee or a percentage of your business, which may include national or regional advertising and training of key personnel. Actually, it may surprise you to know that there are franchised bars around. Investigate their potential and benefits before entering into any franchise association.

A great advantage of a franchise is gaining knowledge and expertise and possibly financing through the parent company. Their national or regional reputation and business record is what you're paying for. This is a good way to learn and enter a new field. The disadvantage is wanting to do things your way and being bound by the parent company's regulations. Make sure their fees or percentage do not consume all of your profits.

How you will set up the legal form of your business will depend on the type of bar you'll be operating.

3

Types of bars

Think of your favorite place to spend some time. Someone, and it could be you, has put a bar in the place that you just thought of. A bar exists in a grotto in Acapulco where the patrons swim under a waterfall to order a drink as their feet dangle in the water. There are bars in former libraries, old fire stations, bank vaults, waterfront warehouses, in historic houses, next to mountain streams, next to your apartment building, and underground, as well as at the top of skyscrapers. No matter where they are or what they look like, every bar has its "atmosphere" or design concept, its "clientele," and its "volume" of sales in dollars. By varying any one of these characteristics, you alter your bar's personality. Let's look at the basic bar types, first examining the neighborhood bar and finishing with the large entertainment center.

Neighborhood bars

The neighborhood tavern or pub is the most popular form of a bar. It exists all across America on Main Street or around the corner from where you live or work. At its best, it is a lively, congenial place, just like the pubs you find throughout England. Your town may only be big enough to support one or large enough to have thousands. It's a place where the regular customers all know each other. They are friendly with the owner and all of the employees. There is a great deal of camaraderie between them. It may have small-scale entertainment for its customers, in the form of video games, pool tables, darts, coin-operated games, or a jukebox. As the owner, you'll find yourself loaning money to your customers, extending credit, cashing checks, and passing on phone messages. It's exactly these personal touches that make so many neighborhood bars successful year after year.

The neighborhood bar becomes a comfortable extension of people's homes, almost like a private club. The hours your bar is open depends on the neighborhood. Most neighborhood bars open between 6 and 11 AM, and closing time varies according to the trade. Whatever hours you choose, be consistent and be on time. If you start varying your hours, the customers will be confused. They may suspect business is bad. A bar is a convenience for its customers, and the owner must adjust to their wishes. You may be assured that the customers will make their wishes known.

Acquiring a beer and wine license is substantially cheaper than buying a liquor license. You may wish to start out with a beer and wine license and add a liquor license later as your business succeeds. Bars that only sell beer and wine are as popular as those that sell beer, wine, and liquor. Stocking a complete bar with liquor requires a greater investment than just stocking beer and wine. "Beer bars" are often your neighborhood bars that appeal to the blue-collar worker and the younger drinking crowd. These customers enjoy small-scale entertainment and will continue to be regulars because an entire evening out will not cost much money.

An old concept in bars is having a return of popularity. It is the brewpub. Its origins date back several centuries to roadside pubs and inns in England. In a brewpub, you manufacture and sell your beer in one location. You have total control over what you make and sell. The aroma of beer brewing and its taste are real crowd-pleasers. At the Brewhouse Grill, beer is made on the premises (FIG. 3-1). The aroma of hops and yeast draw patrons of The Brewhouse Grill up from the beach a short block away.

Beer bars are popular because of the ease of acquiring a low, fixed-priced license from the state as well as the lower start-up costs. There are no restrictions on the number of beer and wine licenses available. Liquor licenses, however, are restricted by the population of a county. Supply and demand can cause wide fluctuations in the cost of obtaining an existing liquor license.

Fig. 3-1. *These attractive copper tanks hold freshly brewed beer.* The Brewhouse Grill, Santa Barbara, California

If you wish to open a bar with a diverse clientele, it is advantageous to acquire a liquor license. A typical full service bar is stocked with an average of 85 different bottles of liquor. With all of these choices, a wide range of tastes can be met. The mark-up on liquor drinks is at least four to five times the cost of the alcohol poured. By comparison, draught beer is sold at between five and ten times its cost, and bottled beer between three and five times its cost. Substantial profits can be made with each type of operation.

You'll find that each type of bar discussed here also exists in the form of a restaurant and bar. These can be small and neighborly, or large and spacious, cost a fortune, or put together on a limited budget. Often a neighborhood bar serves sandwiches at lunch as a convenience to its patrons and hors d'oeuvres around the dinner hour, but no dinners. In making the choice to serve food, take into consideration your competition, location, and the image you want to project. If you are not licensed as a restaurant, check with your state Department of Alcoholic Beverage Control. They will advise you as to the type of license you will need. Their regulations may allow sandwiches, pizza, and other items to be served in a bar. Serving regular dinners requires a restaurant license.

Recently, the awareness of wine as a drink by itself, separate from drinking it with a meal, has seen the emergence of "wine" and "champagne" bars. Here, you are able to taste several kinds of wines and become educated to their differences. This type of bar, small in scale and very easy to operate, demands a more sophisticated clientele, and, therefore, a more sophisticated neighborhood. Wine's popularity is continually gaining momentum. Naturally, wine sales have dramatically increased in the last few years, more than beer and liquor sales together. (See FIG. 3-2.)

Fig. 3-2. *The simple, bright and clean wine and espresso bar of the Daily Grill in Encino, California.*

Nightclubs

Another type of bar is the small nightclub or "cocktail lounge." It may have a split personality. During the day and early evening hours it acts as a neighborhood bar; as the night progresses it becomes the source of active entertainment: dancing or watching live performances.

Large nightclubs spend a great deal of money for promotion. Their goal is to have customers spend the entire evening drinking and enjoying the entertainment. These clubs are expensive to set up, operate, and promote. They make incredible amounts of money—quickly and consistently. Well-trained owners, managers, advertising, and promotion personnel keep these places running in the black. A large population base is needed to draw enough customers. The clientele will consist of regulars and a large transient crowd, who come for a specific show and may not reappear for months. Whereas cover charges in a small bar are nonexistent or minimal, cover charges in a large nightclub are very high. Drink prices are higher as well. Their liquor costs are slightly lower than smaller bars, however, because large clubs use and buy bulk quantities of liquor at a discount.

Dance clubs

The dance club, or bar that features dancing as its main attraction, is very popular. People have been dancing for centuries and will continue to do so. The key is the music. Depending on the size and concept of your bar, the music can be live or recorded and played by a disc jockey. In smaller bars, a jukebox may be all that is necessary. It is cheaper to have a DJ spin the records than to pay for a group to perform. Some clubs use both; a DJ comes on before, between, and after the live show.

Entertainment clubs

"Total entertainment centers" are found in major metropolitan areas. They usually occupy a large building. There is a separate room or floor for each type of entertainment. The larger the enterprise becomes, the greater the volume of business required to keep it profitable. Because these places are so spacious, crowds are a must. It takes creative personnel to keep these huge establishments alive and fresh for the public. As in any bar, the owners strive for repeat business and a packed house.

Returning customers will bring their friends along and will keep you operating in the black.

Minicasinos

As states seek new ways to increase their revenues, many states are allowing video gambling in bars. Typically, no more than twenty machines are allowed in a minicasino. The states issue a gaming license separate from the liquor license. The states exercise strict control as all machines are linked together to a master computer. Receipts are registered through the state and scrupulously accounted. A percentage of the net proceeds (gross receipts less paid outs) goes to the state.

Unified concept

When you are in the bar business, you are also in the entertainment business. No matter what type of bar you own, it should have an overall concept or theme. This is its personality. Your bar will project a mood and a particular feeling. Its character will attract a certain clientele, providing them with pleasure, entertainment, and comfort. The concept or theme must prevail throughout every detail. This begins with the owner and manager's attitude and is carried down through the employees to the customers. It is carried out in the design and decor and often is decided by your bar's location. The concept can be high-tech, old-fashioned, elegant, country-western, tropical, or a whaling saloon. People like new and different places and ideas. It does not have to cost a fortune to create the right concept. The simplest ideas are often the best. Your entertainment should reflect your concept.

Your customers will label your place as a means to remember what it is all about. Consequently, some concepts cross the line between the different types of bars discussed. A bar with a sports theme could be a neighborhood hangout, or one with dancing. It could have sports memorabilia on the walls in a small storefront location, or several satellite dishes pulling in sports programming from around the world showing on several large screen TVs, combined with dancing in a multi-floored complex. The floor can be covered with sawdust or designed as a regulation basketball court. The choice is yours. Keep your theme and design consistent.

Keep abreast of the latest trends in entertainment. Putting these forms to use in your bar is excellent for business. Yesterday's pinball machines are today's video games which will become virtual reality games. The jukebox grew up to be music videos projected on large screen TVs; these have progressed into the karaoke sing-along music video systems. The coin-operated games or jukeboxes can earn you money when you own the machines. If you rent or lease, you share in the profits derived from them. (See FIG. 3-3.)

The size of your bar will be determined by your budget and concept. Size, room design, and the placement of entries and exits are the basis for determining your square footage allotment. This allotment is prepared by the Fire Department and prescribes how many people will be allowed into your room at one time. This is known as your *occupancy rating*. You want to design your room to provide space for the greatest number of people. The higher your occupancy rating, the more money you can expect to generate.

Fig. 3-3. The Shark Club (Irvine, California) is an upscale billiards bar featuring postindustrial design, complete with a shark swimming in a tank.

Estimating volume of business

Your anticipated volume of business should be considered in your initial design and concept planning. It is your choice to keep it mellow or to keep it busy. Decide if you want to make $100 a day or $10,000 a day.

Here are two ways to project your daily volume. The first way assumes you have a lounge act and the room is cleared and reseated for each show. Each seat represents a minimum dollar amount of income. For example, you have 100 seats in your bar. You charge a $6 cover charge to enter, and a two-drink minimum at $4 per drink. You have two shows per evening. If you fill every seat, you can expect to make $2800. (See TABLE 3-1.)

Table 3-1. Estimating Volume of Business.

100 seats × $6 cover charge	=	$600
100 seats × 2 drinks × $4 per drink	=	$800
$600 + $800 = $1400 × 2 shows	=	$2800

The second way applies if you have entertainment that is less formal or no entertainment. Estimate the number of customers you'll expect for one evening. Your estimate can be based on your occupancy rating. On busy nights, your customer count can be twice your occupancy rating because of the customer flow, while on slow nights, it may be half of your occupancy rating.

As an example, and merely for the purpose of the money flow, if you assume that 250 customers will each have at least three drinks, and you charge a $6 cover, you can expect to make $4500 in one night. (See TABLE 3-2.)

Table 3-2. Estimating Volume of Business.

250 customers × $6 cover charge	=	$1500
250 customers × 3 drinks × $4 per drink	=	$3000
$1500 + $3000	=	$4500

Now project these figures for weekly, monthly and yearly volume. Whether you are planning on a shoestring or are generously funded, a successful bar usually far exceeds its preliminary volume predictions.

Purchasing a bar

Your budget, concept, and level of experience will determine whether you buy an existing bar and business, remodel an existing bar, or build from scratch. There is an obvious advantage to buying an existing bar. Its business is well-established. You can walk right in, and by keeping the current employees, start collecting the profits immediately. It is advisable to keep the current crew for a while so you do not alienate your clientele. Your employees are your greatest asset and should be considered a part of your concept. Their personalities may be why the business has been so successful. When buying an existing bar, be sure to include in the purchase agreement that the seller not be allowed to open a competing bar within a certain distance of yours for a specific period of time (five to ten years).

Before you consider buying any bar and before beginning any negotiations, become a customer at the bar and study the current business thoroughly. Then decide how you would improve it and what the improvements would cost. Often, an owner wants to retire or change careers and will give you a good deal. To determine the right price for the business, be sure to consult a local business broker, bar supplier, attorney, or accountant. When figuring the cost, don't forget the goodwill for which you must pay.

As a rule of thumb, bars and restaurants are purchased for the price of one year's gross receipts. You will need someone well qualified in the business to determine the accuracy of reported gross receipts. Key items to check are liquor delivery invoices against actual sales volume. Use a nightclub and bar consultant to advise you if you are not knowledgeable.

When you buy an existing bar, you also inherit a proven location. If you feel remodeling is necessary, be sure to thoroughly investigate the costs. Remodeling an existing bar because you wish to change the concept or to change the clientele can be very expensive. It is, however, cheaper than building from scratch. Complete a thorough inventory before and after you purchase any existing bar. This ensures that you take full possession of everything that is in your contract. Discuss any physical changes or decisions on a new concept with the Fire, Health and Building Departments before purchasing to eliminate any future problems.

To sum up this chapter, decide on the type of bar you want and the desired volume. Then decide whether to buy an existing bar, remodel, or build from scratch. In this respect, consider your finances available, either in cash or by loan.

4

Selecting a location and attracting clientele

Every type of bar has a suitable location. There are two ways of approaching the selection of your location. You can develop a definite theme and then match the concept to a location, or choose a location that will fit your theme. It would not make sense to think of opening a champagne bar in a cattle rustling area. Nipper's, which calls itself a champagne and caviar bar, is situated on Rodeo Drive in Beverly Hills. The wealth and ambience of its location matches its clientele. Perhaps you would like to open a bar in a particular location because you prefer to live and work there. In order to choose the right concept for any location, you need to make a study of the area as well as those who frequent the area. You will be looking for a void in the marketplace that you can fill.

Demographics

The more you know your clientele, the better you can tailor your establishment to suit its preferences. The study of the composition of a population is known as *demography*. Demographic profiles can be obtained from the U.S. Department of Commerce, Bureau of Census field offices, or ordered directly from the Su-

perintendent of Documents, Washington, D.C. This data is derived from census records taken every ten years. Yearly information can be gathered from a variety of other sources: the local chamber of commerce, university and public libraries, city and county planning departments, realtors, trade associations and their publications, large newspaper, television and radio stations' advertising departments, and local advertising agencies. Firms that sell outdoor and transit advertising space can also supply demographic studies. Most of these sources will provide you with this information at no cost. These studies answer the following questions concerning the potential clientele in a given area:

- What is the ratio of males to females?
- What are their ages?
- Are they married or single? Do they have families?
- What are their jobs?
- What are their income levels? More importantly, what kind of disposable income do they have?
- How far do they travel to work?
- How much education do they have?
- Which religions do they practice?

- What are their races and national origins?
- Do they own their own homes or rent? Do they live in apartments or condominiums?
- How much leisure time do they have and what do they do with it?
- Do they travel?
- What types of entertainment do they enjoy?

The demographic study will provide a profile of your potential clientele. Look carefully at their disposable income. Perhaps sales in the area for goods and services total $5 million, but the demographics show $6 million of disposable income is available. In surveying the area, you notice 200 new condos being built. With another 400 people to draw from, there will likely be more than enough disposable income to support your bar.

Focus groups are another way to find out information about your potential customers. Advertising agencies use this format to seek out responses about all kinds of new products and services. You can use the method yourself. Select a variety of customers who frequent bars in the area where you plan to locate. Keep the group limited to no more than ten individuals. Have them meet in a neutral office environment. The best time for a meeting is after work.

You need to compensate them for their time. Typically, focus group participants are paid a nominal sum and provided with a meal for their efforts. The information you gather will be worth the expense. Additional groups should be used to verify common trends revealed through the participants' comments.

Once the participants are in the room, have them sit around a table, with the interviewer at one end. Record the conversations so no notes are taken during the session. Have the interviewer (someone other than yourself, if you are known to the individuals) ask a series of prepared questions. The interviewer needs to be able to keep the discussion on track and moving. Give everyone a chance to answer. Allow all opinions to be aired. Do not reveal your tastes, or defend or criticize ideas. You are researching the behavior and interests of your customers. Remain neutral for best results. Ask the following questions:

- How often do you go to a restaurant or bar to drink?
- How many people do you go out with?
- What is the purpose of going out?
- Are the people you go out with or meet, friends, business acquaintances, relatives, or . . . ?
- Who decides which place you will visit?
- How long do you stay at any one place?
- How many drinks do you enjoy?
- Does your drink selection vary according to the time of day?
- Do you vary your drinks?
- How often do you try new liquors, wines, beers, or drinks?
- What type of entertainment do you enjoy at bars?
- What radio stations (TV stations) do you listen to (or watch)?
- What newspapers and magazines do you read?
- What do you like most about bars?
- What is your favorite place and why?
- What should a bar look like?
- What constitutes good service?
- Do you like to enjoy food while you drink?
- What types of food?
- If you could open a bar, what would it be? Why?
- What would you charge for drinks? For food?

These questions should act as a catalyst. Treat this research seriously. A common mistake is for potential bar owners to miss a niche in the marketplace because they failed to assess it properly. Successes are built on solid business decisions. Incidentally, focus groups should be used yearly with your regular customers as a means to keep your bar running smoothly and to keep up with current customer desires. You can use focus groups to test out new drink/food items, or concepts/changes in your existing bar.

Suppose you are thinking of buying the local neighborhood bar. It sits on the corner. Everyone knows the place in town. All the regulars are friends. The owner wants to retire, and the place looks as tired as the owner who has been there since she opened it forty years ago. There is nothing to it—some bar stools, a couple of neon beer signs, and a jukebox with 50s music. The prices are the cheapest around.

You buy the place. Instead of leaving it alone, you clean it up, add a frozen drink machine, make it airy and bright with a country western theme. Within six months, nobody comes in and you are wondering what went wrong. Now you decide to hold a focus group. You find out the customers miss the old place, did not care how dirty it was, and liked the homey atmosphere. When they think of country western, they think of dancing. They also liked that the owner was always there. She was as much a part of the atmosphere as the old brass bartop you took out.

It's too late to return to the old look, and you are at a quandary as to what to do. Luckily for you, the store next to you becomes vacant, and you decide to break through the wall and add dancing. You never thought about dancing in your original concept. This simple expansion proves successful.

If you decide to buy an existing bar, it is possible to change the current clientele if it is undesirable. There are several ways of doing this. The easiest are to charge a cover or enforce a dress code. You can modify the existing concept by adding some type of entertainment, remodel, or you can open a private club with memberships. In this way, you can control the clientele. Many owners buy a run-down bar in a good neighborhood and completely renovate the place. It becomes a brand new bar, people perceive it as such, and the owner will enjoy tremendous success.

Selecting a location

To select a site, drive around the area. Notice what type of activity takes place there. If the area is filled with steel mills, chances are a beer bar would be very popular with the workers. If the area is surrounded by office buildings, a singles bar with dancing and a live band might work best. Pay particular attention to any new construction of office and industrial buildings, colleges and universities, houses, condos, apartments, hotels, shopping centers, and cultural, entertainment, and sports complexes. Let's examine some typical sites you might consider for your bar. (See FIG. 4-1.)

Central or downtown business districts In big cities, this is usually separated into distinct sections.

- Financial: banks, stock brokerages, and insurance companies
- Governmental: attorneys, courthouses, and city, state, and federal buildings
- Cultural: performing arts theaters and museums
- Commercial: wholesale and retail businesses

These areas are typically active during the day and early evening hours and deserted at night when everyone goes home. Consequently, there is often a daytime parking problem.

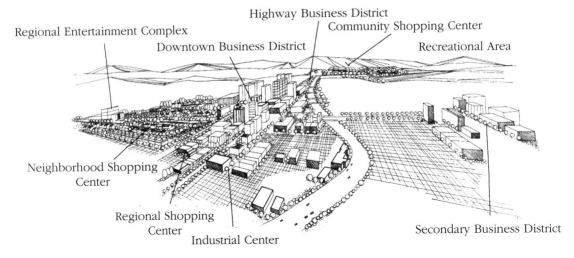

Regional Entertainment Complex
Downtown Business District
Highway Business District
Community Shopping Center
Recreational Area
Neighborhood Shopping Center
Regional Shopping Center
Industrial Center
Secondary Business District

Fig. 4-1. Centers of activity where people can congregate. Sol Blumenfeld

Due to the desirability of these locations, rents tend to be higher than in other parts of the city. Bars might serve lunch for their business customers and provide light food snacks during happy hour in order to attract the after-work crowd. Unless the area is active at night, these bars often close early.

Secondary business districts Located outside of the central business area, they offer more parking, cheaper rents, and are dependent on traffic coming in and out of the downtown area. Small cocktail lounges and beer bars would be most successful here. They provide a stop-off point for rush hour commuters and a gathering spot for local residents.

Highway business districts They often are isolated from the surrounding city or residential neighborhoods. Rents are cheaper than in the city and parking is not a problem. These bars are usually closed during the day, but because of their prime location for commuter traffic, they often open for happy hour and provide entertainment later. A bar with a special theme attraction would do well here, such as a country bar, sports bar, or one with adults-only entertainment.

Planned shopping centers They offer convenient parking and are designed to attract large numbers of people. Generally, the older the center, the cheaper the rent. You may want to consider one of these for your location. Shopping centers may have lease restrictions against a bar without a restaurant attached. Inquire about rent recapture, which provides for a reduction in rent each month for the money you spend on improvements.

Regional shopping centers You will find these in plaza settings or as enclosed malls. They are intended to serve the needs of a large metropolitan area or a number of small cities. A typical center will include several large nationally known department stores surrounded by clusters of smaller retail and entertainment businesses. These environments have taken the place of main streets all across America. The rents are high and parking is planned and plentiful. The clientele has leisure time and money to spend. Singles bars have proven successful in these malls.

Community shopping centers They are designed to serve a local area. Their tenants will probably include a local department store, a drug store, a supermarket, a national fast food outlet and small retail or service businesses. This center may take up an entire city block or run along a street as a shopping strip. Depending on the area, a bar could easily fit into this environment. Parking is convenient; rents are not outrageous.

Neighborhood, convenience, or strip shopping centers These are small clusters of stores that take up a corner or part of a city block. A small bar, a local fast food restaurant, a mini-market, and a dry cleaner might be a typical neighborhood center combination. (See FIG. 4-2.) Beer bars and small lounges with dancing provide a retreat for the locals. They like having a place to go in their home territory. These regular customers are very cohesive as a group. Generally drinks are cheaper than in larger and fancier bars. Parking is limited. Rents vary according to the affluence of the neighborhood. In addition, every city has one or more of the following centers which attract business to the area:

Regional entertainment complexes These complexes consist of performing arts theaters and civic museums located within a downtown area or a distinct part of the city. A bar with a related theme would provide a complement to the activities offered by the entertainment complex. Parking is planned as part of the complex. The clientele would tend to be upscale and sophisticated.

Entertainment districts Small performing arts theaters, movie houses, art galleries, and night spots, such as restaurants and bars clustered together, make up this district. The clientele tends to be young and attracted to small lounges, comedy clubs, singles and dance bars. Specialty bars selling only beer, wine, or champagne would prosper.

Professional districts These are a single large building, groups of buildings, or a distinct area encompassing several blocks within a city, known as an area where professionals do business. Typical districts would be a garment (fashion), interior design, photography, produce, or antique center. A bar serving

Fig. 4-2. The Classroom (Northridge, California) is located in a strip shopping center and close to a university. It offers inexpensive drinks and dancing on a small scale.

lunches and light dinners would act as a central meeting point. (See FIG. 4-3.)

Fig. 4-3. J. Sloan's (Los Angeles, California), in its homey, friendly building on trendy Melrose Avenue, is dwarfed by the Pacific Design Center behind it, home to hundreds of interior design showrooms.

Professional sports complex A stadium or an arena will be the focal point. Depending on the size of the surrounding community, it may be active all year round or only in certain seasons. Here, sports theme bars would be very successful, as will singles and dance clubs. Clientele will be varied. Ample parking is available.

Education centers Colleges, universities, and trade schools dominate this area. Beer bars, coffee and wine houses, and dance clubs will be packed with students if you have wild and crazy promotions and cater to their limited pocketbooks.

Transportation centers Airports, train and subway stations, harbors and marinas are usually surrounded with hospitality services, ho-tels, restaurants, and bars. This transient clientele has a need for company, especially when the location is unfamiliar. Travelers often have hours of free time, and bars with entertainment would have great appeal.

Convention centers Both large and small cities have discovered the economic drawing power of hosting conventions. These complexes must accommodate from several hundred to several thousand individuals. The majority of these people are from out-of-town and they need places to eat, drink, and unwind.

Recreational areas They include parks, rivers, deserts, mountains, lakes, and beaches. These are public places where nature is the attraction. The clientele is varied and transient. Successful bars capitalize on the uniqueness of the area.

Tourist attractions Whether natural or manmade, they have their own drawing power. These require supporting food, drink, and lodging for their customers. Alternative forms of entertainment will attract adult visitors.

Industrial centers Active during the day and virtually deserted at night, they have a major impact on the community by providing jobs and the need for housing, restaurants, and bars. Shot and beer bars with small-scale entertainment will do a booming business. The atmosphere tends to be informal, and all of the customers know each other.

Industrial centers also are the locations of many progressive and avante garde clubs. These warehouse dance clubs feature the latest music and post-industrial decor. Customers like the atmosphere of these open spaces and do not mind travelling into industrial centers at night. Your clientele must feel they are on the cutting edge of music and entertainment.

Evaluating a location

Once a general location is decided upon, you must further evaluate potential sites within that area. Ideally, a site will provide all of the ingredients for success. When you are comparing actual locations, however, certain factors may outweigh the others. For example, the need for covered parking in a wet climate or high visibility along a highway may be more important than cheaper rent at a site hidden from the highway or without covered parking. To help you decide, rate each site according to its desirability for each of the following factors.

Economy Is the general climate of the area strong or in a state of collapse? If your site is near a mining town and the company running the mine is ready to expire, then the whole area could be depressed overnight. If the area is dependent on one business for its economy, find out if the business is subject to fluctuations or strikes. Is a resort dependent on snow or other weather factors? Is the area dependent on tourists? If so, do tourists have the option of arriving by several modes of transportation? What happens if there is a gas shortage or an airline pilot's strike?

Labor How about the availability of labor? Is the labor population the right age for your concept? Are there places for employees to rent? You may be able to offer jobs, but can they afford a place to live, or are rentals available? This is a particular problem in seasonal tourist areas.

Drawing power Does the location attract enough people to support your bar? Is your site close to the central area of activity? This could be an intersection of two highways, next to a baseball stadium, in a cluster of smaller stores around a major store, or on top of a highrise building overlooking the city. Are you along the route to a major city or attraction? The larger the drawing power of the trading area, the greater your potential for customers and sales.

Growth potential Is the location in an area where population or business density and incomes are growing? Is there a definite direction of growth? Is the area due for development or redevelopment, and when? Are there any factors that could slow or stop growth? There might be political opposition to bars in an area, or a ban on new construction, or pending changes in zoning laws. The local planning department can provide this type of information that is not available anywhere, but comes from knowing an area intimately. If a new port or hotel is scheduled to be built right across from your location, then secure this prime spot immediately.

Competition How successful are those who would be your competitors? Is the competition complementary? Do people stop at the bank, do a little shopping, and then have something to eat and drink afterwards? Do they go to a movie and then out to dance later? Are there restaurants and bars clustered together where customers walk in and out of several places in one night? Does this practice draw more people to the area?

Make the competition work for you by offering an alternative. If all of the bars in the area are crowded and have dancing, try lounge entertainment such as a comedy club. If all of the bars serve hard liquor, open up a beer and wine bar with over 100 varieties on hand. Will the competition detract from your business? You would not want to open a beer bar with pool tables right next to another beer bar with pool tables.

If the area can support another bar, open an alternative—a sports-oriented bar that offers large TV screens, each showing a different event. Check out all of your competition at different business hours on different days. Notice what their sales are. Talk to their customers and ask them what type of bar they would like to see in the neighborhood.

Visibility How will people know you exist? Can your bar be seen from the street or highway? Are there any visible obstructions, buildings, or hills that hide your place? Investigate the use of signs, their costs, and any restrictions imposed by the local zoning department. On streets, corner locations are considered the best. In malls, you want to face out towards the street, so you will be visible at night.

Traffic What are the patterns and peak hours of movement? How do people get around—by foot, car, train, subway, bus, or plane? What are the pedestrian and auto traffic counts? Consider the speed the traffic is moving. Are they commuters in a hurry to get home? If they are zooming by on a freeway, then they must be able to see your bar or sign before they pass the off ramp. Is there a stoplight or stop sign nearby that will increase the visibility of your bar?

Accessibility Are you close to mass transportation systems? How easy is it to get in and out of your place? Are you located on the best side of the street? If you want to catch the commuter trade, locate on the side of the street or highway that coincides with the direction of homeward movement. Is your driveway visible and have easy access? Do you have enough driveway space so as not to obstruct traffic? Are there any traffic barriers, median strips, fences, or signs prohibiting left or U-turns? If your place is difficult to get to, customers may just keep on going.

Parking Is there enough parking? Is the parking free or must they pay? If parking is available on surrounding streets or lots, will other businesses' activities interfere with the number of parking spaces available? A popular business or shopping area during the day and early evening could allow plenty of parking at night.

Consider your customers' preferences. Younger clientele may not mind a short walk from their car, while older or suburban patrons may want to park close-by. If you do have a shortage of parking, consider hiring parking attendants. Notice how the climate affects people's parking habits. They might not mind walking in warm weather as much as in cold.

Costs Does the site justify its costs? Will there be a trade-off between higher rent and a smaller space as opposed to lower rent and a larger space at a different location? Will one location require more advertising? Do you have to spend a lot of money renovating the site or bringing it up to the building codes? Can you expand? What about the taxes?

Choosing the right location can only enhance the chances for success. With expertise and investment, you could probably make a success of a ski bum's bar in the middle of the desert. At this crucial point in the development of your bar, no time can be better spent than studying and investigating each potential location thoroughly. Keep in mind how all of the factors interrelate before deciding on the site that will best suit you and attract the clientele you desire.

5

Designing the environment

You have now identified your location and clientele. In going through that process, you determined the type of bar that will appeal to your customers. Today's marketplace demands that a bar have a definite "personality" that is consistent with the clientele desired. This personality or ambience should be apparent in the total design of the bar—starting from the front door to the enveloping atmosphere within. This "unification of design" should even extend to the type of glassware and the choice of bar stools. You want every customer not only to visit your bar for its singing bartenders, the great view, or the dazzling light and sound show (if you have any of these), but also to return, because they like the feel of the place. You want them to have a definite idea of what your bar is like so they can describe it to their friends.

To achieve this goal, clarify your idea in your own mind: a high-energy singles dance club; a sophisticated champagne/wine bar serving imported cheeses, caviar, and chocolates; a friendly neighborhood tavern patterned after a speakeasy; a wacky beer bar that caters to college students; a comedy showcase; or a sports bar that appeals to young professionals. The name you choose for your bar

should reflect your concept, be easy to remember, and as catchy as you can make it. Jukebox Saturday Night (Chicago, Illinois) and The Hop (Fountain Valley, California) are fifties and sixties dance clubs, while The Underground (Los Angeles, California) is a roving (it changes locations frequently) dance club in a different industrial warehouse location each week. Champions (Washington, D.C.) and Jox (Jupiter, Florida) are sports bars, and The Blue Note (New York) is a jazz club. Houdini's (Chicago, Illinois) specializes in magic; the Punch Line (Atlanta, Georgia) in comedy. Or you can use your own name, like Ziggie's Saloon (Denver, Colorado), Fanny's (Kansas City, Missouri), or Jake O'Shaughnessey's (Seattle, Washington).

Now, let your theme guide all of your design decisions.

Atmosphere

People come to bars to meet friends or make new friends, to be seen, to look at other people, to relax, to be entertained, and most of all, to escape. A bar as a place to relax is often the key design factor. That is why so many bars are dark and cavelike. You can walk into one at any hour and the mood is the same. There are no clocks. In fact, time appears to stop. From the moment a customer opens your front door, you should be aware of his or her expectations.

Exterior

The environment starts with the exterior. It should reflect what people can expect to find inside. Your sign should indicate who you are and what you have to offer. It should excite and motivate people to come inside. (See FIG. 5-1.) Make sure your sign is illuminated at night and conforms to state and local zoning regulations.

Fig. 5-1. The unusual circular sign of Cobb's Comedy Pub (San Francisco, California) acts like a target to draw your eye towards it.

As much as possible, keep your building's design and the surrounding grounds consistent with your image. A clean exterior indicates a similar attitude inside. At Henry Africa's in San Francisco, California, the exterior planter boxes are trimmed in polished brass bar rails, just like the ones inside. A rustic barn exterior might indicate a country bar, with customers kicking and stomping inside.

Consider remodeling the exterior to enhance your image. Use your windows to entice passersby, informing them what is going on indoors. Consider opening walls to create windows or extend your space by adding a patio. Make your entry as inviting as possible. Avoid a nondescript exterior unless, of course, mystery is part of the concept. Compare the ugliness of the facade in FIG. 5-2 with the warm, inviting, open door exterior of J. Sloan's, FIG. 4-3.

Fig. 5-2. An example of how not to design an entrance. The drab brick building and security gate gives the impression of a prison.

There was once a bar in Hollywood, California, called The Candy Store. It was a candy store when you first entered. But off to the side was a door guarded by a muscular giant. Once he checked you out and decided you were "okay," you were admitted to the real world behind the candy store—a bar, decorated like a twenties speakeasy.

Interior

Your interior—furniture, layout, surface treatments, and audiovisual sensations—creates a mood that, when combined with good service, will attract your clientele and keep them spending money once they are inside. Your club's atmosphere is one of your primary selling tools.

Lighting is an essential part of your overall design. Its absence or presence enhances or distracts from your ambience. Light creates and accentuates design elements and adds to the mood of your place while giving it purpose and style.

The first decision to make is whether to use daylight or artificial light during the day. Daylight adds a lightness and freshness to a room. It can be restricted to certain areas for maximum dramatic effect. Skylights can be used to highlight plants, a reception or waiting area, or an entire room. (See FIG. 5-3.) Daylight can be brought inside by windows, window boxes, glass doors, glass walls, or bounced indirectly around a room through mirrors and walls. Daylight also accentuates details, but be aware that it also exposes dirty areas. Direct sunlight can quickly fade fabrics on furniture, carpeting, and wall treatments, as well as artwork.

Daylight is very economical, and it is free! There is a certain beauty to daylight as it enters

Fig. 5-3. A skylight softly illuminates the entire bar area of Stratton's (Encino, California). The striking mural sets the tone.

and moves around a room. As nighttime takes over the day, the changing nature of the color of daylight can be a wonderful spectacle to watch. You might want to take advantage of this by careful placement of west-facing windows.

Besides using daylight to cut costs, fluorescent fixtures dramatically reduce energy consumption. In work areas not visible to the public, fluorescent lights give you the most light for the least amount of money. Install these fixtures in restrooms, kitchens, refrigerators, storage rooms, and offices. Check with your local water and power departments for other energy-saving tips. Some departments will provide a free energy evaluation and consultation.

When using artificial light, you can make your lighting fixtures design statements or simply hidden in the ceilings and walls. (See FIG. 5-4.) Many options are available, ranging from tiny (silver-dollar size) quartz halogens to large-scale lighting trusses. Quartz halogen lighting is extremely bright and hot to the touch. Direct viewing into the bulb can cause eye damage. Consequently, it is best used for spotlighting tables and work areas from above. Larger halogen fixtures, when pointed upwards and bounced off a wall or ceiling, act like a floodlight. Halogen bulbs are bluer in color than tungsten bulbs, so they appear whiter to the eye.

Lighting trusses look and serve like the trusses used to span and support roofs and floors in industrial buildings. The trusses are made of triangular metal supports between two horizontal wood or metal beams. They are lighter and stronger than their wooden counter-

Fig. 5-4. The abstract design makes this lighting fixture so dramatic. The bar and restaurant of DC-3 overlooks the Santa Monica Airport in California.

parts. Typically, theatrical spots and floods are suspended or attached to these frames. Nightclubs connect these trusses to motors to raise, lower, and rotate them for dramatic effects.

Every light in public space should be on a dimmer. Different lighting levels during different parts of the day can create interest and mood, just as changing the pace of the music will alter the mood of your customers. During the day, a lighter, brighter atmosphere is often called for. At night, a dimmer, darker mood adds to the romance. Turning down the lights during after-work hours signals the start of the evening. Soft lights and dark areas around tables will create more intimacy, while brighter lights on the bar or dance floor should define these central areas of activity. Use the flickering light of candles or a fire for a calming effect.

The color of light creates moods. Reds are hot and exciting. Pinks and ambers are the most pleasant and appealing. They make everyone look great by warming up their skin tones. Any clear bulb can become any color by covering it with theatrical gels.

A whole range of effects can be achieved with lights. Generally, your primary activity areas should be lit directly, while indirectly lighting unimportant areas. Shafts of light can be created with pin spots or floods to highlight tables, pictures, or entryways. Neon can be bent into almost any configuration and comes in many colors. It is often used as a graphic element for signs both inside and outside the bar and as a way to define areas within the bar. Tivoli or tube lighting (small, low-voltage lights within tubes), used in trees and around architectural elements, adds a festive party atmosphere and draws attention to your place immediately. Twinkling lights always add an aura of romance to any environment when done tastefully. These lights are often used along stairs as a safety feature to accent their edges. (See FIG. 5-5.) Projectors can throw any image on a wall to create static or changing effects.

Fig. 5-5. Placing tube strip lighting along stairs for safety is a good idea. Fantasia

If you have a dance floor, lasers, fiberoptics, matrix walls, strobes, floods, spots, and neon are just a few of the many elements you can use to create programmed highly animated special effects. They can be eye-popping and dazzling with excitement, or sensuous and conducive to romance. (See FIG. 5-6.) Special lighting can also be built-in to floors, ceilings, and walls. Lights in combination with mirrors can alter a space by giving the illusion it is larger and brighter.

When using different intensities of light, make the transition from one area to the next gradual. The walk from your dimly lit bar to a bright bathroom should be interrupted by an intermediate level in the hallway. Be aware of light spill in your design. You do not want a bright flash of light from a door opening from a storage or office interrupting a couple's intimate conversation.

The color of your surfaces, furniture, and employee uniforms also affect the atmosphere. As with fashion, certain color combinations are fashionable one year and out the next. Colors do elicit emotional responses, however. People have strong reactions and attachments to colors. The more intense a color, the louder it speaks, while pastels can whisper and manipulate space subtlety. Colors can be warm (red, orange, yellow) or cool (blue, green, violet). Red is violent, sexual, and stimulating. Yellow is happy and vibrant. Blue tends to be relaxing and pleasing. Green is peaceful and serene, symbolizing growth. Violet and orange are often thought of as spiritual colors. Grey is cool. Black depicts cold, makes a space lifeless, and creates a closed-in feeling. White is very expansive and can be used to create an illusion of greater space.

Fig. 5-6. *Neon lights ring the dance floor and the spaceship, which doubles as a DJ booth. The futuristic styling of the Fantasia nightclub complements the space-age architecture of the Westin Bonaventure Hotel in downtown Los Angeles.*

No one color should dominate, because it becomes irritating and tiring. Your eyes distinguish shapes and contours by the contrasts in the color and forms of objects. If you want something to fade away or "disappear," like overhead air ducts and piping, paint them the same color as the background. Paint objects in a contrasting color to make them stand out.

Darker colors can shrink a large room, while lighter colors can expand a room. Paint a high ceiling black to make it appear lower. Or paint a ceiling or wall a light color to push it away and enlarge the space. Reflective metallic colors create unwanted glare and eye strain. Lots of color creates excitement, but it can also be confusing. Any color should be viewed under the lighting conditions in which it will exist. Large areas of color are reflected on surrounding surfaces, thereby altering their original hue. You can make fluorescent lights either cool or warm by placing different colored gels around the fluorescent tubes.

Sound can be used to convey a mood. If you want to create a noisy, boisterous bar, use hard surfaces everywhere to reflect and bounce the sound around the room. A softer, more intimate mood can be achieved through the use of cork or fabrics on the walls, carpet on the floors, and a ceiling made of acoustical tiles, rough sawn wood, or other sound-absorbing material. The ceiling shape itself can reduce noise by being curved or composed of different levels.

Sound consists of both foreground and background sounds. *Foreground sound* is the dominant sound in a room and is typically created by a TV set, live entertainment, or a DJ playing compact disks or videos. Arrange part of your bar so the foreground sound is greatly reduced, providing customers with a quieter space. You can do this by building booths, room dividers, walls, or a section on a different level.

Background sound comes from the environ-ment both inside and outside of the bar. The natural sounds of water falling, waves breaking, or the wind rustling through trees should be put to a positive use. People find nature's music soothing.

Background music that is programmed to achieve any number of desired effects can be purchased. Tapes can be leased and exchanged for new ones every few weeks from companies specializing in background music. They can program a slow set during the day and increase the tempo over the course of the evening. It is a subtle manipulation of the environment, but it should not be overlooked.

Sometimes, you can find a way to use unwanted sounds to your advantage. For instance, a bar near a railroad can have a neon sign that flashes every time the train roars by advertising shots for a special price. Bars near airports can be connected to the control tower, so customers can listen on headphones to the tower-to-pilot communications while watching the planes land.

Plan your "surface treatments" carefully to coincide with your overall theme and the volume of business. The walls, floors, and ceilings should be coordinated. Plush carpet on the floor of a beer bar is probably the wrong choice. Hardwood floors wear best. Stainless steel, marble tiles, and hardwood parquet make great dance floors. Walls can be painted, wallpapered, covered with fabric, paneled in wood, or mirrored.

Your "fixtures" can make your decor memorable. At the Hotel Utah (San Francisco, California) stuffed animals, bus destination signs, and all types of crazy stuff hang from the ceilings and walls. The gigantic back bar with its graceful arches was brought around Cape Horn from Belgium in the 1850s as part of a brewery promotion. Bill Woodhouse's Whale's Tale in South Dartmouth, Massachusetts, is decorated with beer cans from around the world. Most of them were donated by cus-

Fig. 5-7. *The owner's personal sports memorabilia collection along with donations from customers provided the decorations for Mays' Sports Pub.*

tomers. Mays' Sports Pub in Tarzana, California is filled with all types of sporting memorabilia. (See FIG. 5-7.) Over the years, faithful customers have donated their cherished Yankees uniforms, tennis rackets, Raiders hats, or jockey silks. The owners of the Club Arena in New York City have a unique approach to decor. They change it every six weeks. Artists and designers are invited to create different themes, so a visit to the club is always a fresh experience.

Layout

When designing a bar, you need to arrange the available space so there is a focal point within the room. The center of interest is usually the bar, but it can be the dance floor, a stage, pool tables, or a large-screen TV. The focal point can be emphasized with lighting, different ceiling heights, different levels of seating and activity, and the steps leading to it, or simply by size in relation to the overall space. These principles apply from the smallest neighborhood bar to the largest nightclub.

When the bar runs the entire length of the room, it is obvious what dominates. A dance floor acts like a visual magnet when placed centrally and lower than the rest of the bar. In a lounge, place all seats facing the stage. If you have the option of more space, put the entertainment in a separate area or room so there are two centers of activity—the bar and the entertainment. (See FIGS. 5-8 through 5-11.)

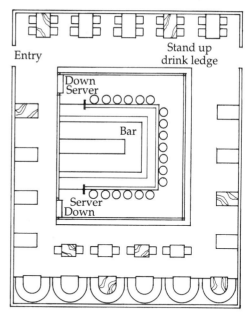

Fig. 5-9. *The island bar is the center of activity. A dance floor or stage with seats could also occupy this central area.* Stephen Moore

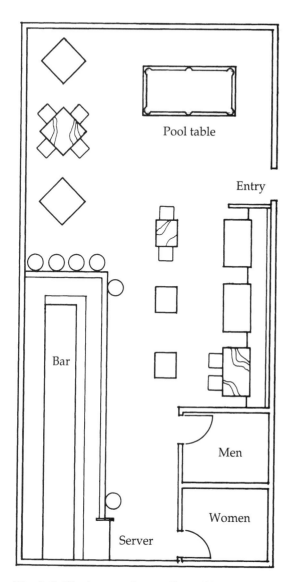

Fig. 5-8. *The layout of a small neighborhood beer bar.* Stephen Moore

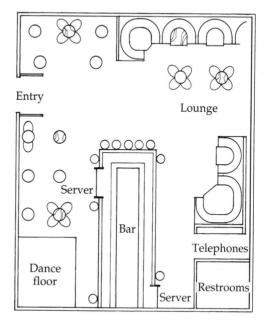

Fig. 5-10. *In this plan, the space is divided by the bar into an entertainment area and an area separated from the dancing and sounds of the music.* Stephen Moore

Island bars are bars surrounded by seating or stand-up drink areas. Usually, an island bar complements a main bar for service during busy times. However, a unique use of island bars is to cluster several island bars close together rather than have a large main bar. Cus-

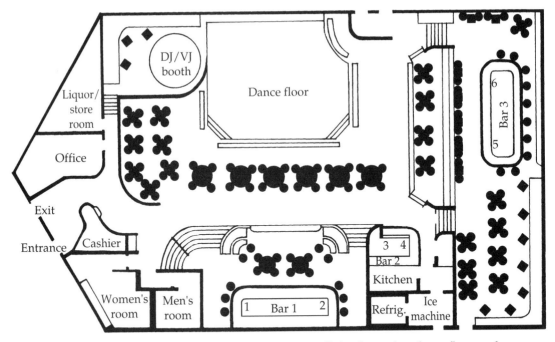

Fig. 5-11. *Fantasia West's floor plan shows its three bars, split levels, sunken dance floor, and numerous stand-up bars. The bar has an occupancy rating of 485 people.*

tomers are jammed together and intimacy is created with very few people.

The layout of the space must also take into consideration the traffic patterns of customers and employees. Traffic patterns are easily controlled, and barroom designs can stimulate or inhibit customers' circulation. Your concept will dictate certain choices. Except in entertainment lounges where table service is emphasized, the bar should always be visible and accessible. Position your bar so a customer wanting a drink does not have to run an obstacle course to reach it. You want to make it easy for people to spend their money.

It is best for control purposes to limit your entry and exit to one door, even though the fire department might require additional exits for emergency uses only. At the front entry, you might need to have a cashier's booth to collect cover charges and a checkroom for coats and hats. All aisles should be large enough to accommodate customers milling about.

As mentioned in chapter 3, the fire department makes the final decision about how many people can be accommodated in your club at one time. It will give you an occupancy rating based on the square footage of the room, the types of seating arrangements, stand-up bars, entries, and exits. Major congestion can be avoided by placing the rest-rooms, phones, and cigarette machines together and away from the bar or central activity area. Typically, they are near the entrance or to one side of the bar. Place a blackboard with chalk next to the phones to keep people from writing on your walls.

The physical layout of the bar itself is covered in the next chapter; however, the location of the servers' stations at the bar can greatly affect service. Ideally, the servers' route to order and pick up drinks should have the least amount of cross traffic. The more space you give the servers to move about, the less chance for spilled drinks. Servers should not have to fight with customers for standing room at the bar. Place their stations at the ends of the bar or provide them with a separate service bar. In a restaurant, a service bar can be away from the main bar or at one end, accessible to the servers through a window.

Ice and liquor need to be close at hand for the bartender. The back of the bar should have a door leading directly to a storage area. This could be a combination liquor room and office or a kitchen with ice machines and refrigerators for beer and wine storage.

The rear area of a bar can include storage, offices, a kitchen, walk-in refrigerators, and employee restrooms. A rear entrance should be used only for deliveries and by management. Employees should always come and go through the front door for control purposes. Keep your back door locked at all times. It is amazing how inventory walks off the shelves and disappears out an unlocked back door.

Seating

Beer bars tend to have an open floor plan with large tables for group seating. A singles bar will want to encourage everyone to keep circulating. This is achieved by means of tiered seating and standing levels, and an arena-style floor plan. The bar or dance floor takes center stage. The different levels keep eyes moving, create little pockets and groupings of people, and make the room more interesting. Include plenty of drink rails near phones, in the restrooms, and throughout stand-up drink areas. Wherever there are drink rails, people will congregate.

Table and chair heights can also be varied. Normal tables are at 30 inches high. When the table height is raised to 42 inches, bar stools can be used instead of chairs (see FIG. 5-12). This arrangement faciliates mingling by allowing

Fig. 5-12. When 42 high-top tables are used in conjunction with bar stools, a person standing next to someone sitting will be at the same eye level. Great for singles bars.

someone standing next to a person seated at a bar stool to maintain eye level contact while talking, which is easier and more comfortable than bending over a regular table. When there is a shortage of seats, several people can stand around and still be a part of the group.

Chairs and cushions can also be used to control the amount of time a person sits comfortably. The larger and softer the cushion, the more relaxed a person will feel. Bar stools with a back and arm- and footrests are the most comfortable. Hard wooden chairs with stiff backs can keep people moving about, if that is your object, and the people are totally unaware of having been manipulated. Avoid wooden chairs with spokes for a backrest. These break easily. Romantic spots can be created with high-backed chairs, booths, curtains, and love seats. Outdoor seating can be used on cool nights with overhead infrared heaters. A wine bar will probably cater to couples, so choose smaller tables. In a lounge environment, choose small tables for drinks and larger ones for food and drink service.

Private booths and small rooms that can be reserved in advance for a fee for 2, 4, 8, or 20 people are an income-generating way to offer an aura of exclusivity to your customers. (See FIG. 5-13.) Private booths can be made private by curtains, or because of their strategic location within the bar. In some cases, they are overhead and have unique views of the interior or exterior environment. Booked for a special occasion, birthday, anniversary, or an office celebration, these spaces can be paid for by the hour or night. When you are not busy, these booths and rooms are closed, thereby visually creating a smaller-sized club.

Fig. 5-13. *A private booth can be reserved and charged for by the hour. At The Shark Club, several private booths ring pool tables, and a small room with two pool tables can also be curtained and booked by the hour.*

Working with local building, health, and fire departments

When acting as your own contractor for all or part of the construction, keep all of your papers and permits in one folder. As you travel from one government office to another applying for licenses or permits, you might be required to show proof that you already have other permits, certificates, or licenses.

The department of building and safety

The building and safety department should be your first stop, as construction can only begin after they have approved your plans. This department's concern is for the safety of the users of any structure, and they will give your building or room an initial occupancy rating, subject to the fire department's final rating. The fire department is concerned with the occupancy rating of a space and can lower, but not raise, the rating given by the building department. This is a key number, especially for busy bars.

Local ordinances specify how occupancy ratings are given, so consult these before designing your space. Submit two complete sets of plans for approval. Plans that are incomplete or have a number of changes will be returned for revision before approval.

The standard for most construction, specifications, and occupancy ratings is the Uniform Building Code. While not the universal standard, it is widely accepted. Local rules obviously will complement this code. Check with the building inspector with whom you will be working for any local variances in the code. The sooner you establish a relationship with an inspector, the more helpful he will be. You want to present yourself eager to abide by every rule. Don't try to avoid or disobey any codes; it can prove very costly when you have to alter everything and rebuild. Further, if an inspector suspects you might be difficult or are cutting corners, obtaining final approval of your finished work can be very difficult.

Plans should be drawn in ink. A floor plan, drawn to scale, should show the building or area to be changed. Show all partitions and exits, doors and windows, steps, ramps, stairways, and elevators, existing, proposed, or scheduled for removal. Identify all equipment and fixtures, tables and chairs, stools, counters, bars, and restrooms. Of particular interest are the heights of the ceilings and the surface treatments of all walls, floors, ceilings, and sinks. The codes indicate clearly what minimum treatments are necessary. The number of restrooms required is based on the number of employees and customers expected. You must comply with regulations to ensure the physically handicapped have access to restrooms, special sink fixtures, sufficient door widths, and ramps to entries, exits, the various levels, and in some cases, work areas of your club.

Ventilation and refrigeration facilities must be adequate and capable of handling the necessary volume of air. The proper hooding of cooking ranges is very important. All food preparation areas need to have hot and cold running water and meet sanitation requirements for sinks and drainboards. The draining of ice machines and sinks and the space used for waste storage also come under close inspection. When approved, signed, and stamped, the department will keep one set of plans on file, and the other will be returned to you. You should keep the plans on the jobsite until construction has been completed. Any revisions must be submitted for approval.

Health department or environmental health service

Depending on the city in which your bar is located, the health department or environmental health service also must approve your plans. Of special interest to the health inspectors are floor and wall surfaces in all rooms where food or beverages are stored or prepared, where utensils are washed, and where garbage is stored. For wall surfaces that come in contact with water, white fiberglass reinforced plastic satisfies most health departments. Fiberglass is easy to clean and inexpensive to purchase and install. Bar tops can be made of numerous materials that wear well and are attractive:

- marble
- copper
- stainless steel
- resin-coated wood
- tile
- laminated plastic

The health department is also concerned with the floor surfaces of restrooms, dressing rooms, locker rooms, and walk-in refrigerators. These areas should be smooth, easy to clean, and impervious to water, grease, and acid. Tile is the most durable and the easiest to clean. Try to choose surfaces that provide traction when wet. Concrete is often used, but it can wear and become pockmarked with age. These chipped areas become fine depositories for mildew and fungus. When considering ceiling treatments, avoid materials that will crumble, possibly dropping on employees and customers or into ice, drinks, and food.

The health department sets lighting requirements for all areas of a building. Lighting requirements vary depending on the activity that takes place. Ventilation systems must be approved and should keep the area reasonably free of heat, steam, smoke, vapors, and other odors so as to provide a comfortable work environment. Provide adequate ventilation over the bar, dance floor, and in the restrooms.

The health department has specific regulations designed to keep flies, rodents, or other vermin out. These might include screening windows, curtains or fly fans at delivery or entry doors, or the proper location of trash containers.

Sinks must be provided near toilets and are recommended in food and bar preparation areas. The health department specifies the exact number of toilets for public and employee use. The need for locker or dressing rooms for employees is also controlled by the number of employees of each sex working each shift.

The health department inspects all equipment and fixtures to ensure that they comply with National Sanitation Foundation (NSF) standards for material, construction, fabrication, and design. This is rarely a problem, as the large manufacturers build to these specifications and place the NSF seal of approval on their equipment.

The installation of this equipment must also meet certain standards. Typically, this involves the proper sealing of pipes and joints. The inspectors will take a close look at all sinks, drainboards, dishwashing equipment, and garbage disposals. Sneeze guards are required when serving food. They protect the food from contamination by customers. In addition, all plumbing, gas, and electrical lines must be concealed as much as possible. All floor drains must be accessible for cleaning and inspection.

All construction, equipment, and fixture installations are subject to on-site inspections during construction. A final inspection and approval is required before opening. After a bar is operating, the health inspector will come by at least once a year and sometimes more often. It is to the bar's advantage to maintain a safe and healthy environment for its patrons and employees. To ensure this, cooperate with your inspectors, follow their advice, and implement your own review and maintenance programs.

Fire department

Present your plans to the fire department at the same time you give them to the building department. Often, the building department requires the fire department's approval before granting its permit. During construction, the fire department will examine the surface treatments to ensure they meet all existing fire codes, paying special attention to any unusual materials used. The inspectors measure the square footage of the bar, egress and access, and the placement of the tables and chairs. These can be arranged in a number of ways, each way requiring a certain amount of area around the tables, depending upon their shape.

Lighting is another important concern of the fire department, particularly the lights at exits. Emergency lights should be installed in case electrical power is interrupted. There are strict codes regarding the use of open-flame candles and their containers. Fire extinguishers and protection devices have to be strategically placed for quick access and will be inspected periodically.

Remember, ensuring the safety of public places is the function of all inspectors. It is their responsibility, as well as that of the proprietor of any business serving the public, to make certain that all requirements have and will be maintained. If a problem is pointed out by an inspector, it should be remedied imme-diately. The adverse publicity and lack of public confidence generated by violations due to negligence can destroy any business. Work with your inspectors from the time you begin to design your bar through construction or remodeling, and continue to do so once you are open for business.

It is advisable to consult your insurance agent during the design stages of your bar for suggestions that might save you money in lower premiums. Perhaps more smoke detectors or better lighting and design of stairs, if planned from the beginning, could eliminate potential accident areas.

The design of your bar is an integral part of your overall marketing strategy. You might have the talent to design your bar entirely by yourself. More likely, you will have a general idea of what you would like, but would benefit from the help of professionals specializing in bar and restaurant design. These consultants will be recommended by manufacturers or suppliers, working for them, or as independent designers and consultants if you so desire. They can be retained to consult on concept development only, or to actually design and oversee the construction and opening of your bar. The supervision of any construction work is a full-time job.

6

Equipment and fixtures

The proper design and placement of the equipment in your bar allows a bartender to work at maximum speed and efficiency. A club's true test of efficiency occurs when customers are five deep at the bar, all the tables are full, and there is a line outside the door. That is when a well-designed bar pays off. The more drinks a bartender can make and sell, the greater your chances of success. Having the right tools available for your bartender can make a tremendous difference in the employee's performance. The areas of the bar that need careful design consideration are the underbar, the backbar, and the remote bar space.

Bar equipment comes in standard sizes, so design your bar accordingly. All of the equipment described can be purchased from bar and restaurant suppliers located in every major city. For larger pieces of equipment, consider leasing instead of buying. With a minimum cash outlay, you can make payments from the bar's income after opening, thereby conserving your start-up money. Generally, equipment is leased for 60 months, with an option to renew or purchase for a fraction of the original cost. Ice machines are usually leased. A 24-hour service agreement can be included in the lease. Soda dispensing guns and glass-washing equipment are often provided at no cost from suppliers when you sign

an agreement to purchase their syrups and detergents. The supplier will also provide free service and repair or replace broken equipment. Before leasing, look at your cash flow, and compare the tax benefits of buying versus leasing. Then choose which method will be best for you.

Leasing is one way for an investor to secure an interest in your bar. The investor buys the equipment and leases to you. Some investors will feel more comfortable having tangible property rather than shares to show for their money. Tax advantages occur for both parties.

The best equipment is manufactured according to standards set by the National Sanitation Foundation. Their seal of approval virtually guarantees a piece of equipment will meet Health Department codes. Stainless steel is highly recommended for any bar equipment. It provides a surface that is easy to clean, durable, and impervious to the ever-present moisture and mildew. All equipment should be purchased new whenever your budget allows. Used equipment can be bought through suppliers, bars going out of business, or at auctions, and should be inspected carefully. Look for cracks in the body of the equipment, along welds and joints. Check to see if replacement parts are available.

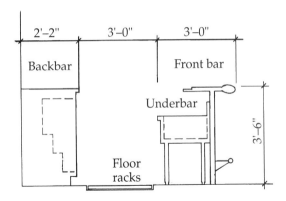

Fig. 6-1. *Profiles and dimensions for an underbar.*
Stephen Moore

The underbar

The underbar is the section of the bar where the bartender makes drinks and cleans glasses.

It is installed against the front of the bar where customers sit or against a server's station. (See FIG. 6-1.) The bartender's workplace consists of a cocktail station, a mixer and blender stand, a sink, a waste receptacle, and a storage area for glasses. Design this working space so the bartender makes the fewest moves. Ideally, everything should be within arm's reach. The height of this equipment is typically 30 inches. The depth will range from 18 to 24 inches and the length will depend on the size of the whole bar. High volume bars should use larger sized equipment as these provide the greatest working area. That means more room at the cocktail station for ice and bottles, and longer drain boards on either side of the sinks to place glasses for cleaning and drying. (See FIG. 6-2.)

Each station should be custom-designed to fit a particular bar's current and future

Fig. 6-2. *Large workstation, ice bin, and pouring mats placed in scupper (gutter) of bar. Notice the bar top extends halfway over the back bottle well. Any more extension and the back bottles would be very difficult to pull out, especially when the height of the bar top is a standard 42 inches from the floor.*

needs. If equipment available from bar and restaurant suppliers fits your needs, then use their designs. If you want optimum capacity and efficiency, however, then it is advisable to work with a manufacturer and develop a station that is best suited to your requirements.

The extra expense will be money well spent. (See FIGS. 6-3, 6-4, and 6-5.)

The following discussion of the design of work stations is based on the needs of a high-volume bar and the fact that the overwhelming majority of bartenders are right-handed.

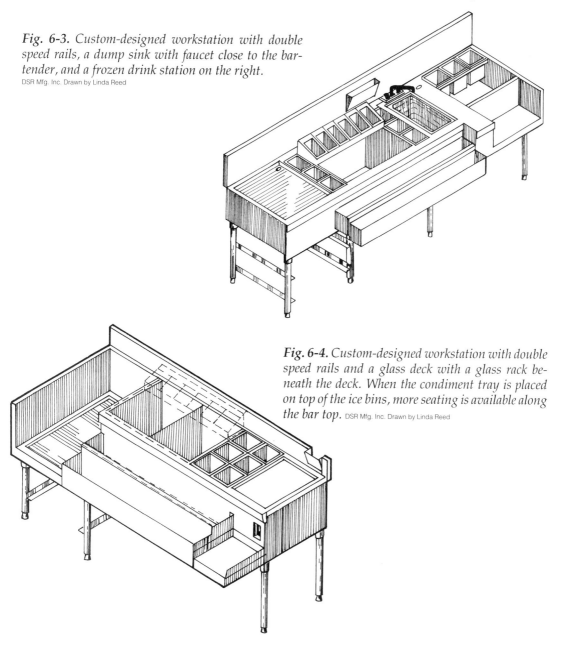

Fig. 6-3. *Custom-designed workstation with double speed rails, a dump sink with faucet close to the bartender, and a frozen drink station on the right.* DSR Mfg. Inc. Drawn by Linda Reed

Fig. 6-4. *Custom-designed workstation with double speed rails and a glass deck with a glass rack beneath the deck. When the condiment tray is placed on top of the ice bins, more seating is available along the bar top.* DSR Mfg. Inc. Drawn by Linda Reed

Fig. 6-5. *Custom-designed workstation built for maximum capacity, compactness, and speed. The soda gun, which is used constantly, is on the left, the wine gun is on the right, and the blenders are on the lower deck.*

The cocktail station

The cocktail station, also referred to as a *jockey box*, has an ice bin, bottle wells, and a speed rack or "rail." You can use an ice bin for both cubed and crushed ice by placing a divider in it. Purchase a cocktail station that has a deep ice bin, 12 to 15 inches, for maximum capacity. The extra-deep ice bin saves bartenders, barbacks, or buspersons from making extra trips to the bar to fill your ice bin. When you are busy, every move you make or every minute you spend waiting for ice and supplies will cost you money. When a bartender does not have a server coming to his station, the garnish tray can be placed at the rear and on top of the ice bin (see FIG. 6-3). That frees extra space on the bar top and provides more seating along the front of the bar.

When a bartender is standing at a typical cocktail station, well liquor bottles are placed to his right in the bottle holders. These are made of rubber or plastic inserts that lift out for cleaning. The bottle wells on the left hold juices and creams that are chilled by the adjacent ice bin. The number of inserts varies with the size of the cocktail station; they can ring the entire ice bin. Twelve inserts, six on either side of the ice bin, is usual (see FIG. 6-2). Eight inserts on either side is even better. When there are fewer than six on either side, a bartender has trouble putting his well liquors close by, and his ice bin starts filling up with juice bottles for lack of space. Health Departments frown on placing containers in an ice bin. In a busy bar, a cluttered or inefficient setup can be very frustrating for a bartender, thus slowing his pace and output. When installing any cocktail station, make sure there is enough room to lift the rear bottles completely out of their wells. The rear wells are often beneath the bar top. To avoid problems, allow at least 12 inches of clearance between the top of the bottle well and the bottom of the bar top, or place the cocktail station a few inches away from the front bar wall rather than flush against it. There are slanted stations that solve this problem by tilting the entire box at a 15–30 degree angle. These are usually custom-made. The slanted design keeps the bartender from bending over as he must at the standard cocktail station.

Directly above the cocktail station and attached to the end of the bar top are liquor, wine, and soda guns. Usually, the soda gun is placed to the left, so a bartender can have a liquor bottle in his right hand and the soda gun in his left (see FIGS. 6-2 and 6-5). By using both hands to mix drinks, the bartender works at top speed. A liquor gun, if used, would be placed on the right side. The wine gun can be placed on either side, as it is used less frequently. The placing of these guns is critical. To ensure speed in usage, make sure the gun lines do not interfere with the bottles being pulled out of the wells.

All soda guns require mixing of syrup and carbonation. This is done either underneath the bar or away from the bar in a back room with lines extending to the cold plate underneath the ice bin. Carbon dioxide lines run from a CO_2 tank to a carbonator beneath the bar. All lines pass through a cold plate resting beneath the ice bin, where they are chilled.

In the past, cold plates were placed at the bottom of the ice bin. When the syrup passed through the cold plate before it reached the gun, it was chilled. If the ice is not melted from the bin upon the bar's closing and the cold plate is not lifted up and wiped clean, fungus develops on the bottom of the ice bin and cold plate. Health Departments object to fungus and molds. As a result, many Health Departments are now requiring a sealed cold plate that is attached to the bottom of the ice bin.

With the cold plate positioned underneath the ice bin, every soda line can circulate within the plate. This arrangement is called the *fast-flow cold plate*. Up to 12 lines can be chilled in this system; therefore, wine, beer, and all of the sodas and mixes can be run through the plate. The cold plate can be eliminated by running a refrigerant line around the soda lines in a special insulated conduit that travels from the tanks to the gun. This is state-of-the-art technology and costs more to install and maintain. Drink quality is improved and more consistent with the chilled lines, however.

Seven or eight button soda guns are available. The lines are used for cola, 7-Up, ginger ale, soda water, tonic, Collins or sweet and sour mix, and plain water. (See FIG. 6-6.) You can buy whatever brands you please to fill your lines. Inside the gun, the syrup is properly mixed with the carbonation. This type of system is known as a *post mix system*.

Some bars use only bottled sodas. Even if bought by the case, it is an expensive way to go, but the rationale is that the drinks taste better, because the carbonation lasts longer and the bottles can be chilled. The quality of bottled sodas is definitely superior to any post mix system. But the use of bottles slows a bartender's speed and requires more storage space than the post mix system. When you run a first-class bar, use bottled sodas for the ultimate in taste and quality.

Attached to the cocktail station is a *speed rack*. It may be permanently spotwelded or hung by screws so it can be removed for cleaning. In the speed rack, a bartender will place additional frequently used liquor bottles. Speed racks should be as long as the cocktail station. They can also be doubled up, with one placed slightly below the other and attached (see FIG. 6-5). These double speed racks should

Fig. 6-6. An eight-button soda gun in its proper position allows the bartender easy access to the ice bin. This workstation is a small one for a service bar that does not do a lot of volume.

only be positioned in places accessible to the bartender. A long stretch can be extremely tiring. The bartender has to reach over the racks, ice bin, and bar top to reach a customer.

If space allows, attach additional speed racks to walls, beer boxes, or sinks that are adjacent to the work station. When space limits the size of the cocktail station, and thus the number of bottle wells, consider using *insulated speed racks* . All or part of the speed rack is insulated and packed with crushed ice. The juice or mix bottles are placed in the ice. A perforated bottom lets the water drain out.

If the standard speed racks are attached to the front of the ice bin, line each with a towel. The towels will absorb the water from the melting ice that falls into the racks and drips on your bartenders' feet. Bartenders should not have to endure wet feet each shift. Rinse and hang the towels to dry at the end of each day.

The mixer station

Right next to the cocktail station, or built into it, is the blender or mixer station. This unit is usually on the bartender's right. It holds mixers and blenders on the lower shelf. A mixer is used instead of hand-shaking drinks and is especially useful when making cream drinks. It is the same machine that makes malts in ice cream shops. If you want to sell alcoholic ice cream drinks as specialty items, this is the gadget to have.

If space is critical, buy the blender and

skip the mixer, because the blender is the real workhorse for a bartender. Get the strongest and heaviest-duty commercial machine you can find. These blenders take considerable abuse. The best machines will last for years without repairs. They crunch ice cubes and make frozen Daiquiris and Margaritas in short order. Your typical blender holds one liter. If you plan to specialize in frozen drinks (without using a frozen drink machine) then buy the one-gallon size blender.

Just above the blender shelf is another shelf. A bartender usually places small items used for making drinks, such as a bottle of Bitters, salt, sugar, nutmeg, a hand-mixing glass and strainer or even a pot of coffee on a hot plate.

A variation of the mixer station is the *frozen drink station*, which combines a mixer station and a separate ice bin for crushed ice. This ice bin takes the place of the upper shelf of a normal mixer station. (Refer back to FIG. 6-3.)

The ice cream station

Because of an increased demand in ice cream based drinks, many bars are including an *ice cream station* in the underbar. It consists of a storage bin for one or two five-gallon containers of ice cream and a dipper well with a faucet.

The dump sink

Many designers of cocktail stations also place a *dump sink* either between the cocktail station and the mixer station, or in lieu of the upper shelf of the mixer station. (Refer back to FIG. 6-5, and note the dump sink with faucet in the upper right corner of the work station.) That saves steps for the bartender when the only other sink might be several feet away. This sink is used constantly to rinse out blender and mixing canisters. Sometimes a *melt-down hose* or *fill faucet* is added as part of the sink. This flexible and retractable hose is directly connected to the hot water heater and is used to melt the ice bins very quickly, especially when a glass breaks in the ice.

The server's station

Directly facing the bartender's work station is the *server's station*. Beneath the bar top is a shelf for supplies and directly underneath it is a trash bin. The server needs an area to place her tray, put together her drink orders, and store her checks and tabs. An adding machine, credit card imprinter, and authorization machine may also be in this space. A server's station placed at the end of the bar allows for uninterrupted seating across the front bar. It also provides easy access for the servers, who would normally have to fight with customers into and out of the station if it were placed in the middle.

If the server's station is at the front of the bar, metal bars or a wooden partition can be attached to the bar to physically separate the work area from customer seating. The top of the bar usually holds a garnish tray, containers for straws and napkins, and a receptacle for drink tickets. (See FIG. 6-7.)

Some bars are utilizing a pass-through ice bin for the server. This is an extension of the bartender's ice bin that goes through the bar's vertical wall. A server ices all of her glasses, and the bartender only pours the liquor. That greatly speeds up an operation that does a large volume of business.

On either side of the bartender's work station are the *draft beer* and *house wine* faucets. The wine is run using nitrogen to push it through the lines. Beer is best pushed with CO_2. These faucets can be located anywhere in the bar, but the closer they are to the bartender, the easier his job.

Draft beer kegs can be stored in remote refrigerators or in a tap box. A *tap box* or direct draw beer dispenser is a small refrigerated container that holds one to three kegs. CO_2 lines must enter the box. The faucet and tap

Fig. 6-7. Server station with all supplies stocked.

extend through the bar top into the box. It is a compact system, less expensive than cooling kegs in a walk-in refrigerator. The placement of these boxes must take into consideration the need to change the kegs, however, which are heavy and awkward to move. Naturally, a keg will run out in the middle of your busiest time. Make sure there is enough space to maneuver a keg without disrupting the flow of business. (See FIG. 6-8.)

The glass washing/storage station

To the left or right of the cocktail station is the *glass washing station*. This has three or four sink compartments with drainboards on either side. Dirty glasses are placed at one end. Before washing in a four-sink unit, the ice, garnishes, and straws are removed by dumping

them into a sink only used for this purpose. This dump sink has a strainer in the bottom to let the ice melt through and prevents the garnishes and straws from passing into the drain. When full, the strainer is lifted out and emptied. With only three sinks, a separate dumping pan is placed between the drainboard and the backsplash. Another solution to the dump problem is to place a funnel with a strainer on top of one of the stoppers of the sinks. The drain line beneath glass washing equipment should be straight with no "S" or "J" bends that clog and back-up.

In the first sink of this unit is a glass washer. This unit is submerged in hot water with a cleaning solution added by hand or from a faucet dispensing system. The glasses are cleaned as they are rubbed against the bristle brushes. In motorized units, the brushes

Fig. 6-8. Backbar beer dispensers with direct draw kegs in refrigerators below. Kold-Draft

spin when the machine is turned on. The motorized versions are quick and efficient. These units are usually leased from the same company that supplies the cleaning and sanitizing chemicals for the sinks. After cleaning, a glass is passed through the rinse water in the second sink. Then it is submerged and rinsed in the third sink, which contains a sanitizer. The glass is then placed on the corrugated drainboard to dry. This three-part cleaning cycle is the most sanitary way to clean glasses.

Glasses can also be washed in an area away from the bar, in a kitchen or storage area, although that may present logistical problems, because they have to be moved back and forth. In a busy bar, all glasses are constantly in use. If they are not washed right at the bar, you may need to have a larger supply in order to keep up with the demand.

Automatic glass washing units no larger than a home dishwasher are also available. These are installed in the underbar or in a back area. (See FIG. 6-9.) Compact and fast, they eliminate the three-sink system. Some Health Departments will require a three-sink system as a backup if the glass washer fails. When the majority of glasses are washed away from the bar, the use of an automatic system is even more beneficial.

Attached to the front of the drainboards are rings or bars to hold towels. The area underneath the drainboards is always used for storage, trash bins, or as a place to put the compressor that runs the carbonation and soda guns. Some glass washing units even come equipped with a small refrigerator or a special insulated compartment to hold ice as a back-up.

The storage of glassware needs careful consideration during planning stages. The bartender needs to have enough glasses at his disposal to get him through a busy night. The placement of the sinks and drainboards next to a bartender's pouring station allows glasses to be stored and to dry at the end of the drain-

Fig. 6-9. *Automatic glass-washing unit at Victoria Station's service bar. The open front liquor storage cabinets are an excellent way for customers to see the types of liquor offered.*

boards. When kept right next to his well, the glasses are within easy reach. If the washing area is not close by, then shelves or tops of liquor storage cabinets next to the cocktail station can be used.

Health codes demand that glasses dry on surfaces that provide air circulation. That means a corrugated surface. Towels do not meet health codes because when a glass is inverted on a towel, no air circulates, allowing bacteria to grow. Plastic netting is commonly used but does allow mildew to grow, and it is hard to keep clean. Check with your Health Department to see if they permit its usage. Special racks can be built to hold trays of glasses. Overhead racks are a good alternative for stemmed or footed glassware. (See FIG. 6-10.) These racks

can be hung directly over the bar or above the bartender's head. Build these racks with enough room between the rows so the glasses in one row do not touch the glasses in the next row. This eliminates breakage that frequently occurs when the glasses are removed.

The other alternative is to purchase a cocktail station that has a glass deck attached as an integral component. The decks should be on the bartender's left. They can be recessed to allow stacking of a large number of glasses. Beneath this deck are rack slides to store additional glasses on trays or in glass bins used with automatic glass washing equipment. (Refer back to FIG. 6-4.) When this glass deck is combined with an overhead rack to store stemware, the cocktail station's efficiency is greatly increased.

Fig. 6-10. A small bar with great glass storage overhead, on the bar, and on the shelves at the backbar.

The overbar

The overbar area can be built to house storage cabinets for backup liquor, wine bottles, supplies, or shelves holding open liquor bottles a bartender will use to pour from. That frees up the backbar for more refrigerators and makes effective use of the total volume of space, particularly when floor space is at a premium. Add locks to the doors of the cabinets for securing the bottles when the bar is not in use and when you are closed (see FIG. 6-11). Build these cabinets with glass or open fronts. (Refer back to FIG. 6-9.) Displaying liquor, beer, wine, and champagne bottles makes your customers aware of what you have in stock.

The backbar

The backbar area can be used for liquor bottle displays, the cash register, refrigerators, glass and liquor storage, beer and wine taps, and other drink machines. A brilliant use of the backbar area as a display area is shown in FIG. 6-12. Here the area underneath the backbar top is open and filled with ice to show and chill bottled beers, wines, champagnes, wine and martini glasses and beer mugs.

Backbar displays

Liquor bottles are usually on shelves, on top of refrigerators, or on backbar storage cabinets. (See FIGS. 6-13 and 6-14.) Customers sitting at or approaching the bar can see which brands are for sale. Displaying several bottles grouped together (refer to FIG. 3-2) makes your eye immediately notice the similarities and the cleanness of the display. The same technique is used when part of the bar faces the exterior. (See FIG. 6-15.) By displaying your wines, beers, mineral waters and liquors in such an at-

Fig. 6-11. Locking overhead cabinets act as a backbar when your bar is the island type. Stratton's, Encino, California

Fig. 6-12. Backbar area with creative and effective chilled bottle and glass display uses space beneath the top. Marix, Encino, California

Fig. 6-13. Interesting use of backbar space with a mirror in the arch. Mirrors appear to deepen and expand space. The Parkway Grill, Pasadena, California

tractive manner, you give passersby and waiting customers a chance to leisurely browse through your inventory. The alternative is the huge backbar display seen in FIG. 6-16. Both methods have their place.

Backbar refrigerators

Backbar refrigerators can be self-contained units with locking doors. They come in all sizes and lengths and are used to store bottled beer, wine, champagne, juice, cream, garnishes, and other items. By purchasing clear glass doors for your backbar refrigerators, you again have the opportunity to display what you are selling. (See FIGS. 6-17, 6-18, and 6-19.) Some of the shelves in the refrigerators may hold beer and wine glasses or a separate glass chiller can be part of the underbar or backbar. If the backbar area lacks space, a beer box can

Fig. 6-14. Attractive backbar display. Note the use of wood cabinets, marble arm rest at bar, and Tiffany lamps. Henry Africa, San Francisco, California

Fig. 6-15. Backbar doubles as exterior display at the Daily Grill in Encino, California. (Refer to FIG. 3-4 to see their backbar wine display.)

Fig. 6-16. *An impressive and massive backbar.* The Elephant Bar, Santa Barbara, California

Fig. 6-17. *Backbar refrigerator with see-through glass doors.*

Fig. 6-18. *Lower backbar refrigerators with glass doors and locks. A beautiful way to let customers browse.*

Fig. 6-19. Bar top incorporates a clear glass display of fine wines and champagnes.

be used as the bar refrigerator. It opens from the top and the bottles are stacked on their sides inside. There is a separate space for the other chilled items.

Beverage machines

Most places have an automatic coffee brewing machine on the backbar. Larger bars may keep this in an area away from the bar. These machines require a connection to the cold water supply. They can have multiple burners to hold several pots of coffee or hot water. The coffee is available in a variety of blends, packaged in the exact amount necessary to make a perfect pot. But if you really want to impress your customers, buy your own coffee beans and grind them fresh daily. Make sure they are aware of your effort or it could be a waste of time.

In addition, you may want to have an espresso machine. They add a certain touch of

Fig. 6-20. Cash register with four keys for separating sales, a standard in bars for years.

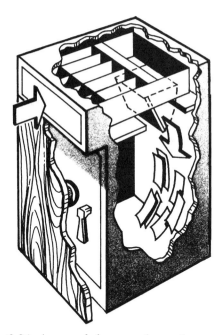

Fig. 6-21. A concealed money-drop safe. Korden, Inc.

class to a bar and can be purchased in a wide assortment of metal finishes. (Refer to FIG. 3-4 to see espresso machine and coffee bean grinder.) Espresso machines can make a strong espresso drink, cappuccino, and even hot chocolate.

If you choose to have frozen drinks as a specialty item, consider buying or leasing a frozen beverage machine. Five gallons of Strawberry Daiquiris or Piña Coladas can be put in the machine and soft frozen very quickly. A glass is placed under its tap and out comes the slushy mixture. At the end of every night, the remaining drink mix is stored for reuse, and the machine is emptied and cleaned.

Cash register

The cash register needs to be in an area visible to the customers at the bar. Unless the front bar top has plenty of room, putting it there can take up valuable customer seating and counter space. Usually, the register is on the backbar.

Registers can be simple machines or computers tied to central terminals. No matter how complex, they all do the same things. They record and add whatever is rung. The difference is that the computer registers can keep track of each type of drink sold, act as a time clock, and even dispense liquor.

Computer registers may have numerous keys with preset prices for specific drinks or liquors. Preset keys save time and money. A register such as the one in FIG. 6-20 has four keys for ringing sales and comes with one or more cash drawers. A multidrawer register lets each bartender account for his own bank. The more hands in each drawer changing money, the greater the possibility for mistakes. Registers with special money drops into locked boxes or concealed safes can also be obtained for greater cash security. (See FIG. 6-21.)

Some computer systems have terminals away from the bar where a server can place drink orders that will print out at the bar's terminal. Drinks are already prepared by the time the server arrives to pick them up, a very speedy system for a large club. Each order can be assigned to a specific table and reorders billed to that table's check. These systems are particularly useful in a restaurant and bar operation.

The cost of any register goes up with the number of different operations it can perform. Sales volume, the number of controls, and the accounting records you want your system to keep all should be considered before you buy a register. A simple machine could be all you need for a small bar, while the computer models are more appropriate for a large establishment.

Point of sale (POS) information is becoming more affordable for even a small operation. The information available is particularly useful in allowing an operator to judge which products are selling, when they are selling, who is selling these items, and the prices being charged. Each employee can be monitered for sales and cost percentages. Electronic cash registers (ECR) can also provide increased security by only allowing a particular key to activate a certain cash drawer or only perform certain functions. A void key should be only in the hands of a manager, whereas the bartenders can order, ring up, and dispense. Some registers will allow the drawer to open only after the drink has been rung up on a ticket. If your register is tied to a liquor dispensing system, only after the method of payment is entered into the machine will the drink be dispensed.

Many ECRs will permit only a specific key or security ID number access to the program to change prices. Most ECRs will allow different prices for the same drinks according to the time of day. An added advantage that is extremely useful is the magnetic stripe reader, which scans credit cards and automatically dials the bank's telephone number for approval codes. All information is printed on the sales ticket or voucher.

Reports are generated from the machine in a "Z" printout, or the data can be integrated with your own software accounting program. Reports are also available mid-shift to assist you in evaluating your operations. The more capable the machines, the greater the cost. If you can use the reports, the information will lead to leaner labor costs by:

- Adjusting scheduling times for peak sales.
- Reducing inventories that tie up cash.
- Noticing trends in sales.
- Monitoring liquor pouring percentages to maximize profits.

Computers and desktop publishing

By purchasing a computer for your bar, you will enable yourself to generate reports, do your accounting, keep track of your inventory, payroll, and notice trends much easier than doing the work by hand. Build the price of a good computer system with plenty of memory in its hard drive, and a laser printer into your overall budget. It will be money well spent. With your laser printer and the appropriate software, you can print up or at least create the graphics necessary for many of your printing needs: advertisements, promotional flyers, daily menus, calendars, drink menus, and drink specials.

Remote equipment

A bar may have an area or room behind the bar for the ice machine, post mix soda system, and a walk-in refrigerator. You'll need additional ventilation and air exchange systems for these rooms due to the heat buildup from these machines. Check with your local building department for requirements.

An ice machine needs to produce enough ice for the busiest night. It is easy to figure your ice needs. Take your occupancy level or average customer count, and multiply by three pounds of ice per person. A bar with a 100-person occupancy level should buy an ice machine with a 300-pound capacity. Large operations often have more than one machine. One produces cubes and the other flaked ice. The flaked ice machine is smaller in capacity than the cuber, and this ice is used only for frozen drinks or chilling wine bottles and glasses. Flaked ice makes a highball too watery. Some machines produce both.

You will also want to consider the type of cubes the machine produces. The shape of the ice affects how the glass is filled, how much of it is filled, and how easy it is to pour liquor into it. Certain large shapes of ice cause splashing and waste liquor. The ¾-inch cube or cubelet is the most popular size, with or without holes. Solid cubes are your best bet, as holes will fill with liquid, thereby increasing the amount of liquor and mixes you pour. Pillow-shaped ice cubes or half-circle cubes are the easiest to scoop; and they stick together less because of their slippery edges. In some machines, the grid that makes the ice can be changed to alter the shape and size of the cubes. Some compact units are designed to fit into the underbar and be used in combination with another ice maker for all of a bar's ice needs. A small ice crusher can fit within your bartender's work area. It is ideal for making special drinks requiring flaked ice where you do not have the space for a large machine.

All bars need some type of refrigeration. Just how much depends on the size of your operation. You will be storing beer kegs, wine, bottled beer, cases of fruit for garnishes, juices, and other perishable items in your walk-in refrigerator. Walk-ins should be purchased from a local refrigeration manufacturer or distributor. They will be familiar with local health and building codes and are available for quick service. When using draft beer and wine guns, placing the walk-in cooler directly behind the backbar can shorten the lines running to the bar and cut down on installation problems and costs. Free-standing refrigerators or a beer cooler can be purchased if a walk-in is not needed.

In larger clubs, this area behind the bar may also include a trash compactor and a room that holds the automatic liquor dispensing system. (See FIG. 6-22.) Automatic liquor dispensing systems come in two forms. In the first, liquor is dispensed by a liquor gun with 12 to 18 buttons, each for a different type of liquor. In a more complicated computer controlled system, a faucet dispenses the liquor. Each system needs a separate room to house

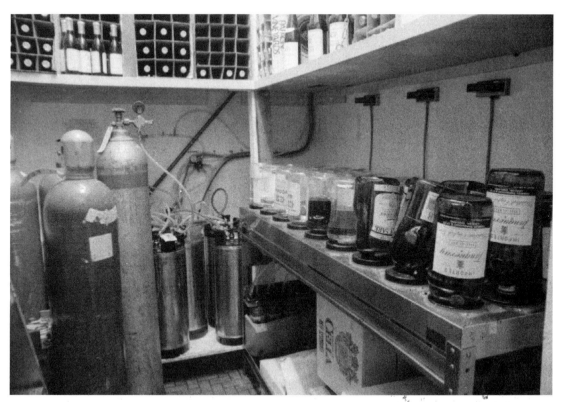

Fig. 6-22. Automatic liquor dispensing system.

the bottles. Each bottle is placed upside down on a rack or table with a line running to the gun or faucet. A pump pushes the liquor. Each system is calibrated to measure an exact amount of liquor for each drink. This calibration should be checked frequently for accuracy. The "shot" can be changed at any time (i.e., from a one-ounce pour to a one-and- one-eighth-ounce pour).

Liquor costs are brought down through buying in larger quantities, such as 1.75 liters, and by strictly controlling your pouring. A liquor gun is recommended for high-volume and service bars, while the computer system works best for hotels and bars in large restaurants. Using an automatic dispensing system destroys the human element and the tradition of the bartender physically pouring your drink, and customers often feel they are being cheated out of a full shot. Customers like to see which bottle is being poured. However, it is difficult for a person to compete with the accuracy of an automatic dispensing system. The choice of methods is a function of how you want your bar perceived. Liquor control systems are particularly valuable for the cost-conscious owner.

Construction reminders

The following items should be checked carefully when making plans to build a bar from the ground up:

- Place chase pipes (6"–8" diameter) underneath bar floors for beer draught and soda lines. These pipes hold the plastic lines that transfer these liquids from a storage room to the bar. If you forget these you will have to find room for them in a crowded underbar.

- Make sure electrical plugs fit above the height of the underbar equipment to be installed.

- Attach strip plugs underneath the bartop. Plug in Christmas light bulb fixtures (night-lights for kids) to help illuminate the ice bin, coffeemakers, and other items difficult to light.

- Have a separate electrical circuit for your cash registers and bar refrigerators. Your registers will not be subject to power failures due to overloads from other areas of your bar.

- Place floor drains underneath or close to jockey boxes. Reaching drains in the middle of a back bar will require breaking up the floor to run your drain pipes flush with the floor. This is costly and aggregates mold problems around drains and complicates proper equipment placement.

- Make sure you have a small cold water line in place for your coffee, espresso, and bar ice machines.

- Provide a hot and cold water faucet for blender stations, allowing bartenders to wash out their blenders quickly.

- Plan to provide space for a small water heater for a satellite or service bar.

- Plan space for trash cans behind your bars.

- Underneath each jockey box you'll need a "T" off the main cold water line for water for your CO_2 compressor and an electrical outlet right where each compressor will be plugged in. The compressor only has a 2½" cord.

- In addition, place a ½" gate valve where your chase line conduit comes into the bar. This saves running lines all over the bar just to get to your carbonator.

- Plan on one carbonator for every two bar stations, if there are more than two stations in one bar. If one carbonator stops working on a busy night, you'll have the other carbonator and its station working.

- For best results, keep carbonators dry (sometimes required by inspectors to be 6" off the floor). Carbonators do not have to be underneath the underbars, and can be stored where syrups are, away from the bar area. They do need a water and power source closeby.

- Carbonators should be unplugged whenever the water is being turned off. The carbonator has a float valve, similar to those in toilets, and when the water level drops and the carbonator kicks in, the pump will burn out due to a lack of water.

- Plan for storage, walk-in refrigerators, glassware and bottle storage at the bars.

- Allow a minimum of 44" clearance between the back bar and the front bar.

- Provide a clear 36" access space to each bar area to meet disabled and handicapped employment codes.

Glassware

Glassware is fragile equipment that must be replaced often. You will be amazed at how many glasses disappear or are broken each week. The style of glasses chosen should be consistent with your overall concept. Glasses determine the strength of your drinks because their size affects the amount of liquor and mix poured. Glasses also reflect your merchandising skills. Fancy glasses can upgrade the image of a drink. Certain glasses can also look and feel heavier, thus giving the illusion of a larger drink. Some glasses have flared inner bowls that appear to hold more than they actually do.

Space for storage behind the bar can also affect your choice of glassware. Some bar owners choose one type of glass to be used for all drinks. That is only recommended in rare instances where the ambience of the bar is geared to the bizarre. Most bars have a variety of glass sizes. Recommended glass sizes for drinks are in TABLE 6-1. One glass can be used for several types of drinks. For example, sours, blended cream drinks, Daiquiris, and Margaritas can all be served in a wine glass.

Table 6-1. Recommended Glass Sizes.

Glass	Size (Oz.)	Stocked at Bar*
Beer	10–12	36
Brandy snifter	12	12
Bucket/double old-fashioned	15	36
Champagne	5½	12
Cocktail/martini	4½	12
Coffee mug	9	12
Collins/soft drinks	10–12	36
Chimney/cooler	16	36
Cordial	1	12
Highball	8–10	72
Hurricane/tulip	14–22	24
Margarita	5½	24
Old-fashioned	7–8	48
Rocks	6–7	48
Sherry	3	12
Shot	1½	12
Sour	4½	12
Wine	8-9	24

* The number recommended is for stock ready-to-use at the bar to serve 50–75 people during a busy two-hour period. You might decide to have some glasses used for more than one type of drink. Adjust your stock accordingly.

Glassware comes in three basic styles with varying degrees of quality in each. Tumblers are glasses with no stem or foot. Footed glassware has a base with a short bubble or design leading to the bowl of the glass. Stemware has a long stem that attaches to the bowl. You will probably select some of each style. Certain drinks de-

Fig. 6-23. *Footed and tumbler glassware, stemware, and specialty glassware.* Libbey Glass

mand certain glasses. Wine, champagne, and martinis are served in stemware. A brandy snifter is always footed. Beer can be served in a variety of glasses and mugs. (See FIG. 6-23.)

Inexpensive glassware breaks and chips easily and may cut a customer or employee. A chipped or cracked glass should be discarded immediately. The heavier and more expensive glasses wear better, because they are heat-treated, have a nice weight and feel to them, and rarely break, even when dropped.

A bartender's tools of the trade

A bartender uses many tools to mix and pour drinks properly. Most are made of plastic or stainless steel for long wear. Each work station should have a complete set of these tools with backups available if an item is lost or broken.

The first essential items are ice scoops. Two sizes are used. A large scoop saves time when filling large containers with ice for transfer to the bar. Smaller scoops kept in the bartender's ice bin are used to put ice in the glasses. Hands should never be used for this purpose. An ice pick is used to break up chunks of ice and also to prepare garnishes.

A pouring mat is placed in the scupper (gutter) or on top of the bar. (Refer back to FIG. 6-2 and see FIG. 6-24.) This mat collects excess liquid that may spill when the bartender mixes drinks. It can also hold a shot glass or strainer at one end. It is made of rubber or plastic and easily cleaned. A stainless steel perforated insert can also be used. At the end of the scupper is a drain where excess liquid flows (see FIG. 6-25.)

Fig. 6-24. Stainless steel perforated pouring mat.

Fig. 6-25. Perforated pouring mat drains excess liquid.

Shot glasses or jiggers are used to measure liquor before it is poured into the glass. These come in a range of standard sizes from ½ to 2 ounces, in ⅛-ounce increments. Jiggers are made of stainless steel and have two different-sized cups connected at the middle. (See FIG. 6-26.) Shot glasses have lines placed around them indicating the measured amount. These double as serving glasses when a liquor is ordered straight up or neat.

Pour spouts are placed in liquor bottles when they are opened. The pourers help to control the liquor flow by forming a steady stream. The smaller the pour spout, the slower it pours. For purposes of control, different sizes can be placed on different bottles. (See FIG. 6-27.) The well liquors might have speed pourers, the backbar liquors medium pourers, and certain liqueurs slow pourers. The stainless steel pourers have plastic or real corks. The real corks wear out and must be replaced periodically. Plastic pourers come in several colors, allowing coding of bottles. Also available are even-measured pour spouts that only release an exact quantity of liquid.

Pour spouts need to be cleaned regularly, at least once a week to eliminate sugar build-up. Fruit flies are often attracted to sweet liqueurs and can end up in a patron's drink. Pourers with fruit fly traps should be used if you have a problem. Some health departments require their use.

There are also plastic containers with removable colored-pour spouts that are used for juices and other mixes. (See FIG. 6-28.) The necks can be removed and a colored cap screwed in place for storage in a refrigerator. These are easy to clean. Buy the ones with the textured necks that provide a good grip when a bartender's hands are wet.

A mixing glass, strainer, and metal hand-shaker are used to mix certain cocktails. The

Fig. 6-26. Shot glasses and jiggers.

Fig. 6-27. *Different pour spouts. From left to right: medium, fast, slow, and premeasured.*

Fig. 6-29. *Mixing container and strainer. When used together, drinks can be chilled or blended by hand.*

Fig. 6-28. *Juice containers with pour spouts and caps.*

mixing glass is a sturdy, thick, clear glass used for hand-stirring and chilling Martinis, Kamakazis, Manhattans, and other mixed drinks. Drinks are stirred with the barspoon. A metal strainer placed over the rim of the glass keeps ice and fruit from going into the serving glass when the liquid is poured. Before the magic of whirling blenders, all drinks were hand-shaken. Some bartenders prefer to mix drinks the old way, and carry on this tradition by placing the metal hand-shaker over the mixing glass to hand-shake sours and cream drinks. (See FIG. 6-29.)

Another carryover from the old days is a wooden muddler. This is used to crush a sugar cube with bitters for an Old-Fashioned. Because granulated sugar is widely available, this tool is not an absolute necessity.

Once drinks are made, they are gar-

nished. Garnishes are cut on a small plastic cutting board rather than a wooden one, as wood surfaces collect mildew, splinter, and are not recommended by Health Departments. A sharp knife and an ice pick are used to cut and slice fruit. (See FIG. 6-30.) A small pair of tongs is helpful for retrieving olives and onions from jars. These condiments and garnishes are placed in a plastic condiment tray with removable sections. This fruit tray has a hinged lid to keep moisture in and protect the contents. In addition, holders for napkins,

Fig. 6-30. *Cutting board with examples of how to cut garnishes.*

straws, and fruit picks are placed next to the garnish tray on the bar at the servers' and bartender's station. A ticket holder is a handy item.(See FIG. 6-31.)

Fig. 6-31. Ticket holder.

Other items that come in handy and should be kept behind the bar are several wine openers and corkscrews. (See FIG. 6-32.) Some are pocket-sized and include a knife for cutting the bottle's seal, a lever that rests on the lip of the bottle, and the corkscrew. The larger version is a cork remover. Its arms rise 180 degrees as the screw turns into the cork. When the arms are pushed down, the cork rises out of the bottle. Avoid buying any corkscrews that do not use some kind of leverage to help extract the cork as these are often difficult to use. Wine and champagne ice buckets, whether on a stand or on the table, add to a customer's enjoyment of a nice bottle of wine or champagne.

A hand can opener, a large "church key," and several beer bottle openers, both the hand-held and mounted kind, are frequently used. A funnel is used to transfer mixes from one container to another.

Serving trays should have cork surfaces providing some traction for glasses to keep them from sliding. Some trays come with a

Fig. 6-32. The Screwpull, a superb and unique wine cork extractor is simple to use and requires no screwing and turning—just two moves of the upper handle and the cork is out.

cash caddy. This is a place for servers to organize and keep their money. Tip trays can be used when checks or change are presented.

Ashtrays should be placed throughout the bar. Some bar owners buy larger ones on the belief that they will not disappear. Others use the standard small black glass ashtray. Have plenty on hand, as they constantly break and mysteriously disappear.

A first-aid kit is essential for any bar and should be readily accessible to all employees. A small kit should include several sizes of band-aids, butterfly closures, a couple of rolls of adhesive tape, scissors, tweezers, sterile gauze pads, an elastic bandage, an antiseptic cream, solution, or swabs, antibiotic ointment, ammonia inhalants, and a manual on first-aid and emergency procedures. Visual posters that demonstrate the Heimlich maneuver to aid choking victims, and a chart that shows respiratory and circulatory emergency procedures are essential.

You should have at least one safe. Two is ideal, each in a separate location. Safes are rated according to their resistance to fire and burglary. The exact type of safe you require depends on the amount of money stored in it and the requirements of your insurance. You should also consider a safe that will store your computer disks and records and prevent them from melting in the event of a fire.

A small fire extinguisher should be placed in a convenient place behind every bar.

An important detail of the bar is the floor mat the bartender walks on. It should be a rubber or plastic material that can be easily removed for cleaning. It acts as a cushion and helps to relieve the strain on the bartender's legs and back.

Care should be taken with each purchase of equipment for the bar to ensure its quality and durability. The bar's equipment has to withstand a tremendous amount of use. Buy quality merchandise the first time; it will last longer. Install this equipment correctly, and your investment will pay for itself over and over again. Use the checklist in TABLE 6-2 to aid you in purchasing equipment and supplies.

Table 6-2. Opening Bar Equipment and Supplies Checklist.

Adding machine
Ashtrays
Backbar refrigerator
Barspoon
Beer bottle opener
Beer draught system
Beer refrigerators
Blenders
Buckets for transferring ice
Can opener
Cash registers
Checks & check holders
Cocktail station
Coffee, cream & filters
Coffee maker & pots
Condiment/garnish trays
Condiments
Credit card imprinter & vouchers
Detergents and cleaners
Dustpan with long handle
Espresso machine and condiments
Fire extinguishers

Frozen drink station
First-aid kit
Floor mats
Frozen drink machine
Frozen drink station
Fruit
Fruit juicer
Funnel
Glassware
Glass washing system
Glassware storage—racks or trays
Hand washing sinks
Ice buckets & stands for wine/champagne service
Ice cream station
Ice machine
Ice pick
Ice scoops
Knives
Liquor, beer, wine
Liquor, wine, or soda guns
Matches—printed with logo
Mixer & blender station
Mixing glasses & cans with strainer
Mixes and fruit juices
Mop & broom
Paper napkins—printed with logo
Pens & pencils
Plastic juice containers
Plastic netting
Plastic swords & picks
Plastic trash cans & liners
Pouring mats
Pour spouts
Safes
Salt & sugar containers
Salt shakers for spices
Scratch pads
Serving trays
Soda mixing system
Spices & flavoring—cinnamon, chocolate, nutmeg
Straw & napkin holders
Straws
Sweetners
Tongs for garnishes
Towels
Trash compactor
Waste/dump sinks
Wine opener & corkscrew
Wooden muddler

7

How to obtain financing

After you have scouted locations, checked out the competition, and have a concrete concept for your bar, you may wonder where all the money will come from. If you are personally blessed with all the funds necessary to begin, you are lucky. Most prospective bar owners need additional funds for start-up costs to add to their working capital, for expansion, or for the purchase of new equipment. You can solve your financial problem by bringing in partners in exchange for a percentage of the profits, or borrowing funds from a lending institution. Whether the financing is short-term or long-term depends on what the money will be used for.

Preparing a business plan

The first step to securing any outside money is to prepare a solid business plan. The business plan summarizes the financial facts and figures. Future income and profits are projected. The plan is a valuable analytical tool in guiding your operation and as a means to attract investors and lenders. It shows how and where the money will be spent, and how it will generate a return. The plan should be neatly typed and organized for easy comprehension. It is a good idea to present your plan in a folder. Colorful renderings, graphs, charts, and photographs add visual interest. This simple detail indicates a professional attitude and goes a long way toward making a good first impression.

When looking for capital, begin the plan with a cover letter stating the amount requested and your proposed terms. Then give a brief summary of your business. Include the name of the bar, the location, and a physical description of the premises, as well as an actual layout or blueprint. If the bar already exists, then include photographs with a clear overlay of remodel changes. Discuss the concept, the market, and the competition. State the financial goals of the bar. Follow this with a short description of the management's experience, including the owners and key employees. Next, list the financial needs and how the funds will be utilized. Conclude by projecting profits and the return on the investment. The remaining sections of the plan should elaborate in detail this summary.

Next comes the *market analysis*. Explain how your concept fits in with current bar trends and how it will succeed in the marketplace. The goal here is to convince lenders that your ideas are innovative and backed by creative marketing experience. Discuss the total market environment in the area of your location and any trends in business and population growth. Investors seek growth-oriented businesses that are not affected by minor upheavals in the national business cycle.

Potential lenders want to know how you will attract customers to your bar. Impress them with innovative promotions and powerful advertising. Here is the perfect place to explain your pricing concept, and based upon expected customer flow, your projected profit margin.

Next, describe exactly how the bar will be run, from the type of ownership, to the management, to the hierarchy of the employees and their job responsibilities. Include resumes of key personnel. Lenders and investors know that even though your business plan is solid, the experience of management and its proper implementation of the plan is a major factor in the success of any business.

The final part of the plan deals exclusively with finances. If your establishment is already in operation, prepare financial statements for the last three fiscal years. If not, provide projections. For the first year, give month-by-month projections. Be realistic with your figures. These projections should include a profit and loss statement. To do this, take your operating expenses (rent, labor, supplies, utilities, insurance, advertising, etc.), add the cost of beverages and other items (food) sold, then subtract this total from your projected gross sales. This is the bottom line and shows either a profit or a loss. Additional funds can be re-

quested in either case for remodeling or expansion, or for the infusion of money to generate new business.

The *cash flow chart* is next. This pinpoints the difference between expenditures and income for a given period. It takes into account expenditures for loan principal reduction, owners' withdrawals and reserves for taxes. The cash flow projections should provide ample money to repay the loans you are requesting.

Now provide a capital expenditures budget that explains how all of the money for your business will be used. Make a distinction between your own capital and the loan money. The lenders need to know how their money will be allocated. Itemize purchases of equipment, improvements to the existing bar, building, and the cost for acquiring new facilities.

An existing business requires a balance statement. This determines its net worth. To derive this, take the bar's assets (all property and inventory that can be converted into cash), and subtract its liabilities (all monies owed including debts of property, equipment, and inventory). (Refer to FIG. 7-1.) In the left column are the assets. List everything your business owns, including items you still owe money on, and their current market value; that is, what you could sell them for today, not what you bought them for previously.

Your liabilities are recorded in the right column. Here you list the business's debts and what is owed as of the day you fill out this sheet. Take the total of the assets and subtract the total liabilities. This equals your net worth. The two columns balance when your assets are equal to your liabilities plus your net worth.

Sample business plan

The following is a sample business plan for a proposed bar called THE CATCH.

```
┌─────────────────────────────────────┬─────────────────────────────────────┐
│   ASSETS   What you own.            │   LIABILITIES   What you owe.        │
│                                     │                                     │
│ CASH Money in your checking &       │ ACCOUNTS PAYABLE Your balance due   │
│   savings accounts & cash at        │   on goods &                        │
│   home                    ━━━━━━     │   services, credit cards, charge    │
│ TIME DEPOSITS Money in certificates │   accounts, medical,                │
│   of deposit              ━━━━━━     │   dental & health care    ━━━━━━     │
│ STOCKS & BONDS U.S. Savings bonds,  │ NOTES & CONTRACTS PAYABLE           │
│   Treasury notes, stock             │   Cash loans on secured & unsecured │
│   & money market funds    ━━━━━━     │   agreements. Balance due on        │
│ REAL ESTATE Any interest in         │   contracts for cars, appliances,   │
│   improved or unimproved property,  │   furniture, etc.         ━━━━━━     │
│   crop, water or mineral rights,    │ REAL ESTATE LOANS Balance due,      │
│   trust deeds and mortgages ━━━━━━   │   including any liens     ━━━━━━     │
│ LIFE INSURANCE Cash surrender value │ TAXES All Federal, State Income &   │
│   or equity, not the face           │   Property taxes due and past       │
│   value                   ━━━━━━     │   due. Social Security taxes due if │
│ ACCOUNTS & NOTES RECEIVABLE Money   │   self-employed           ━━━━━━     │
│   owed you for                      │ OTHER LIABILITIES Unpaid interest,  │
│   goods & services & signed         │   law suit settlements, past        │
│   promissory notes        ━━━━━━     │   due accounts, etc.      ━━━━━━     │
│ CARS & RECREATIONAL VEHICLES use    │                                     │
│   current resale                    ├─────────────────────────────────────┤
│   value                   ━━━━━━     │ TOTAL LIABILITIES         ━━━━━━     │
│ PENSION & INDIVIDUAL RETIREMENT     ├─────────────────────────────────────┤
│   ACCOUNTS ━━━━━━                    │ NET WORTH                           │
│ OTHER ASSETS Cash valuable items.   │     TOTAL ASSETS          ━━━━━━     │
│   Home furniture, appliances &      │                                     │
│   electronic equipment    ━━━━━━     │     LESS TOTAL LIABILITIES ━━━━━━    │
│   Art, antiques, jewelry  ━━━━━━     │                                     │
│   Clothing, furs, sports equipment  │     EQUALS NET WORTH =     ━━━━━━    │
│                           ━━━━━━     │                                     │
│   Tools & equipment       ━━━━━━     ├─────────────────────────────────────┤
│   Partnership interests   ━━━━━━     │ ASSETS = LIABILITIES + NET WORTH    │
│   Other                   ━━━━━━     │                                     │
├─────────────────────────────────────┤                                     │
│ TOTAL ASSETS              ━━━━━━     │                                     │
└─────────────────────────────────────┴─────────────────────────────────────┘
```

Fig. 7-1. *Personal or business balance sheet.*

LOAN APPLICATION SUMMARY

Applicants
Bob and Ray Miller (Brothers)
3106 Pacific Coast Highway
Malibu, CA 90001
(213) 555-7021

Business
THE CATCH
1200 Pacific Coast Highway
Malibu, CA 90001

Type of Business
Full Service Bar: Liquor, Beer, Wine

Size of Business
Annual sales of $575,000.

Ownership
Copartnership

Availability of Funds from Applicants
Ray Miller is contributing $80,000 cash. Bob Miller is contributing $20,000 cash. Bob Miller's home equity will provide collateral for the loan. Bob will be General Manager and the working partner. Ray will continue his law practice, which nets $175,000 a year. Ray will contribute legal and business advice, in addition to cash reserves, if needed.

LOAN REQUEST

Amount
$100,000

Terms

Eight years with no prepayment penalty.

Interest Rate

Current lending rate at 10% per year.

Debt/Equity Ratio

$100,000/$100,000 = 1/1

Collateral

1. Secured interest in liquor license.
2. Secured interest in lease.
3. Personal guarantee by owners.
4. Second deed of trust on home of Bob Miller.

Other Conditions

1. Borrowers will assign life insurance in the amount of the loan and during the term of the loan.
2. Borrowers will maintain hazard and loss of income insurance with losses payable to the lender in the event the entire business is interrupted.
3. Borrowers will provide annual financial statements to lender.

Purpose of Loan

The loan, together with owners' equity, will allow Bob and Ray Miller to purchase a liquor license, equipment, make improvements, secure a lease, and open a bar called THE CATCH.

(See TABLES 7-1, 7-2, and 7-3.)

RESUME

Name

Bob Miller
1538 Edgewater Lane, #201B
Malibu, CA 90001

Phone

(213) 555-6706

Education

University of California, Los Angeles
B.A. in Business Administration, 1977

Employment

The Bicycle Cafe, Santa Monica, CA, 1990 to present
Position: General Manager of 250-seat restaurant and bar with annual sales of $2.2 million.

The Sunset Club, Hollywood, CA, 1982 to 1990
Position: Manager of concert nightclub.

Churchill's, West Los Angeles, CA, 1980 to 1982
Position: Assistant Manager, Bartender, Waiter of 150-seat restaurant and bar.

Personal Credit References

Security Bank, Santa Monica, CA
Auto Loan No. 1331-00245
Home Loan No. 08-579

Great Western Bank, Malibu, CA
Checking Account No. 121245
Savings Account No. 369895

(See TABLE 7-4.)

RESUME

Name

Ray Miller

Address

3106 Pacific Coast Highway
Malibu, CA 90001

Phone

(213) 555-7021

Table 7-1. Business Plan— Use of Funds and Source of Funds.

Use of funds	Source of funds		
Expenses	Loan	Equity	Total
Opening costs lease deposits, insurance, legal, taxes, advertising, zoning variances, licenses, pre-opening expenses	$10000	$10000	$20000
Liquor license	0	40000	40000
Inventory	15000	0	15000
Leasehold improvements	0	50000	50000
Fixtures & equipment	50000	0	50000
Working capital	25000	0	25000
Totals	$100000	$100000	$200000

Table 7-2. Business Plan—Use of Funds for Leasehold Improvements.

Leasehold improvements	Cost
Air conditioning/heating	$8000*
Plumbing—rough stubbing for two restrooms	6000
Electrical wiring and fixtures	6000
Paint	2000
Carpentry—bathrooms, entry, liquor room/office, front and back bar	15000
Exterior sign and lighting	4000*
Exterior	2000
Tile—bathrooms, sloping drains, bar, grease traps	3000
Floors (carpeting or tile)	3000*
Smoke and fire detectors, emergency lighting	1000*
Total	$50000

* Items depreciated.

Table 7-3. Business Plan— Use of Funds for Fixtures and Equipment.

Fixtures and equipment	Cost
Two 30-inch jockey boxes with cold plates and blender stations	$2000*
Two post-mix soda systems with 7-button guns, 50-foot line, and a carbonator	2000*
One 6-foot three-compartment sink with speed rack in front and 20-inch drainboards on both sides	750*
One 6-foot self-contained 4 keg utility cooler refrigerator	2000*
One 3-door vertical storage front loading refrigerator with laminated doors and top	2500*
One 2-foot glass froster with 80 mug capacity	1000*
One 4-foot flat top bottle cooler	1000*
One ice machine with 500-lb. capacity	2000*
Two computer cash registers	3500*
One computer with laser printer	2000*
Glasses	1000*
Miscellaneous bar supplies, blenders, coffee machines, mixers	1500*
One direct draw, 2-keg beer box and taps	1750*
Back bar top and cabinets	500*
One 25-foot front bar, top and foot rail	4000*
Ten bar stools at $200 each	2000*
Forty bar chairs at $200 each	8000*
Twelve bar tables and bases at $200 each	2500*
One satellite dish and 2 TVs	10000*
Total	$50000*

* Items depreciated.

Education

University of Illinois, Chicago
J.D. 1984

California State University, Los Angeles
B.A. in English 1981

Table 7-4. Business Plan—Bob Miller Personal Financial Statement.

Assets	Value
Cash in checking account	2500
Savings account	20000
Life insurance	150000
Real estate	175000
Automobile	20000
Other personal property	20000
Total	$387500

Liabilities	Amount
Accounts payable	4000
Auto payments	12000
Mortgages on real estate	90000
Total	$106,000

Assets – Liabilities = Net Worth, or $281,500

Table 7-5. Business Plan—Ray Miller Personal Financial Statement.

Assets	Value
Cash in checking accounts	8000
Savings and certificates of deposit	85000
Life insurance	300000
Real estate	350000
Automobile	30000
Other personal property	35000
Total	$808,000

Liabilities	Amount
Accounts payable	12000
Auto payments	22000
Other installments	8000
Mortgages on real estate	275000
Total	$317,000

Assets – Liabilities = Net Worth, or $511,000

Employment

1984 to present

Self-employed attorney, Portland, OR, and currently Los Angeles, CA, specializing in real estate law.

Personal Credit References

Oregon State Bank, Portland, OR
Auto Loan No. 152785-641
Savings Account No. 93058

Bank of America, Malibu, CA
Home Loan No. 80823-18635

Checking Account No. 67011
Savings Account No. 403697

(See TABLE 7-5.)

BUSINESS PLAN

THE CATCH
1200 Pacific Coast Highway
Malibu, CA 90001

Ownership

Copartnership: Bob and Ray Miller

Type of Business

THE CATCH will be a sports-oriented neighborhood bar with full liquor, beer, and wine service. It will be located in The Malibu Colony Shopping Center currently being built one block from the main entrance to Malibu Beach and opposite a state-owned beach parking lot. Other pertinent information is as follows:

- Hours of operation: 11 AM to 12 AM (Monday through Tuesday) and 11 AM to 2 AM (Wednesday through Sunday)
- Size: 2000 square feet
- Seating Capacity: 100
- Decor: Sports memorabilia, hats, helmets, gloves, rackets, shoes, nets, etc., and photos of famous athletes.
- Entertainment: 2 TV monitors, 1 large-screen TV, and a satellite dish to show sporting events from around the world

live, repeat telecasts of famous games from THE CATCH's video library, interactive sports programming games and live programming through the Sports Bar Television Network.

- Happy hour: 3 PM to 8 PM "Catch of the Day" fish fry.

- Clientele: 21 years and older from neighborhood residents (approx. 10,000), beach goers (on peak days 2,000 on foot), and auto traffic from Pacific Coast Highway (California Department of Transportation estimate on off-season days, November through May, 15,000 cars a day; and peak season days, June through October, 40,000 cars a day).

- Competition: The restaurants with bars within two miles of THE CATCH's location are: Jeff's, Seashadow's, The Outrigger, and The Blue Whale. Jeff's and The Blue Whale have dancing. The Wine Bistro, three blocks away, only serves beer and wine with cafe food. Each restaurant is located along Pacific Coast Highway, none as close to Malibu Beach's main entrance as THE CATCH. Every restaurant and bar is busy each day of the peak season, and Thursday through Sunday during the off season.

- Market potential: The growth potential is tremendous. The Malibu Colony Shopping Center will have 12 retail and service shops and parking for 100 cars. THE CATCH will occupy the corner store. The Edgewater, a 300-unit townhouse project, two blocks away, was recently finished and is occupied by 500 new residents. The Edgewater Phase II, with 250 more units, is currently breaking ground. Neighboring Pepperdine University is buying land adjacent to The Edgewater to build dormitories for 400 students. THE CATCH, with its satellite TV reception, Sports Bar Television Network programming, and sports-oriented concept should attract crowds of all ages.

THE CATCH plans to sponsor surfing, wind surfing, and volleyball teams, along with golf tournaments and fishing trips. THE CATCH plans to hire buses to take patrons to various professional sport events in the Los Angeles area, such as football, baseball, basketball, soccer, and ice hockey. THE CATCH has already lined up several professional athletes and celebrities to be "bartenders" on Celebrity Bartender Night every Monday. There is no bar in the area that can match THE CATCH's concept.

- Management: THE CATCH will be under the direction of Bob Miller, who has 12 years experience as General Manager, Bartender, and Waiter in several Los Angeles restaurants and bars. Bob is thoroughly trained with inventory, record keeping, and all aspects of the bar business. The owners are both residents of Malibu. Ray Miller, past president of the Malibu Chamber of Commerce, is still active in that organization and other community service clubs.

(See TABLES 7-6, 7-7, and 7-8.)

EXPLANATION OF PROJECTED PROFIT AND LOSS STATEMENT

Gross Sales

Due to the beach location, opening sales are expected to be good. The strongest months will be the summer months and December. Sales are expected to decline during January through April, picking up again as the weather warms up in May. Second year sales should average $55,000 a month, as the neighboring area continues to develop.

Table 7-6. Business Plan—Weekly Projected Cash Flow for THE CATCH.

HOURS: 11 AM to 12 AM Monday–Tuesday
11 AM to 2 AM Wednesday–Sunday

Average drink prices: $3.25 per drink
Average spending per person: $8 per person or 2.5 drinks per person

Day	Number of Customers	× $8 =	Income
Sunday	225		$1800
Monday	100		800
Tuesday	100		800
Wednesday	100		800
Thursday	150		1200
Friday	300		2400
Saturday	400		3200
Total	1375		$11,000

daily average	=	$ 1571
weekly average	=	$11000
monthly average	=	$47666 (1 month = 4.333 weeks)
annual average	=	$572000, or $575000 for 52 weeks)

Cost of Sales

Remain at 20 percent constantly.

Gross Profit (or Gross Margin)

The difference between sales and cost of sales.

Expenses

These are itemized below:

- Payroll: See Weekly Employee Work Schedule, should hold at 18.8 percent of gross sales. Will hire mostly Pepperdine University students.

- Payroll taxes: 12.5 percent of payroll to cover employer's share of FICA, unemployment, and worker's compensation.

- Owner's salary: Owner will draw minimum salary necessary to live in the beginning, increasing draw as the business establishes itself.

- Administration and general: Accounting fees and other office expenses.

Table 7-7. Business Plan—Weekly Employee Work Schedule and Payroll.

Payroll	Weekly employee work schedule						
	Sun	Mon	Tue	Wed	Thu	Fri	Sat
Hours Open	11:00 AM–2:00 AM	11:00 AM–12:00 M	11:00 AM–12 M	11:00 AM–2:00 AM	11:00 AM–2:00 AM	11:00 AM–2:00 AM	11:00 AM–2:00 AM
Bartenders							
	21 hrs.	14 hrs.	14 hrs.	16 hrs.	23 hrs.	25 hrs.	25 hrs.
Shift hours	1 10–5	1 10–12	1 10–12	1 10–6	1 10–6	1 10–6	1 10–6
	1 2–8			1 6–2	1 5–2	1 5--2	1 5–2
	1 6–1				1 6–2	1 6–2	1 6–2
$6 per hour	$126	$ 84	$ 84	$ 96	$138	$150	$150
Servers							
	21 hrs.	8 hrs.	8 hrs.	12 hrs.	18 hrs.	25 hrs.	25 hrs.
Shift hours	1 10–6	1 4–12	1 4–12	1 10–2	2 5–2	1 10–6	1 10–6
	1 2–8			1 6–2		1 5–2	1 5–2
	1 8–1					1 6–2	1 6–2
$4.50 per hour	$ 94.50	$ 36	$ 36	$ 54	$ 81	$108	$112.50
Subtotal	$220.50	$120	$120	$150	$219	$262.50	$262.50
Asst. Mgr							
* Owner	$125	$125	$125	*	*	*/$125	*/$125
Total	$345.50	$245	$245	$246	$219	$387.50	$387.50

Total = $2075.50 per week × 52 weeks = $107,926 or $108,100 used for year.
$108,100 divided by $575,000 gross = 18.8% (Labor as a percentage of gross sales.)
* Owner manages and owner salary is not included in payroll figures. Owner salary and draws listed under a separate category.

Table 7-8. Business Plan—Projected Profit and Loss Statement.

	Jun	Jul	Aug	Sep	Oct	Nov	Dec	Jan
Gross sales	45000	55000	60000	55000	50000	45000	60000	40000
Less cost of sales	9000	11000	12000	11000	10000	9000	12000	8000
Gross profit	36000	44000	48000	44000	40000	36000	48000	32000
Expenses								
Payroll	8460	10340	11280	10340	9400	8460	11280	7520
Payroll taxes	1058	1293	1410	1293	1175	1058	1410	940
Owners' salary	3333	3333	3333	3333	3333	3333	3333	3333
Admin./general	2000	2000	2000	2000	2000	2000	2000	2000
Rent @ $2/sq. ft.	4000	4000	4000	4000	4000	4000	4000	4000
Equipment	0	0	0	0	0	0	250	250
Bar/misc.	1000	1000	1000	1000	1000	1000	1000	1000
Music/entertain.	300	300	300	300	300	300	300	300
Taxes/licenses	1000	1000	1000	1000	1000	1000	1000	1000
Utilities	3000	4000	4000	3000	2500	2000	2000	2000
Insurance	1200	1200	1200	1200	1200	1200	1200	1200
Advertising	3500	3000	3000	2000	2000	2000	2000	1000
Repairs/maint.	500	500	500	500	750	750	1000	1000
Depreciation	975	975	975	975	975	975	975	975
Interest	833	828	822	816	810	804	798	792
Total expenses	31159	33769	34820	31757	30443	28880	32546	27310
Net profit before income taxes	4841	10231	13180	12243	9557	7120	15454	4690
Profit year-to-date	4841	15072	28252	40495	50052	57172	72626	77316

	Feb	Mar	Apr	May	Total	Percentage
Gross sales	40000	40000	40000	45000	575000	100
Less cost of sales	8000	8000	8000	9000	115000	20
Gross profit	32000	32000	32000	36000	460000	80
Expenses						
Payroll	7520	7520	7520	8460	108100	18.8
Payroll taxes	940	940	940	1058	13515	2.4
Owners' salary	3333	3333	3333	3333	39996	7
Admin./general	2000	2000	2000	2000	24000	4
Rent @ $2/sq. ft.	4000	4000	4000	4000	48000	8
Equipment	250	250	250	250	1500	0.3
Bar/misc.	1000	1000	1000	1000	12000	2
Music/entertain.	300	300	300	300	3600	0.7
Taxes/licenses	1000	1000	1000	1000	12000	2
Utilities	2500	2500	2500	2500	32500	5.7
Insurance	1200	1200	1200	1200	14400	2.5
Advertising	1000	1000	1500	2000	24000	4
Repairs/maint.	1000	1000	1500	2000	11000	2
Depreciation	975	975	975	975	11700	2
Interest	786	780	774	768	9611	1.8
Total expenses	27804	27798	28792	30844	365922	63.2
Net profit before income taxes	4196	4202	3208	5156	94078	16.4
Profit year-to-date	81512	85714	88922	94078		

- Rent: Based on lease of $2.00 per square foot per month.
- Equipment: Replace equipment as needed. This should increase to 2 percent after second year in operation.
- Bar and miscellaneous supplies: Replace glassware, linen, laundry, napkins, matches, fruit for garnishes, etc.
- Music and entertainment: Tapes and compact discs for audio and video library, monthly payments for Sports Bar Television Network.
- Taxes and licenses: Various permits for Health, Fire, liquor license, music copyright royalties, etc.
- Utilities: Air conditioning being highest during summer months.
- Insurance: Approximately $3.50 per square foot per year.
- Advertising: Heaviest during first six months, and includes sponsorship of local teams, banners, small ads in local papers, and fliers. Second year should level off at 3 percent of gross sales.
- Repairs and maintenance: Reserve for wear and tear, cleaning crew comes 3 times a week. This will increase as equipment grows older.
- Depreciation: $65,000 of fixed assets, leasehold improvements, equipment, and fixtures are depreciated over five years on a straight line basis at $11,700 a year, with a salvage value of $6500 or 10 percent of cost at the end of five years.
- Interest: Interest on loans of $100,000, amortized over eight years at a fixed rate of 10 percent interest.

Total Expenses

Sum of above.

Net Profit as Income

Difference between total expenses and gross profits, before income taxes.

(See TABLE 7-9.)

EXPLANATION OF PROJECTED CASH FLOW

Cash Sources

See below.

- Equity: The owners will put $100,000 cash into the bar.
- Loan: Requested loans from equipment suppliers and banks.
- Net profit: Taken from Projected Profit and Loss Statement, a source of cash.
- Depreciation: Depreciation of fixtures, equipment, and leasehold improvements. Because it was deducted as an expense before net profit and is a non-cash expense, it is added back as a source of cash.

Total Cash Sources

Sum of the above.

Disbursements

Itemized below:

- Liquor license: Cost of acquiring a liquor, beer, and wine license.
- Improvements: See Use of Funds—Leasehold Improvements.
- Fixtures and equipment: See Use of Funds—Fixtures and Equipment.
- Opening inventory: Purchases of liquor, beer, and wine to stock the bar.
- Opening costs: Lease deposits, legal, advertising, pre-opening parties, etc.

Table 7-9. Business Plan—Projected Cash Flow.

	Pre-opening	Jun	July	Aug	Sep	Oct	Nov	Dec
Cash sources								
Equity	100000							
Loans	100000							
Net Profit	0	4841	10231	13180	12243	9557	7120	15454
Depreciation	0	975	975	975	975	975	975	975
Total	200000	5816	11206	14155	13218	10532	8095	16329
Disbursements								
Liquor license	40000							
Improvements	50000							
Fixtures/equipment	50000							
Opening inventory	15000							
Opening costs	20000							
Loan payments-prin.	0	684	690	696	701	707	713	719
Owner's draw	0	0	0	0	0	0	0	7000
Income taxes	0	1936	4092	5272	4897	3823	2848	6182
Total	175000	2610	4782	5968	5598	4530	3561	13901
Net cash flow	25000	3206	6424	8187	7620	6002	4534	2428
Cumulative cash flow	25000	28206	34630	42817	50437	56439	60973	63401

	Jan	Feb	Mar	Apr	May	Total
Cash sources						
Equity						100000
Loans						100000
Net profit	4690	4196	4202	3208	5156	94078
Depreciation	975	975	975	975	975	11700
Total	5665	5161	5177	4183	6121	305658
Disbursements						
Liquor license						40000
Improvements						50000
Fixtures/equipment						50000
Opening inventory						15000
Opening costs						20000
Loan payments—prin.	725	731	737	743	749	8595
Owner's draw	7000	7000	7000	7000	7000	42000
Income taxes	1876	1678	1680	1283	2062	37629
Total	9601	9409	9417	9026	9811	88214
Net cash flow	(3936)	(4248)	(4240)	(4843)	(3690)	42444
Cumulative cash flow	59465	55217	50977	46134	42444	42444

- Loan payment: Principal reduction of $100,000 loan, eight-year amortization at a fixed rate of 10 percent interest.
- Owners draw: Both partners taking draws after first six months. Draws to increase when business stabilizes after first year of operation.
- Income taxes: 40 percent of net profit placed as a reserve for income taxes.

Total Disbursements
Sum of the above.

Net Cash Flow
Difference between monthly cash flow and disbursements including $25,000 reserved for working capital after the bar opens.

Cumulative Cash Flow
Sum of monthly cash flows. Cumulative year-end cash surplus is $42,444, which includes $25,000 of beginning working capital.

Investors

At this point, if it is decided new capital is needed, several sources can be approached. The question should be whether to borrow, which will incur a debt and add to your operating expenses, or to take in a partner or partners, who will provide the necessary cash. An investor can become a part of the business by acquiring an equity (percentage) interest. Otherwise, the investor receives no percentage of the business, only interest on the money loaned.

When looking for investors, talk to your relatives, friends, and the people you work with: suppliers, customers, and coworkers. Other helpful sources are bankers, accountants, insurance brokers, stock brokers, attorneys, business journals, and newspapers.

The Internal Revenue Code provides numerous tax advantages for investments in businesses, including favorable treatment for capital gains and losses. This means a lower tax rate on income earned or lost from investments as opposed to higher tax rates on personal income. Depending upon your investor's tax status, their investment can be structured in a variety of ways to help them and you. Look for ways to be creative. Maybe someone wants to invest in your bar and desires to have something substantial to secure their money. Arrange for them to purchase your equipment and then lease it back to you. You profit by not putting out the cash, and they profit by writing off the depreciation on the equipment and taking the investment tax credit. Some bars provide management positions to qualified individuals who put up some start-up capital for a percentage of the profits. It is also possible for key personnel to take a percentage of the profits in lieu of a larger salary. Always be positive when seeking investors and your enthusiasm will attract the money you need.

Your personal financial statement

Before approaching any bank, prepare a personal financial statement. As in your business plan, you need a balance sheet and an income and expense statement, which is the same as a Profit and Loss statement for a business. When loaning money to new ventures, most lenders require the borrower to have at least 50 percent of the capital. These lenders also want to know that your current income can repay the loan if the business fails. It is the same process you would go through to obtain a new car loan. Prepare your Personal Balance Sheet as in FIG. 7-1. Although similar in form, a business and a personal balance sheet differ only in the categories listed.

FROM _____   TO _____

INCOME Money paid to you.	EXPENSES Money you pay out.
NET SALARY OR WAGES Gross received minus any	MORTGAGE/RENT _____
Federal or State Income Tax, Disability, etc., withheld _____	PROPERTY TAXES _____
COMMISSIONS, TIPS, BONUSES _____	OTHER REAL ESTATE LOANS _____
NET BUSINESS OR PROFESSIONAL INCOME _____	HOUSE REPAIRS & MAINTENANCE _____
INTEREST & DIVIDENDS FROM STOCKS,	UTILITIES _____
SAVINGS & OTHER NOTES _____	FOOD _____
NET INCOME FROM RENTAL PROPERTY _____	TRANSPORTATION Car repairs, oil & gas, parking, public
ROYALTIES, RESIDUALS & TRUST INCOME _____	transportation (bus, subway) _____
BENEFIT INCOME Social Security, Pensions, Veterans,	CREDIT & CHARGE ACCOUNTS _____
life insurance, unemployment, disability _____	INSTALLMENT CONTRACTS _____
OTHER Sale of Assets, etc. _____	INSURANCE Real & personal property, life, health, car, etc._____
	INCOME TAXES Federal, State, Self-employment,
TOTAL INCOME _____	Social Security _____
LESS TOTAL EXPENSES – _____	OTHER TAXES Gift or Estate _____
EQUALS AMOUNT	PERSONAL CARE Clothes, laundry, hair & eye care, health,
AVAILABLE FOR	medical, dental _____
SAVINGS, INVESTMENTS	EDUCATION _____
OR NEW DEBTS _____	ENTERTAINMENT & RECREATION _____
	SAVINGS _____
	LEASE PAYMENTS Car, appliances, furniture _____
	ALIMONY & CHILD SUPPORT _____
	CHILD CARE _____
	DUES & MEMBERSHIPS _____
	CONTRIBUTIONS _____
	TOTAL EXPENSES _____

Fig. 7-2. Personal income and expenses sheet.

Next, use FIG. 7-2. The income and expense statement is a way of looking at the money you receive (income) and the money you spend (expenses). This can be done for any period of time, usually for the month, quarter, or year. After totaling your income, subtract your expenses. The extra money remaining is of great concern to those looking over your finances. This statement becomes an excellent tool for developing and adjusting budgets and simply looking at how and where you spend your money. Whenever an expense varies, such as family entertainment, use the average amount.

Equipment companies

Before approaching any bank for financing, many equipment suppliers and manufacturers will finance the purchase of their equipment. This option is a very viable source of financing for bar owners and should not be overlooked.

The banks

Banks make the majority of loans. For the most part, they loan conservatively, viewing any new business as a high risk. The loan officers take a close look at your personal financial statement and your personal credit record. Loans to new businesses require a closer inspection than established, profitable ones. If you do not have any history of personal credit, such as credit cards or a charge account, it is advisable to establish credit first before approaching any bank about a loan. Then start talking to several banks until you find a suitable loan rate and terms.

In the beginning, a short-term loan may be easier to receive. Repayable in less than a year, a short-term loan can be used to cover a temporary shortage of capital, to purchase new inventory at a discount, or to prepare for a seasonal rush of business. This is a good way to establish credit and build a positive lending relationship with a bank. Later, when larger funds are needed to expand, your ability to repay has been proven, and your bar's success and growth add to your borrowing power.

Short-term rates tend to be higher. Because banks lend money based upon where they obtain their money (mostly from deposits), a borrower pays more than what the bank pays out to its depositors in interest. The prime rate is a good indicator of the interest rate a borrower pays. The prime rate is the rate the banks pay to borrow money from the federal government. Banks typically quote rates one to four points higher than prime for small businesses.

Long-term loans for start-up costs, working capital, equipment, or construction, come as *secured* or *unsecured*. As part of the loan agreement, salaries, other debts, draws by partners, and dividends to shareholders, might be limited. A compensating balance, which is a cash reserve in the bar's bank account, may also be required. If you do not qualify for an unsecured loan, try obtaining an equipment loan or an equipment leasing loan, which uses the equipment as security or collateral. A secured loan is usually backed by personal or business assets. For a bar owner, this can be the lease, the inventory, the real estate, or the equipment of your bar.

Long-term interest rates are generally lower than short-term rates. Banks lend money based on their long-term deposits and funds, which are less susceptible to short-term fluctuations in the prime rate. Generally, these loans are fixed-rate, however, it is becoming a common practice when the economy is unstable or the inflation rate is running rampant, to make adjustable-rate loans. This ties the rate of interest to a predetermined index, such as the six-month U.S. Treasury bill rate or the prime rate. At specified time periods, usually quarterly or every six months, the interest rate is adjusted according to the movement of the index.

Adjustable rate loans often have a limit as to how much the rate can change at each adjustment period and over the entire length of the loan. As your borrowing power increases, you can negotiate for lower interest rates on loans. When just starting out, expect to pay a higher rate.

Allow at least a week for smaller loans and several weeks for larger loan processing. Each loan officer can sign-off loans up to their limit. Beyond this limit, loan approval goes to an officer of the bank or the bank's loan committee. Naturally, the fewer individuals who must approve the loan, the shorter the time required for you to receive an answer.

Make a point to get to know the loan officers in your bank. Invite them to your bar so they can observe your operation. Establishing a good relationship with these people can only help in future financial endeavors.

Commercial finance companies

If the banks turn down your loan request, commercial finance companies often take the risk. When your business is new, has a sudden reversal, needs to expand quickly, or has a large debt already, commercial finance companies loan money based on the collateral offered, rather than your financial condition.

They often lend beyond the net worth of the borrower. A bank rarely does this. Expect to pay a higher interest rate.

Typically, commercial finance companies loan money for two to five years secured by your new or used equipment. Sometimes the loan is secured by your lease or real estate you own separate from your bar business. These finance companies look for creative ways to make loans.

Life insurance companies

Anyone who has whole, not term, life insurance, can borrow up to 95 percent of the cash value of the policy. Naturally, interest is charged. This interest can be deferred as long as the borrower continues to pay the policy premiums. When the policy is needed, and the loan has not been paid, the amount of the loan is subtracted from the policy payout. Also consult your life insurance company about mortgage loans on real estate. Their rates correspond to the banks' prevailing interest rates.

Consumer finance companies

Consumer finance companies also provide loans when banks will not. They loan for personal or business needs and are secured by your personal property or real property. Consumer finance companies look for credit stability in their borrowers. To exceptionally creditworthy individuals, they offer unsecured loans. Again, plan to pay higher interest rates.

Savings and loan companies

Savings and loan companies have traditionally specialized in real estate loans. Recent federal and state laws have allowed these companies to expand their financial services. They look at the applicant's personal and business financial statements, examining them closely for the ability to repay. They loan up to 75 percent of a property's appraised value for 25 to 30 years. Interest rates with savings and loans are competitive with banks.

If you own a home with a fixed-rate mortgage and have built up equity, try to obtain a variable rate loan at a lower interest rate. You can pull the equity out of your home and use it to help finance your bar. If interest rates have gone down, your monthly mortgage payments can be less. For example, you purchased a home 10 years ago for $125,000. You put $25,000 down and financed the remaining $100,000 with a fixed rate loan of 12.5 percent interest fully amortized for 30 years. Your monthly payments are $1067.26. Now you want to open a bar and your home is worth $175,000. You have built up $50,000 in equity, and the bank will loan up to 75 percent or $131,000 of the appraised value of your house. You decide to refinance your home with a new variable rate loan of $125,000 starting with a 9.5 percent interest rate. Your monthly payments are less than before at $1051.07, and you have the additional $25,000 to help finance your bar.

U.S. Small Business Adminstration

Established by Congress in 1953, the Small Business Administration (SBA) has been a tremendous help to many businesses. The SBA guarantees intermediate and long-term bank loans. It makes direct loans when the borrower has been turned down by two banks in a city of 200,000 or more, or only one bank in cities with less than 200,000 people. Direct loans are for under $150,000, and the interest rates are similar to banks'. The terms vary according to the amount and intended use of the money. The SBA was set up to assist those who have exhausted all of the normal routes to financing.

The 7a Loan Guarantee Program under the SBA guarantees loans under $500,000 or up to 90 percent of a bank loan, whichever is less. The borrower is expected to contribute from one-third to one-half of the business's financial needs. Whenever possible, collateral in the form of fixed assets, real estate, or inventory is used to secure the loan. The SBA does have special programs for minorities, economically disadvantaged groups, and Vietnam veterans. These groups may qualify for lower collateral and capital requirements.

The SBA has numerous other programs to assist businesses that need financial help. Among them are natural Disaster Recovery Loans for businesses damaged by an official natural disaster declared by the President, the Secretary of Agriculture, or the SBA. Small Business Investment Companies (SBICs) and Minority Enterprise Small Business Investment Companies (MESBICs) are licensed and regulated by the SBA. The SBICs and MESBICs receive matching funds from the federal government to invest in small businesses. The SBA also offers literature and seminars on all aspects of business at little or no cost.

When approaching the SBA, have your financial statements well prepared, including your business plan. While the SBA will be less stringent on their requirements than a bank, they still look for the ability to repay. SBA interest rates tend to be the same or less than the banks'. The SBA also offers longer terms to allow your business to stabilize and maintain a profit.

When approaching investors and lending institutions for financing it is very important to be thoroughly prepared. Make sure your research is complete and your business plan is solid and accurate. Be confident, and you'll obtain the funds you need.

8

Regulations and licenses

Your bar must comply with laws at the federal, state, county, and local levels. These laws cover everything from the manufacture of alcohol to the wages of the workers who serve it. These regulations have undergone changes over the years since the ratification of the Constitution gave the Treasury Department the power to levy and collect taxes in 1787. Even today, these laws are being revised and updated, so it is the responsibility of any bar owner to keep abreast of changes in legislation. It is also the owner's responsibility to acquire adequate insurance for the bar and its property. This chapter is devoted to information about the different levels of regulations and the types of insurance needed. Please be advised that these regulations are constantly changing and vary from state to state, and city to county. This chapter also discusses the social responsibilities that come with selling alcohol in your community.

Federal laws

The first Internal Revenue law, The Act of March 3, 1791, gave the Secretary of the Treasury, under the newly evolved Internal Revenue Code, the power to tax stills and spirits.

This right of taxation eventually caused an uprising in western Pennsylvania in 1794 called the Whiskey Rebellion. This rebellion was quickly subdued by George Washington and provided greatly needed revenue for the newly organized states.

The taxing of liquor and brews has since been repealed and reinstated numerous times, but never again so vehemently challenged. During the American Civil War, what is now known as the Bureau of Alcohol, Tobacco, and Firearms (BATF) was created for the express purpose of law enforcement, industry regulation, and collecting liquor taxes for the Treasury Department. In this century, the biggest blow to the industry came on January 16, 1920, when the Eighteenth Amendment to the Constitution went into effect. This was the start of Prohibition that officially outlawed the manufacture, sale, transportation, importation, and exportation of intoxicating liquors for beverage purposes.

Abuses in the industry continued until the ratification of the 21st Amendment that repealed the 18th Amendment. As a result, the Federal Alcohol Administration (FAA) Act of 1935 was established. Liquor, as defined by this act, is any fluid or substance, either distilled or fermented, or a beverage with alcoholic content. The FAA regulates all interstate and foreign commerce relating to the quality of alcoholic products and their taxation. These regulations cover manufacturing processes, use of materials, aging, packaging, labeling, adulteration, and advertising of all liquor.

The FAA must approve the contents of all liquor and requires that an analysis appear on product labels: identity and quality of product, age (for distilled spirits only), net contents, the manufacturer, bottler, or importer of the product, and the alcoholic content of products (for beer when required by state law and for wines containing more than 14 percent alcohol by volume). The Internal Revenue Code prohibits any seller of distilled spirits to alter the contents of any liquor bottle by adding distilled spirits, water, or any substance to the original contents. It is also against the law to possess any bottle so altered. Bottle sizes are controlled by the Treasury. States can limit which bottle sizes are sold within their boundaries, however.

Strip stamp or alternative seal

The strip stamp seals a liquor bottle as a final approval that this product has been made according to federal regulations. It is a red and white or a green and white paper strip stamp tax that goes over the cap and seals it. This ensures that the bottle has not been opened or tampered with prior to purchase for the consumer's protection. This stamp or seal is the means by which the Internal Revenue Code collects its tax. Once opened, a portion of the strip stamp or alternative device must remain attached to the container while any contents remain. The BATF can seize any bottles with altered contents or suspected altered contents, or with missing strip stamps or seals.

As of July 1, 1985, the strip stamp formerly required by the BATF has been replaced by a tamper-resistant closure, such as a perforated, break and twist off cellophane or plastic cap or a paper seal. The closure and seal after this date becomes the manufacturer's responsibility rather than the BATF. No liquor bottles can be reused or refilled in any manner for any reason. Nor can the liquor be emptied from its original container into another container and then resold. (When using frozen drink machines, the slush comes out of the machine and then the alcohol is added; the alcohol is not added to the slush mixing in the machine. When premixing Margaritas or other popular drinks in gallon quantities, mix in the alcohol in the individual glass right when the drink is made, not in the larger quantity.)

Obtaining a retail dealer license

A retail dealer is defined as any person engaged in the selling of alcohol used as a beverage who sells to the public. The Internal Revenue Service (IRS) requires two dealer forms be filed. First, an Employer Identification Number must be obtained by filing IRS Form SS-4. Next, a dealer must file IRS Form 11, Special Tax Return and Application for Registry, available at any IRS or BATF office, for each place of business on or before July 1 of each year. This empowers the federal government to levy a special occupational tax. The dealer receives a Special Tax Stamp as a receipt of payment, which allows the federal government to keep track of all retail dealers. This is not a liquor license. Additional state and local licenses must be acquired before retail sales can begin. Your Special Tax Stamp must be available for inspection at your place of business by any BATF officer during business hours. If lost or destroyed, contact your local Internal Revenue center for a "Certificate in Lieu of Lost or Destroyed Special Tax Stamp."

The Special Tax Stamp is not transferable. Any change of location requires a new IRS

Form 11—Amended Return—to be filed within 30 days from the time operations begin at the new location. Any change of ownership or control of a bar also requires a new stamp and application. The exceptions to this are persons related to or legal representatives of a deceased dealer, a husband or wife who takes over the business from his or her living spouse, a trustee in cases of bankruptcy or an assignee of creditors, and the partner(s) remaining after the death or withdrawal of a member of the partnership.

Anyone meeting these requirements need only file IRS Form 11—Amended Return—showing the basis for taking over the business. The old stamp, along with the form, must be sent to the IRS. It will be amended and returned. This must be done within 30 days from the date of change of ownership. Any name change of the business does not require a new stamp or application when the original owner or owners remain the same.

A Retail Liquor Dealer sells either distilled spirits or wine and pays a tax of $54 a year. A Retail Beer Dealer pays $24 a year. If a dealer chooses to operate on a seasonal or temporary basis, an application as a Limited Retail Dealer is filed. A Limited Retail Dealer of distilled spirits pays $4.50 per month. A Limited Retail Dealer of beer or wine is taxed $2.20 per month. If a dealer has a traveling bar such as in a boat, airplane, or train, this person is classified as a Dealer at Large, and pays $54 a year.

Depending on state and local laws, retail dealers may purchase distilled spirits from the following: owners of distilled spirit plants (manufacturers), wholesale dealers, persons legally appointed to dispose of bankruptcy assets, and other retail dealers going out of business and selling their entire stock.

You, as a retail dealer, must retain all invoices and bills for all distilled spirits, wines, and beers purchased. BATF officers can inspect any retail dealer's records and liquor stock at any time. If you have questions concerning these forms or regulations, consult your regional office of the BATF as listed in TABLE 8-1.

Tied-house interests

The FAA has numerous regulations relating to tied-house interests between industry members (wholesalers and manufacturers of alcoholic products) and retail dealers. Tied-house interests occur when industry members exert influence over their markets by having an interest in a bar, furnishing things of value, providing free warehousing, display and distribution services, assisting in acquiring a license, paying for advertising, guaranteeing loans, extending credit, or demanding a quota of the retailer's purchases.

Certain exceptions do exist. Industry members can legally provide, sell, or loan a variety of services or items. Product displays, such as wine racks, barrels, or kegs, may not exceed $100 per brand in use at any one time in any one retail business.

Inside signs and other promotional items, such as napkins, clocks, and calendars, are allowed. These items are limited to no more than $50 per brand per calendar year per retail establishment. Glassware and tapping accessories may be sold to a retailer at a price not less than the cost. The purchase price must be collected within 30 days. Limited samples may be given if the retailer has not purchased the brand previously from that industry member.

Educational seminars may be given by the industry member at the retail dealer's or industry member's place of business. Each state has further rules and laws as to what constitutes a tied-house interest. Legal interests in one state may be illegal in another. For instance, in some states, the installation of a beer-tapping system by a beer manufacturer or wholesaler may be an illegal tied-house action. Tied-house regulations are to ensure a

Table 8-1. BATF Addresses.

Office	Region
Federal Office Building 550 Main Street Cinncinnati, OH 45202	*Central* Indiana, Kentucky, Michigan, Ohio, West Virginia
Federal Office Building 2 Penn Center Plaza Philadelphia, PA 19102	*Mid-Atlantic* Delaware, District of Columbia, Maryland, New Jersey, Pennsylvania, Virginia
Federal Office Building 230 South Dearborn Street Chicago, IL 60604	*Midwest* Illinois, Iowa, Kansas, Minnesota, Missouri, Nebraska North Dakota, South Dakota, Wisconsin
Federal Office Building P.O. Box 15 Church Street Station New York, NY 10008 (6 World Trade Center, 6th Floor)	*North Atlantic* Connecticut, Maine, Massachusetts, New Hampshire, New York, Puerto Rico, Rhode Island, Vermont, Virgin Islands
Federal Office Building P.O. Box 2994 Atlanta, GA 30301 (3835 Northeast Expressway)	*Southeast* Alabama, Florida, Georgia, Mississippi, North Carolina, South Carolina, Tennessee
Federal Office Building 1200 Main Street Dallas, TX 75202	*Southwest* Arkansas, Colorado, Louisiana, New Mexico, Oklahoma, Texas, Wyoming
Federal Office Building 525 Market Street, 34th Floor San Francisco, CA 94105	*Western* Alaska, Arizona, California, Guam, Hawaii, Idaho, Montana, Nevada, Oregon, Utah, Washington

free and open marketplace, protecting bar owners as well as their clientele.

The exception to the tied-house rules are microbreweries and brewpubs. These small breweries are allowed to manufacture and sell their beer on the same premises if they produce less than 15,000 barrels a year. Currently, 46 states allow brewpubs. Some states require food to be served with the beer.

OSHA

Every bar must comply with OSHA, the federal Occupational Safety and Health Act of 1970. OSHA determines that it is the general duty and responsibility of every employer to maintain a place of employment that has safe and healthful working conditions. A state is allowed to develop and run its own occupational safety and health program, provided it includes federal requirements. Consult your state OSHA board or local building and safety inspector for details.

Taxes

Each bar must report its income to the IRS, as well as collect the Federal Income, Social Security, Unemployment, and Disability taxes for each employee. See Chapter 16, Maintaining Records, for further information.

Wages

The Fair Labor Standards Act (FLSA), or the federal minimum wage law, outlines many regulations besides the minimum wage and overtime rates. You are required to comply with the FLSA if your bar or any business it controls has total revenues of more than $362,500 gross annual sales, exclusive of excise taxes at the retail level. If your sales are less than $362,500, state laws prevail. For a new business, until it has been in operation for one year, the first quarter's receipts will be used to determine its annual volume. Enforcement of the FLSA is directed and carried out by the offices of the Wage and Hour Section, Employment Standards Division of the U.S. Labor Department. The FLSA, while defining minimum wage and overtime laws, does not require employers to grant pay raises to employees or provide fringe benefits, such as health insurance, paid vacations, paid holidays, sick pay, days off, or rest periods. It does not require an employer to give any reason or notice for discharge or severance pay. In addition, the federal minimum wage law does not provide for a limit on the number of hours a person sixteen years or older may work each day or each week. Many of these issues are preempted by state laws or are left to negotiations between employers and employees or their representatives.

In order to determine how many hours an employee has worked, a definition of what constitutes "work time" must be established. From the time an employer requires an employee to be on duty until this employee is relieved of his duty, minus any official breaks, is considered work time. When an employee is entirely relieved of his duties during a meal period, that time is not considered work time. These meal breaks do not require an employee to leave the premises. Allowing an employee to continue working after his or her shift, even voluntarily, is considered work time. If the employer does not intend to compensate the employee for this additional work, the employee must be told before starting the work. Employee meetings or training programs that are voluntary are not considered work time. On the other hand, if the employer requires that employees attend, the time spent is work time. When an employee receives or is waiting for medical treatment or diagnosis at the employer's request during the employee's regular working hours, the employee is considered to be working.

A "work week" is defined as a regularly occurring period of 168 consecutive hours or seven consecutive 24-hour periods. This week can start on any day or at any hour as long as it is a fixed week starting and stopping at the same time every week. Overtime is computed for each week only, never by averaging two or more work weeks to achieve a lower number of weekly hours worked. Work weeks are separate from pay periods as pay periods can be daily, weekly, biweekly, bimonthly, monthly, quarterly, or any other period of time.

Overtime

An overtime rate of one and one-half times the employee's regular hourly rate is required by the federal minimum wage law after the employee has worked a 40-hour work week. For instance, if an employee works 40¾ hours in one week at a rate of $6 per hour, that additional three-quarters of an hour is paid at the overtime rate of $9 per hour.

To determine overtime rates for a salaried employee, an hourly rate must be calculated. This rate is figured by dividing the rate of salary by the amount of hours in an expected work week. As an example, a weekly salary of $500 divided by 50 hours gives a regular rate of $10 per hour. After working the regular 50-hour week, overtime hours are paid at $15 per hour. When the salaried employee is paid monthly, multiply the amount by 12 months and divide by 52 weeks to arrive at a weekly salary. If an employee works at more than one bar owned by the same individual(s), overtime must be paid if this employee's combined hours worked total more than 40 hours in any one week. This applies even if the payrolls are compiled separately or the names of the bars are different. If the owners are different, however, no overtime need be paid.

Under the federal minimum wage law, executives, managers, and administrative personnel are exempt from the minimum wage and overtime laws when they qualify in one of two ways. In the first way, all of the following conditions must be observed:

- The management of a company, department, or subdivision of the company is the employee's primary duty.

- This employee is engaged in the regular direction of two or more employees.

- This employee has the authority and can recommend the hiring, firing, promotion, training, or transfer of another employee.

- The regular use of freedom of judgment or opinion while working is a part of this employee's job.

- This employee receives a salary of at least $155 per week.

- Nonmanagerial duties do not take up more than 40 percent of work time unless this employee is the only person in charge or owns at least 20 percent of the business. (Only one person per establishment can be the sole-charge manager.)

In the second way, an employee who is paid $250 or more per week (not including board or lodging), for primarily performing managerial duties while supervising two or more employees, qualifies and is exempt. Management trainees are not exempt from overtime or minimum wage laws.

State and local laws vary widely according to minimum wage, maximum work weeks, and overtime. For food and beverage employees, many states provide for the payment of overtime based on 8-hour or 12-hour work days, 48-hour work weeks, 7 consecutive work days, or no overtime compensation. According to the FLSA, when there is a conflict between federal or state and local laws, the law that is best for the employee prevails. Thus, if the state minimum wage is higher than the federal, the state wage must be paid. If the state's maximum work week is 48 hours before overtime applies, the federal's maximum work week of 40 hours will take precedence.

In some businesses, instead of paying overtime, employers allow their employees time off and credit from regular work hours. The Department of Labor provides this means of substitution only if the time off is taken and used before the end of the pay period when the overtime was worked.

Hiring students

The FLSA allows the hiring of full-time students at a special rate of 85 percent of the current minimum wage. The following conditions must be met:

- An employee is considered a full-time student when attending a bona fide school or institution while receiving the majority of instruction during the day.

- The confirmation of student status should be established by the school.

- Full-time students can work no more than 20 hours a week at the special rate except during vacation periods when 40 hours a week is permissible.

- All hours worked over the limits must be paid at least the standard minimum wage.

Up to six full-time students can be employed by applying to the Regional Office, Wage and Hours Division of the Department of Labor for a certificate. If you wish to hire more than six students, authorization is needed first. You cannot reduce a student employee's wage who was hired prior to your receiving a certificate to employ students.

Once you have applied for a certificate, you do not have to wait for approval to begin employing students. With the application, you must describe your business and the total number of hours of employment during the last 12-month period. Typically, the Labor Department will allow you to pay up to 10 percent of your employees the reduced full-time student wages. If you want this percentage to be increased, consult your local Wage and Hours Division office. Exceptions have been granted. When students are paid the federal minimum wage, there are no restrictions to the number of students you can employ nor do any of the above rules and regulations apply.

Tip credits

A tip is any amount over and above any charges to the customer given to an employee at the customer's initiative. Because the employee receives compensation in the form of gratuities, an employer can pay an hourly employee less wages. A tip credit is the amount of this reduction.

Under the FLSA, an employer can take up to a 40 percent tip credit provided the employee's wage is at least the minimum. For example, using the tip credit, with a minimum wage of $4.25 per hour, the wage becomes $2.55 paid by the employer and $1.70 credited as tips received. The following criteria allows an employer to use the tip credit:

- Employees must receive at least $30 in tips per month on a regular basis.

- The employer must be able to prove the amount of tips earned by the employee.

- Tip credit cannot exceed the 40 percent allowed.

- The employer must inform tipped employees of the tip credit laws and provide payroll records showing the amount of tip credit claimed.

- Employees must be able to keep all of their tips if the employer uses the tip credit against their wages. This ensures against an employer keeping any portion of employees' tips to pay for shortages, uniforms, breakage, or other expenses.

Service charges kept by the employer cannot be considered tips and, therefore, cannot be used as part of the tip credit. Service charges are additional amounts added to the bill of a customer to compensate the house for the use of labor and facilities. This revenue is part of the gross sales receipts of the bar and subject to sales tax in certain states.

In cases of overtime, the tip credit remains the same. Only 40 percent of the regular hourly rate and not 40 percent of the overtime rate can be credited. This credit can be applied to all the employee's hours worked as long as the time spent opening, setting-up, cleaning, and closing are part of the job that includes earning tips. When an employee works two or more jobs at your bar, such as a disc jockey and a bartender, and the job of the disc jockey normally receives no tips, then only those hours worked behind the bar can be used for the tip credit.

Meal credits

In addition to tip credits, an employer can deduct a reasonable amount for meals from an employee's wages. Suppose you provide a meal each day for employees that costs you $4.

You can deduct 50 cents per hour from an eight-hour work day. The reasonable cost of a meal does not include any profit. It is best to figure the direct cost of the food and its preparation only.

The Department of Labor looks at meal credits very seriously. Several requirements must be met before a meal credit can be deducted. The employee must:

- Be allowed to make a voluntary choice as to whether or not to accept the meal credit and its amount.
- Cannot be coerced to accept the meal credit as a condition of employment.
- Retain the option to not accept the meal credit from time to time.
- The employer must keep records of each employee meal eaten and its value.

The burden of proof rests with the employer to justify any deductions. Where state laws conflict, the lesser amount allowed for a meal credit must be deducted. Certain states require additional proof that a meal has actually been consumed. The use of cash register receipts or another form of documentation may be necessary.

Uniforms

The Department of Labor has established rules and requirements regarding the use of uniforms and their maintenance. You can require your employees to wear a specific uniform other than regular street clothes. If you provide the uniform, you can deduct the cost of the uniform from the employee's paycheck if you pay him or her more than the minimum wage. This deduction cannot bring the employee's wage below the minimum, however. Thus, if the minimum wage is $4.25 and the employee is paid $5 per hour, a deduction of no more than 75 cents per hour is allowed until the costs are recovered.

No deductions can be made if the employee is paid only the minimum wage. An employee must be reimbursed for the maintenance of a uniform when paid the minimum wage. This reimbursement is one hour's wages per week and is not considered taxable income to the employee. Employees who work part-time and are paid only the minimum wage are to be reimbursed at the rate of 67 cents a day for cleaning and maintenance. When the uniform is of the wash and wear variety, and can be done with the employee's regular laundry, no reimbursement is required.

Civil rights

The federal Civil Rights Act of 1964, Title II, provides that all persons, regardless of race, color, religion, or national origin cannot be discriminated or segregated against. They must be able to enjoy all the goods, services, advantages, and accommodations of any public place. When you create certain house policies for dress or standards of conduct, you cannot exclude any person without a just cause. Never discriminate for any reason, as a lawsuit can result. Post your house rules and be sure they are enforced fairly and consistently.

All of the various laws that have been discussed are current as of the time this book was written. Laws are constantly changing. The advice of an attorney or an accountant should be considered whenever an important decision is to be made, particularly in regards to minimum wage laws. If the Department of Labor investigates your bar, it can be very costly to pay back wages because of improper computations or documentation of wages and the various credits. An investigation can be prompted by a complaint from an employee, a competitor, a union, or simply a routine check. It is wise to review all of your policies periodically to ensure they are up-to-date and conform with federal, state, and local ordinances.

State laws

The states began the regulation of the distribution of alcoholic products after the Twenty-first Amendment took effect in 1933. Although the federal government still controls the contents, manufacturing, and advertising of liquor, each state determines how liquor is sold within its borders and where it is warehoused.

Some states became the sole distributor of all products. In these states, known as *control states*, there are no wholesalers. The retailers buy directly from the state. The states have a monopoly on all liquor sales thereby creating a great source of revenue.

In others, known as *license states*, the state governs the industry by imposing heavy regulations and licensing requirements on manufacturers, distributors and retailers. (See TABLE 8-2.) The sole purpose of state licensing is to prohibit illegal activities and tied-house interests stemming from a dominant manufacturer, wholesaler, or distributor. The states were able to establish these controls because the Tenth Amendment allows for: *"The powers not delegated to the United States by the Constitution, nor prohibited by it to the States, are reserved to the States respectively, or to the people."*

Thus, the states possess the power to regulate liquor in their own way. Some states restrict the types of alcohol and the bottle sizes that can be sold. Others restrict the days and hours of operation and set limitations on the times and days deliveries can be received. Some states control liquor and wine but allow the counties to control malt beverages or beers. Others allow each county or municipality to decide whether liquor can be sold or consumed in its own district. If the decision is yes, the area is known as a wet area. If it is no, the area becomes a dry county or city. A dry county may allow the sale of alcohol only in private clubs.

It is obvious that laws on different levels overlap. You need to know which state, county, or municipal law codes apply in your area. Contact your state alcohol beverage control board or liquor control commission to receive a copy of your state's laws. A large public law library will have these as well as the latest local laws.

When researching the laws that apply to a specific location, a new bar owner should find the answers to the following questions:

- What is the legal minimum drinking age?

- What types of identifications are acceptable to verify a person's age? Can I ask for more than one ID?

- Can I serve a double or triple shot in one glass? Can I have a Happy Hour?

- What happens when a customer drinking in my bar leaves and gets into an accident and causes injuries to himself and others? Are I and my employees responsible?

- What is the minimum age of someone I can hire to work in my bar? Does serving food change the minimum age requirement?

- Do my employees have to pass any health tests?

Table 8-2. Control and License States.

Control States	License States	
Alabama	Alaska	Mississippi (Retail)
Idaho	Arizona	Missouri
Iowa	Arkansas	Nebraska
Maine	California	Nevada
Michigan	Colorado	New Jersey
Mississippi (Wholesale)	Connecticut	New Mexico
Montana	Delaware	New York
New Hampshire	Florida	North Dakota
North Carolina	Georgia	Oklahoma
Ohio	Hawaii	Rhode Island
Oregon	Illinois	South Carolina
Pennsylvania	Indiana	South Dakota
Utah	Kansas	Tennessee
Vermont	Kentucky	Texas
Virginia	Louisiana	Wisconsin
Washington	Maryland	Wyoming (Retail)
West Virginia	Massachusetts	District of Columbia
Wyoming (Wholesale)	Minnesota	

- Are there any restrictions placed on how I can advertise and what I can say in my ads?

When it comes to alcohol, every state and locality in the United States has different laws regarding what is and what is not legal. To compound the issue, these laws are constantly changing.

Obtaining a liquor license

Generally these licenses are of two categories: On-premise sales (liquor sold can only be consumed on the premises) and on and off-premise sales (liquor sold can be consumed on the premises and taken off the premises in a package). Licenses specify whether you can sell only beer, wine, or beer and wine, or liquor, beer, and wine. In some states, licenses are required to operate a "locker system" of liquor dispersement. This occurs in dry states when a private club stores liquor purchased by its members. The club then sells or provides everything else needed for cocktail service.

The easiest way to purchase a license is from an existing owner. The buyer can either take over the business and property including the liquor license or buy the license only and transfer it to his own property. Licenses often can be transferred from county to county within a state. Licenses for sale are easily found in local newspaper ads, trade publications, or business brokers' listings. Purchase prices for existing licenses fluctuate widely on the open market depending upon supply and demand.

The state or county releases new licenses based upon population growth (varies from an increase of 1,500 to 2,500 persons per year), usually within a county. A fixed price is set and then sold to a qualified buyer. If the number of applicants exceeds the number of licenses released, a lottery is held. A license purchased from a state or county alcohol board is less expensive than one bought on the open market. The cost of a license and transfer fees vary from state to state. Licenses must be renewed each year at a fixed rate, which is only a fraction of the original cost.

To apply for a license, consult your local or state alcohol control board. This board may direct you to also register with the local city clerk. Evidence of ownership or lease agreements and an opening date for your bar are needed. The board may wish to see a floor plan of the bar to determine areas of liquor sales and consumption. Most states require an applicant, including all parties concerned (partners and officers of corporations), to be fingerprinted and present when applying. Licenses issued for partnerships, corporations, and franchises must submit information concerning stockholders, corporate seals, articles of incorporation, recorded partnership agreements, and certification of any tied-house interests.

In many states, escrows are required when liquor licenses are transferred. An escrow company is a neutral third party to the transaction that holds all considerations until both parties agree on all terms. These considerations are all monies, notes, or properties to be exchanged for the transfer of the license and the business. It is advisable to include in the purchase agreement that the sale is subject to the approval and issuance of a liquor license. In other words, a rejection of your license application will put an end to the deal. Judgments against the license or back taxes owed must be settled or the purchase price adjusted in escrow. A title company should be hired during escrow to verify claims against the license or property. The title company conducts a search through the county records for any recorded claims.

Financial statements will be required as part of your application. In addition, proof of tax permits, business licenses from the various federal, state, or local agencies, a copy of the escrow instructions, and verification of consideration will be needed. You may be responsible for "posting" a sign that serves as a notice of intent to transfer or operate the license at your location. This allows neighbors or surrounding businesses to object to the licensing board if they have cause.

In some states, the application requires a list of the existing schools, churches, hospitals, public playgrounds, military bases, youth facilities, parks, courts, libraries, or private residences nearby. It is best to avoid locations in close proximity to any of the above. Even if the license is approved, future problems can result if objections are raised concerning litter, loitering, noise from within your bar, parking problems, and crowds. Some states require proof of a mailing to all property owners within a certain radius of the bar's location stating the proposed hours of operation. Be sure to check zoning regulations at the state and local government levels. Once the license is acquired, it must be put into operation within a limited time period or forfeiture can result.

Certain states place a special excise and gross receipts tax on alcoholic beverage sales. Permits to collect sales or excise taxes must be issued by the state before the license can be used. Often these tax permits will demand deposits in advance based upon projected sales. Be sure to inquire at all stages of your application process whether you are meeting the necessary tax requirements.

The time needed for approval of the application varies from state to state. There is usually a waiting period of 30 days to allow the board to investigate the applicant and provide adequate time for any protests. In some states, a temporary license is granted, giving the immediate right to serve alcohol. Applications are denied for a number of reasons, the most common being the location of the proposed bar. Sometimes, people feel a bar will create a public nuisance or a law enforcement problem. When reviewing the application, the licensing agency considers the number of existing licenses in the area. If the applicant is not the true owner, is a chronic alcoholic, or has a police record, the application can be denied. Whenever a license is denied, the applicant has the option to demonstrate his or her need for the license.

Once a license is in operation, it can be revoked or fines can be levied in lieu of actual suspension. This occurs when an employee or owner does not obey the federal, state, or local laws and regulations.

Local laws

Local jurisdiction prevails where the state has granted it the power. A business license must be applied for before you can begin business operations. The purpose of this license is to collect taxes on your sales at the local level. If the name of your business uses any name other than your own you must file a fictitious business name statement. Before the city clerk will grant a business license, you must pay a newspaper of general circulation in the area to publish your fictitious business name statement. This informs the public of the owners and the legal form of the business. (See FIG. 8-1.) Many banks require proof of publication of the fictitious statement before they will allow you to open a business bank account using a fictitious name.

The following persons are doing business as: The Catch, 1200 Pacific Coast Highway, Malibu CA 90001. Bob Miller, 1538 Edgewater Lane, #201B, Malibu CA 90001. Ray Miller, 3106 Pacific Coast Highway, Malibu CA 90001. This business is being conducted by co-partners. BOB MILLER AND RAY MILLER. This statement was filed with the County Clerk of Los Angeles County on July 1, 1999. New fictitious business statement July 5, 12, 17, 21, 1999.

Fig. 8-1. Fictitious business statement.

Also on the local level, you must comply with all codes of the Building and Safety, Health, and Fire Departments. Inspections of your bar are made periodically to check for violations. Any violations must be corrected within a specified period of time to the satisfaction of the department or your business license may be revoked. When a change of ownership occurs, notify these departments to verify that existing permits are still valid.

Insurance

Insurance protection is an essential cost of operating a bar. A customer or employee accident, fire, theft, or a loss of business due to damage can destroy a business if you have no insurance. There are insurance companies that specialize in covering bar operations. Rates vary according to building structure, surroundings, value of property, and fire protection systems.

Certainly coverage is needed for property damage, which includes the building, inventory, equipment, and fixtures. Property can be insured for its full replacement or current cash value, which allows for depreciation. This is either *named peril* or *all risk* coverage. Named peril calls out the coverage for fire, smoke, explosion, vandalism, and other hazards. All risk covers these and much more, including damage from water, riots, earthquakes, and even volcanic activities.

There are a number of personal liability coverages you should carry. A *general comprehensive liability* protects from losses due to claims for bodily injury and property damage as a result of an accident. More specific coverages should be in the form of *personal injury liability* against law suits due to false arrest, libel, slander, detention, defamation of character, and personal injuries. *Contractual liability* coverage is to insure against agreements the bar has with equipment leasing or other ser-

vices where the companies providing the services or equipment are not liable for malfunction or injury. *Fire liability* protects against damages to other buildings from a fire that started on your premises. *Automobile liability* will insure you against damages or injuries that employees sustain while driving their own cars or company-owned cars for business reasons. *Crime coverage* protects against loss of property, inventory, or money resulting from robbery, theft, and vandalism. If your bar has an unusual amount of glass, insurance can protect you from losses due to vandalism. Workers' compensation, mandatory in some states, pays for medical and rehabilitation costs resulting from work-related injuries and loss of pay to employees. Another important form of insurance is *business interruption* or *loss of income* insurance. This reimburses for expenses, revenue, and profits lost due to a halt in business resulting from a fire, large theft, or the illness of a key employee.

Employee health and life insurance packages can provide a variety of medical, dental, optical, and death coverages. Often individual plans are provided by owners to key employees. If your employees are union members, you may be required to contribute to benefit packages as part of the collective bargaining agreement. *Product liability* protects from claims against any of your drinks, food, or other merchandise that may be defective. Depending on the dram shop laws in your area, *liquor liability* or *third party liability* insurance protects from losses resulting from customers who become intoxicated and cause injury or damage to others and their property, either within or outside of your bar.

Consult with your local insurance agent for the best and most comprehensive package for your type of establishment. Check with your local restaurant and bar associations to see if a cheaper group rate is available.

Social responsibilities

Beyond any legal regulations, your bar has a social responsibility to the community it serves. Alcohol awareness should be the number one priority of a bar owner. The abuses of alcohol and drunk driving are issues that concern everyone. Alcohol is a powerful commodity that must be dispersed intelligently. By providing services such as complimentary snacks, hors d'oeuvres, or offering food items for sale, you are reducing the chances that a patron will leave your premises in an inebriated condition.

The creation and implementation of a sensible policy of denying liquor to guests who have had too much to drink can help save lives. You can provide transportation for these people instead of allowing them to drive. The idea is not to discourage drinking; after all, your bar is in the business of selling alcohol. The idea is to encourage the recreational use and sensible limitations of alcohol while establishing your bar as a place in the community for fun, relaxation, entertainment, and social interaction in a healthy environment. (See Chapter 15, Management, for more information on alcohol awareness training.)

Think globally and act locally. The recycling of glass, paper, and metal cans is easy to do and benefits everyone. The controlling of your waste is another way to control your costs. Contact your waste removal company on ways to separate these products, along with your local beer distributor on ways to recycle beer bottles. Liquor, mix and beer bottles need to find a new home instead of your trash bin. The owner of the Sagebrush Cantina in Calabasas, California, started his recycling program and decided to expand it as a center for the entire community. His program became a model for other restaurants and bars.

Cardboard is easily recyclable. As with all recyclable materials, all you need to do is find out who will pick it up; they will inform you of the best way to prepare it. In the case of cardboard, the boxes are flattened and baled and paid for by the ton. The recycled cardboard is used for the middle weave of the typical three-part section of a new piece of cardboard.

Paper is abundant in any business today and is easily recycled. Consider using coasters in your bar instead of, or in conjunction with, napkins. Your coasters are reusable and bar menus can be printed on them. Print your menus on recycled paper. When photocopying, use both sides of the paper and reuse old copies for scratch paper.

Encourage your employees to suggest ways to cut down on waste and implement their own ideas. Let your customers know what you are doing to help the environment. A great program would be to coordinate a tree planting in your neighborhood, or sponsor a canyon or beach cleanup. Customers can contribute, your bar can donate money, and everyone can become involved in the plantings or cleanups.

Simply opening a business and withdrawing money from a community is not enough. Giving back to the area that has supported you and made you successful is vital. It can take the form of environmental needs or an issue that is close to your heart, such as raising money for children with cancer. The important issue is to spread your goodwill and take the first step. Others will take note and follow in your footsteps.

9

Selecting, pricing, and merchandising liquor

The alcoholic beverages you offer your customers are selected from an endless variety of liquors, wines, beers, and liqueurs. The selection, pricing, and presentation of your drinks will affect your profits, concept, and clientele. The way you purchase and control this inventory also directly influences your profits.

Liquor selection

The quality and quantity of the liquor you offer your customers depends on the concept and location of the bar you have in mind, your anticipated volume, and the type of clientele you hope to attract.

Most bars offer their customers three or four different levels of quality in liquor. The first level is the *well*, or liquor you will serve when someone orders a scotch and water and does not specify a brand. Well liquors are placed at the bartender's work station. The well is generally out of the direct view of customers. When the bartender is pouring, however, everyone at the bar can see the label on the bottle. Your largest sales will be of well liquors.

The *call* brands are the next level of liquors. These are the brands that customers request by name. Your call liquor will cost you more than

the well brands and, consequently, you will have to charge more for call drinks than for well drinks. Often these bottles will be placed in the speed racks in front of the well or on the shelves of the backbar, facing your customers.

Premium and super premium liquors are requested less frequently, cost more to purchase, and cost the customer more. These top-quality brands should always be prominently displayed on your backbar.

You need to decide which brands will constitute your well, call, premium, and super premium liquors. There are no hard and fast rules that apply, and you can always change your brands whenever you please. Upon opening, however, the brands you serve will come under close inspection by your customers. What you serve them reflects what you think of them. They will be comparing your brands and prices with the other places they frequent. The most important selections you will have to make are the types of liquor offered in your well. For these and all of the other choices, you will need to take into consideration what your competitors are serving and how their concept and price structure compares with yours. Decide whether you wish to compete with them by upgrading your well, by maintaining the same quality and serving the same brands, or by serving brands of a lesser quality than theirs. By all means, make a careful analysis of the total situation.

Consider the drinking habits and the ages of your clientele. If you are opening a dance club where the customers are young and not very knowledgeable about liquor, you would probably decide to serve very inexpensive well brands to keep your costs down and maximize your profits. Younger customers tend not to request specific brands and they usually like their drinks with sweet mixes. On the other hand, if the clientele will be older, serve a better well and charge a little more for it. These customers expect a good well drink and will be able to tell the difference between Brand X and the brands they are familiar with. An older crowd tends to drink liquor on the rocks or with water or soda, so the taste and quality of the liquor is not disguised and thus becomes more important.

Because the majority of drinkers will order well or house brands, do not think that if you have a cheap well you will sell more call or premium drinks. On the contrary, a good well will add to your reputation. Do not under any circumstances offer a cheap well with high prices. You can really damage your business that way. Do not underestimate your customers. Unless they are inexperienced drinkers, they will be able to taste the difference if not feel it the next day. The better you know your clientele and its taste, the better your chances for success. When in doubt, opt for the higher quality.

If you really want to take a lot of pride in your well, offer what is called a *premium* or *super* well. Serve the quality brands in your well that most bars consider call or premium liquors. You can cut down on your inventory this way, because your better liquors are now in the well instead of on the backbar. You have eliminated the less expensive brands. You can price your premium well competitively or drop the

price below the competition's and promote your bar as having the classiest well liquor in town at the lowest prices. You can even serve a super well while selecting only a few call and premium liquors for the backbar. That will cut down on your inventory even more, and it could allow you to serve drinks at lower prices all across the board. This is a good idea for a very small bar lacking in space. You can also limit your selection of liquor when your bar generates a large volume of business because its concept—and not its drinks—will draw a crowd. An example is a nightclub that specializes in lounge entertainment.

You also need to select your well according to the means of the people you will be serving. A middle-priced well of familiar liquor or a premium well would fit in nicely for a bar in Beverly Hills. A back country saloon in South Dakota or a tavern close to a college campus, however, could get by with a less expensive well. A premium well would be out of place and beyond the pocketbook of your customers.

Another factor to consider when choosing your well is the volume of business your bar sustains. If you are out in the country, you may not have as many customers as a bar located along a busy highway or in a large city. Your best bet is to choose the more popular lower to medium-priced brands. You will still make money, since most of your other operating expenses will not be as high.

Once you have decided on the quality of your well liquor, you need to consider the quantity of liquor on your backbar. Again, that depends largely on the concept of your bar and your clientele. There are bars that stock hundreds of bottles of liquor. The backbar of Kincaid's Bayhouse (Burlingame, California) has over 800 bottles (see FIG. 9-1). The bartenders use an old sliding ladder to reach the bottles. These bars make it a point to carry just about every type of liquor ever bottled. They never want to be caught without a customer's

Fig. 9-1. The incredible 800+ backbar bottle display at Kincaid's Bayhouse in Burlingame, California. It's called the Bayhouse because it faces out onto a gorgeous view of the San Francisco Bay.

choice. The backbar display is awesome and impressive.

That is the extreme. The majority of bars stock three or four call and three or four premium brands to back up their well choices. You can tie up a tremendous amount of cash in your inventory with oddball specialty brands that may only be called for once a year. What you want to achieve in your call and premium selections is a well-rounded inventory, so that if someone asks for a liquor you do not have, you can suggest an equivalent. In this way, you will not lose that customer.

Whenever possible, if you have a regular customer who prefers a particular brand, keep it stocked. Once you are open, this type of personal service to your clientele will build your bar a loyal following. Have your bartenders keep you informed if customers repeatedly request a brand that is not in your inventory.

As an owner or manager, you will be informed by your liquor distributors of new products before the national advertising campaigns begin. These sales agents are kept abreast of developments by the liquor manufacturers. You can always tell when a liquor company launches a new campaign or product by the requests from your customers. You want to anticipate their requests and be prepared.

Your well liquors will consist of scotch, bourbon, vodka, gin, rum, tequila, and brandy. Also include sweet and dry vermouth and triple sec as part of your well. Your call and premium spirits are usually aged longer and may be of a higher proof than your well liquors. Most liquor comes in either 80 or 86.8

proof. Several popular brands are also available in 100, 110, or 151 proof liquors, and they should be stocked, too.

Proof is the percentage of alcohol in a spirit. It is indicated by the use of the degree symbol (°) after the number. The numerical system used in the United States that indicates proof, doubles the percentage of alcohol present; therefore, a 100 proof liquor contains 50 percent alcohol by volume. Different countries use different proof systems. The proof on the label conforms to the system of the importing country, however, regardless of how the manufacturing country labels its bottles.

What to stock

The following is a brief discussion of the different types of liquor your bar should stock. From this list, which is not meant to be comprehensive, you can assemble those brands that are popular in your area. Ask your local distributors and compare their recommendations to what you see stocked in your competitors' bars. Also ask your local liquor stores what brands they sell the most. The Liquor Handbook (Jobson Publishing, New York) publishes an annual reference that lists by state and by major cities in the United States numerous statistics on liquor sales and trends. It is available for reference at the business libraries of major universities.

Scotch whiskey

Scotch is made by fermenting and then distilling grains. In Scotland, *malt scotch* whiskey is made entirely from sprouted (malt) barley. A smoky flavor in the finished product results from the barley being dried over peat fires. Glenfiddich and Glenlivet are excellent examples of malt scotch. When malt scotch is blended with spirits made from other grains, mostly corn, the whiskey is known as *blended scotch*. You will want to stock several of these. Bal-

lantine's, Cutty Sark, Dewar's White Label, J&B, and Johnnie Walker Red are good examples. Premium blends, which are aged longer, and are made with a higher quantity of malt, include: Chivas Regal, Haig Pinch, and Johnnie Walker Black. At the top of the line, you might stock a bottle of Ballantine 17- or 30-Year or Chivas Royal Salute.

Irish whiskey

Made in Ireland of blends using malted and unmalted barley and other grains, Irish whiskey has a lighter taste different from scotch because the smoke is avoided in the drying process of the grains. Irish whiskey is often requested as a shot or in Irish Coffee drinks. Have at least one of these brands on hand: Dunphy's, Jameson, Murphy's, or Old Bushmills.

U.S. whiskey

Bourbon is straight or unblended whiskey that is a distinctively American product. It takes its name from Bourbon County, Kentucky, where early distillers made a mash with corn as the main ingredient. Today, bourbon must have 51 percent corn in its mash. The sour mash process involves aging the bourbon in charred oak kegs. Bourbon drinkers will ask for these brands: Ancient Age, Early Times, Jim Beam, and Old Grand-Dad. Higher proof "sippin" bourbons are Old Weller (107°) and Wild Turkey (101°). Maker's Mark is a premium bourbon made in the smallest licensed distillery in the U.S.

Whiskey made in Tennessee is referred to by aficionados as Tennessee whiskey, and not bourbon. Before the liquor is placed in barrels for aging, it is filtered through charcoal, which mellows the taste. Jack Daniel's Black Label, also a sour mash, is a must in any bar, and George Dickel Old #12 would round out this category.

Rye whiskey must use 51 percent rye grain in its mash. Old Overholt is the most requested brand. Rye and ginger ale is the most common drink made with rye.

Blended whiskey is a mixture of at least 20 percent straight whiskey and other neutral grains. The result is a lighter taste. These liquors are most often mixed with some type of soda, for example "7 & 7," popular with younger drinkers. This is Seagrams 7 Crown mixed with 7-Up. Kessler and Calvert Extra are other examples of blends.

Canadian whisky

Note the lack of an "e" in the spelling. These blended whiskies use a combination of corn, barley, wheat, and other grains to achieve their popular light taste. Canadian Club (CC), Seagram V.O., and Crown Royal are requested frequently. If you also stocked Black Velvet and Canadian Mist, you would have more than enough Canadians on your backbar.

Vodka

Vodka is the leading type of liquor sold in America. It is produced from neutral grain spirits and is bottled without aging. The goal of most vodka manufacturers is to produce a clear neutral spirit, without the strong taste or aroma of other liquor. Vodka mixes easily with fruit juice, soft drinks, and other spirits, thus its popularity. It is an extremely versatile ingredient and is used in countless drinks such as the Bloody Mary, Screwdriver, Greyhound, Black Russian, Martini, and Gimlet. Most brands come in a variety of proofs. The number one U.S. brand is Smirnoff. Many of the foreign brands are popular when chilled and served neat as shots. The Soviet Union makes Stolichnaya; Sweden, Absolut; Finland, Finlandia; Canada, Silhouette; and Poland, Wyborowa Wodka. A variation of straight tasting vodka are flavored vodkas. You'll find a variety to choose from: pepper, lemon, citrus, and other herbs or fruits.

Gin

This clear spirit has a colorful past stretching back three centuries to its origin in Holland. Then, as today, the dominant flavor of gin came from juniper berries with subtle hints of other herbs, seeds, roots, and spices. Bottled without aging, its aromatic qualities give gin its characteristic fragrance. The Martini, Gin and Tonic, Tom Collins, and Gimlet are cocktails known the world over. To make these drinks with the best gin, stock your bar with at least one of the U.S. brands: Gordon's, Seagram's, Gilbey's, or Fleischmann's, and with at least two of the British imports: Beefeaters, Tanqueray, Bombay, and Boodles.

Rum

Where sugar cane grows, rum is sure to follow. Made from the cane's molasses, rum is aged and blended. The aging changes the color and often the depth and mellowness of the final product. White or silver rums are the youngest, and gold or amber come next, with a minimum of one year of aging. The añejos are aged four years or more and usually served neat or sipped over ice. Puerto Rico is the world's leading rum producer and no bar should be without its Bacardi Silver and Bacardi 151°. Jamaica's Myers's Original Dark Rum is another must. Rum is second only to vodka as a popular ingredient of mixed drinks. You will use rum to mix with juice, soft drinks, and an endless list of tropical concoctions: the Daiquiri, Frozen Fruit Daiquiri, Piña Colada, Chi Chi, Mai Tai, Planter's Punch, and Zombie, to name but a few.

Tequila

Mexico is the only country that produces Tequila spirit and only in an official designated region around the town of Tequila. The blue agave plant grows there. Its juice, fermented and distilled, gives tequila its flavor. Similar to rum, tequila comes in white, gold, and añejo varieties. The white or silver labels are rarely aged. Gold receives a little aging, and añejo at least a year. Jose Cuervo Gold and Cuervo 1800 are requested most often, with Sauza running third. Tequila is used in Margaritas, the Sunrise, and straight as a shot. The drinking of a shot of tequila involves a routine religiously followed. First a dash of salt is placed on the back of the hand and licked off, then the shot is downed in one gulp followed by biting into a lime wedge.

Brandy

In the United States, almost all domestic brandy comes from California. Made from grapes and aged at least two years, it is almost always served in a snifter as an after-dinner or late-night drink. Christian Brothers, Korbel, or Paul Masson would complement your other liquors in the well or on the backbar.

Fruit brandies are made all over the world with every type of fruit imaginable. Unless you are trying to appeal to a very special crowd, stock domestic products. They are cheaper than the imports and the overwhelming majority of your customers will not notice the difference. Put apricot, blackberry, and cherry brandy on the backbar. They are served over ice, in a cordial glass for sipping, or blended with a sweet and sour mix for "sour" drinks.

Triple sec

Triple sec is a neutral spirit flavored with oranges and should be a part of your well. Stock a generic brand, as it is primarily used as an ingredient in mixed drinks, such as Margaritas and Kamikazes.

Sweet and dry vermouth

Vermouths are actually considered wines. You can buy fancy Italian and French vermouths, if you choose, but domestic ones will do just fine. Dry vermouth goes into Martinis, and Sweet vermouth goes into Manhattans and Rob Roys. Stock only a bottle or two, as vermouths are used sparingly.

Liqueurs

Liqueurs are also called cordials. They are distilled spirits flavored with a variety of ingredients: fruit, herbs, spices, flowers, nuts, seeds, roots, cream, and even other liquors. This category of spirits can be very trendy. What is in one year may be out the next. Those listed below have been around for many years, however. Their proofs are as varied as their flavors, and they are usually lower than other liquors. They are served neat in cordial glasses and snifters, or used as ingredients in many mixed cocktails.

Popular liqueurs you ought to have are imported. You can also purchase many generic brand domestic liqueurs. They cost less, but their taste will not compare to that of the imported brands. Some bars pour the imported brand only when a customer specifically calls for it, and keep a domestic on hand to be used like a well brand. You will probably order a whole line of liqueurs from one dealer. Taste them. Each line tastes a little different. The U.S. brands are Arrow, DeKuyper, Leroux, and Hiram Walker. The Europeans make the Bols line.

Amaretto This has an almond and apricot base. Amaretto di Saronno (Italy) is considered the original and the best, often served by itself or in the Godfather cocktail.

Anisette This is licorice-flavored. Buy a domestic. Also based on the anise seed are Ouzo (Greece), which is considered a brandy, and Pernod (France). Pernod has the distinction of turning a yellowish cream color when mixed with water.

Baileys Original Irish Cream (Ireland) This has a chocolatety coffee-coconut taste.

Fresh dairy cream, used in Baileys, is processed in such a way that it does not spoil without refrigeration for quite a while. Thus, it can remain on your shelf for quite some time. Baileys started a whole new fashion for cream liqueurs. These are usually served in a snifter, on the rocks, mixed, or with coffee.

Benedictine (France) This is one of the oldest herbal liqueurs. Made by the Benedictine monks, it is treated like cognac and relished by itself. Its brother is B & B (France), which is about two-thirds Benedictine and one-third brandy.

Campari (Italy) This is a bittersweet spirit often served in a cordial glass as an aperitif to stimulate the appetite. The majority of your customers will ask for it with soda or tonic and a squeeze of lime.

Chartreuse Another French concoction of more than 130 herbs, it is produced in various proofs and colors. You'll want the green potent version at 110°.

Coffee-based liqueurs These are very popular when mixed with coffee or used in a Black or White Russian. Kahlua (Mexico) and Tia Maria (Jamaica) are the best. No bar should be without these.

Cointreau (France) A stronger version of triple sec in flavor and proof, it is almost always served in a cordial or snifter glass late at night or after a meal.

Creme de Banane This adds a banana taste to cream and specialty drinks.

Creme de Cacao This is a chocolate liqueur with a hint of vanilla. Put both the clear (white) and brown (dark) bottles on your backbar. There are many cream drinks that use either dark or white cacao, such as the Brandy Alexander, Golden Cadillac, Grasshopper, King Alphonse, Pink Squirrel, and Velvet Hammer. For your chocoholic customers, you might want Cheri-Suisse (Switzerland) with its chocolate-cherry taste, or Vandermint (Holland) with its chocolate-mint flavor.

Creme de Cassis A sweet, reddish-purple derivative of black currants, it is mostly used in a White Wine Kir and a Kir Royale (champagne with a touch of cassis).

Creme de Menthe The flavor comes from peppermint. You'll want the white or clear bottle and the green one on your shelves for Grasshoppers and Stingers. Peppermint flavor is also featured in the ever popular Peppermint Schnapps.

Creme de Noyaux or Creme de Almond This is a reddish liqueur used in the Pink Squirrel.

Curaçao This is an orange or blue spirit with a taste of oranges. If you make a lot of tropical fruit drinks, curaçao comes in handy, particularly in a Blue Hawaiian.

Drambuie (Scotland) This has a scotch base and a delicate mixture of herbs and honey. Served alone on the rocks or in a snifter, it is also used with scotch in a Rusty Nail.

Frangelico (Italy) This is another popular late night drink. Hazelnuts provide the dominant flavor.

Galliano (Italy) This is the sweet and syrupy yellow ingredient of the Harvey Wallbanger. It has a vanilla-licorice taste.

Grand Marnier (France) This has a cognac base with orange peel used for flavoring. It is usually sipped in a snifter and sometimes mixed with other liqueurs in special drinks.

Metaxa (Greece) This is a brandy-based liqueur served as an after-dinner drink. It is occasionally mixed with other liqueurs.

Midori (Japan) The original green honeydew melon liqueur, it is principally used in the Melonball as well as the Midori Daiquiri and Margarita.

Rock and Rye (U.S.) This is whiskey-based with fruit flavorings. Whole or partial fruits are often placed inside the bottle. It is served by itself, neat, or on the rocks.

Sambuca Romana (Italy) This has a clear

licorice taste derived from the fruit of the elder bush. It is almost always served neat and downed in one gulp.

Sloe Gin Coming from the sloeberry, which is actually a plum, this brilliant red liqueur is used in the Sloe Gin Fizz, the Singapore Sling, and mixed with orange juice in the Sloe Screw.

Southern Comfort (U.S.) This has a peachy bourbon taste. It is very sweet and comes in 100 proof. The Sloe Comfortable Screw is one of its many uses.

Strega This is another strong Italian after-dinner, late-night sipping liqueur.

Tuaca (Italy) This is a sweet backbar item that is savored by itself, over ice, or in coffee. Vanilla is the dominant flavor, augmented by many herbs and spices.

Finally, select several cognacs, champagnes, sherries, and aperitifs to round out your liquor and liqueur choices.

Cognacs

Cognac derives its name from the Cognac region of France, which is the only place in the world where it is produced and bottled. It becomes progressively more expensive with age. Minimum ages are stated on the label. If the label reads VS, VSP, or has three stars, the cognac is at least two years old. When VSOP, VSEP, VSO, or VO appears, it is at least four years old. Special names like Cordon Bleu, Napoleon, XO, Extra Anniversaire, etc., indicate a minimum of six years' aging and as many as 20 years. A cognac of exceptional age is labeled Age Inconnu, which means Age Unknown. One younger and one older cognac should be stocked for a small neighborhood bar, while a well-rounded backbar would include Courvoisier, Hennessey, Martell, and Remy-Martin.

Sherry and aperitifs

Sherries are fortified wines. They have extra alcohol added. Dry sherry, such as Dry Sack (Spain), is an aperitif, generally served before a meal. Sweet sherry is good after a meal. Harvey's Bristol Cream (Spain) is a sweet sherry. Dubonnet (France) is kept in the refrigerator and often served neat or on the rocks with a twist. It is a sweet aperitif wine.

Port

Sweet, aged wines from the Porto region of Portugal, ports warm the soul. Some are aged in the bottle, and others in wood. Typically served at room temperature in a sherry glass, after a meal, with dessert, coffee, or Stilton or cheddar cheese.

You should know what every bottle you are selling tastes like and how it can be used. The alcohol beverage manufacturers are constantly developing new tastes and brands, hoping to set a trend and establish a new drink sensation. It does happen, and you need to be aware of it. Part of the fun of running a bar is introducing people to new drinks and tastes. Your bartenders and servers are your frontline sales agents. They should be trained to suggest to your customers a great new drink or a new liqueur placed on the backbar.

Beer

The more extensive your beer and wine selections, the more refrigerator space you will need at the backbar and for storage. In a high-volume bar, you need to have enough space to keep several cases of the most popular beverages cold. You can always transfer from the storage refrigerator to the backbar as the bar's stock is depleted. You will need more space for beer storage than for wine storage. You will want to keep cold several kegs of each draft you carry as well as several cases of your bottled beers. When selecting your beer, try to achieve a balance between domestic and imported brands, regular, lite, dry, and dark beers. There are two different types of beer, lager and ale. Lager beer is fermented with the yeast at the bottom of a cold brewing tank. Before packaging, it is aged or lagered for at least a few weeks. Ale is fermented with yeast at the top of a warmer tank, and is not aged.

The lager beers are the pilsners, which are light, dry, malt, bock, and steam beers. The pilsners are the typically mild, amber colored, best-selling American beers such as Budweiser, Coors, Michelob, Miller's High Life, and Stroh's. Light beers are pilsners with about half to a third of the calories. The reduction in calories come from less alcohol or grain used in the fermentation process. Dry beers start with slightly less grains than regular beers, and spend more time in the mashing process; therefore, eliminating any aftertaste, which is their distinction. Malt beers or malt liquors have a higher percentage of alcohol. Colt 45, Champale, and Schlitz Malt Liquor are some of the popular brands. Anchor Steam Beer of San Francisco originated the steam beer process, a combination of lager yeasting and ale temperatures, resulting in an ale-like beer.

Premium beers are everywhere in the marketplace, among them Heineken (Netherlands), Dos Equis, Carta Blanca and Corona (Mexico), Becks (Germany), Watney's (England), and Kirin (Japan). Ales have more flavor and more alcohol. Porter is a dark and heavy beer not widely brewed. Stout is even richer and darker than porter with a higher alcohol content. Ireland is the home of Guinness, probably the best-known stout in America.

Choose several of the most popular beers in your area. If a local brewery is nearby, carry their beer also. The closer you are to the source, particularly with draught beer, the fresher it is. If you are unsure about carrying a brand, place a small order for a case or two and see how your customers like it. Whenever any of your stock is slow in selling, run a special on it by offering it at a reduced price. Try always to keep your inventory current. Replace slow sellers with newer brands. Federal regulations do not require alcoholic content of beer to be listed on the label. Some states only allow 3.2 percent or 5 percent beer. This percentage is usually expressed in terms of alcohol by weight, but can also be figured by volume or proof. Volume percentages are half proof percentages and about 80 percent weight percentages.

Wine

When selecting your wines, you have the option of purchasing bottled wine in a wide variety of types and price. You can even have house wines, just as you have well or house liquors. The quality can vary. House wines are typically bought in bulk in gallon or four-liter containers to reduce costs. If you choose to run your house chablis and rose wines through guns or faucets, you will need extra refrigerator space to store the wine containers for your system and back-up bottles for refilling. You may decide to only serve house wines and skip the bottles, for lack of space or interest. Customers are drinking more and more wine than ever. Many bars sell premium wines by the glass at prices that far exceed what one would pay for a regular drink. It depends on your concept and the clientele you are serving.

For white wine, have two generic brands, one sweet and one dry, which you can buy in bulk. Consider Chablis, Chardonnay, or White Zinfandel. Then stock at least four varietals in bottles, two fruity and two dry, choosing among Chenin Blanc, Gewurztraminer, French Colombard, Grey Reisling, Johannisberg Reisling, Sauvignon Blanc, Fume Blanc, Semillon, and Pinot Chardonnay. Have a generic Rose to serve as a house wine. The best red wines are dry in taste. If current trends continue, you will undoubtedly sell far more white wine than red. A generic Burgundy can be used as a house wine. Then purchase bottles of at least two of these varietals: Cabernet

Sauvignon, Chianti, Gamay Beaujolais, Merlot, Pinot Noir, or Zinfandel.

Have a few sparkling wines for special occasions. These should include a house champagne in both 750-milliliter bottles and small 150- or 187-milliliter (6.34-ounce) bottles for individual servings. There are countless domestic and foreign brands from which to choose. Many of the French champagne makers have sister wineries producing domestic sparkling wines in Napa Valley, California. Mumms, Moet et Chandon, Piper Heidsieck, Dom Perignon, Tattinger, and Korbel are a few of the many outstanding champagnes available. In addition, have at least one of the more expensive champagnes on hand for your customers' special occasions and celebrations.

Pricing drinks

The only way to make money in this business is to react and adapt constantly to the changing marketplace that surrounds your bar. That means adopting a price structure for your drinks that is competitive and maximizes your profits. Your pricing should be appropriate for your concept and clientele. Once you are open, keep tabs on what other bar owners are doing; you might see an idea that will work for you or stimulate you in a different way.

Each drink should be made the same way every time it is requested. In order to standardize drinks, a drink recipe book should be prepared and used when training your bartenders. Keep a copy behind the bar for reference.

There are two ways to approach drink pricing when you are in direct competition with other bars for the same customers. You can have the same prices they do, or your prices can be radically different. Lower prices are good for certain promotions. If your competition lowers their prices to match yours, however, you better have something else going for you. There are times you will want to price your drinks higher:

- Your concept is so unique that people will gladly pay the extra money (you operate the only comedy club in your area).
- You have a captive audience (a bar overlooking an active volcano).
- You are in a resort area where business is seasonal.

Sometimes, a unique location, such as a revolving bar on the top floor of a hotel or office building, can justify your prices. A private club frequently charges higher prices as part of its ambiance. Customers will pay almost any price to drink as long as they feel they are getting their money's worth.

Another simple way of setting drink prices is based on the cost of each ingredient, added together, and multiplied by a markup factor. The markup factor is the selling price of the drink divided by the cost of the drink. Typically, the cost of a drink is 20 to 25 percent of its selling price, which assumes a 5× or 4× markup factor. Beer and wine costs run higher at 33 to 50 percent, resulting in a 3× or 2× markup multiplier. In a liter there are 33.8 ounces. (See TABLE 9-1.) If you are pouring 1½ ounces in each drink, and a liter costs $15, then the liquor cost is $0.67 per drink. (See FIG. 9-2.) Add an additional 15 percent for miscellaneous bar supplies: ice, soda, fruit, straws, etc. Multiply by a factor of 5, and the drink price comes to $3.85.

Table 9-1. Number of Shots in a Bottle.

Shot glass	Number of shots			
Size in	Fifth	750 ml	Quart	Liter
Ounces	25.6 oz.	25.4 oz.	32 oz.	33.8 oz.
¾	34.1	33.9	42.6	45.1
⅞	29.2	29.0	36.6	38.6
1	25.6	25.4	32.0	33.8
1¼	20.5	20.3	25.6	27.0
1½	17.1	16.9	21.3	22.5
1¾	14.6	14.5	18.3	19.3

$$\frac{33.8 \text{ oz.}}{1.5 \text{ oz}} = 22.5 \text{ shots per liter}$$

$$\frac{\$15 \text{ liter cost}}{22.5 \text{ shots}} = \$0.67 \text{ cost of liquor per drink}$$

$0.67	cost of liquor poured
+ .10	cost of miscellaneous supplies
= .77	total cost of drink
x 5	multiplier for drink price
$3.85	selling price of drink
or	
$4.00	when rounding all prices to nearest $0.25 increment

Fig. 9-2. Pricing by ingredients.

You can get even more exact than the 15 percent used above for miscellaneous supplies by determining the exact cost of every olive, fruit, juice, or special mix added to each drink. When figuring the price, round off to the nearest nickel. At most bars, however, prices are standardized for each category of drinks. All well drinks might be $3.25; all call drinks, $3.75; all premium drinks, $4.25; all blended drinks, $3.75, etc. Many bar owners price their drinks in increments of 25 cents. That makes calculation easy when servers are adding several drink prices. All prices should include any sales tax. The tax can be deducted later.

Volume is another factor to consider when pricing drinks. The cost of a popular drink will lower slightly when the liquor poured is pur-chased at volume discounts. A lower drink price might produce greater volume and greater profits. Look at the figures and notice how a reduction in price combined with an in-crease in volume leads to larger gross profits. (See TABLE 9-2.)

If you are offering entertainment, the stan-dard practice is to increase all drink prices by a set amount. Usually, 50 cents to $1 is added on to the regular price of each drink to pay for the entertainment. If you are charging a cover charge at the door, however, this admission fee pays entertainment costs, and drink prices almost always remain the same.

The hours you are open can also help de-termine your prices. If you are open from 10:00 AM to 2:00 AM, you might have day prices un-til 6:00 PM or 7:00 PM and higher prices at night. Generally, if your bar is a nightclub only open from 8:00 PM to 2:00 or 4:00 AM, the shorter operating hours will dictate that your prices be higher.

Another factor to consider when setting prices is the economy of your area. An affluent community can afford higher prices while a depressed area cannot. A bar close to a college, catering to students, will be cheaper than a bar in the same city with a downtown business clientele.

Pricing as a function of merchandising

Drink prices can be affected in two other im-portant ways. Both involve drink merchan-dising or the way drinks are presented. Let's

Table 9-2. Volume Pricing.

Price of Drink	×	No. Sold	=	Sales	—	Cost of Drink	×	No. Sold	=	Cost of Sales	=	Gross Profits
$3.00	×	300	=	$ 900	—	($0.50	×	300	=	$150)	=	$ 750
$2.00	×	500	=	$1000	—	($0.50	×	500	=	$250)	=	$ 750
$1.50	×	700	=	$1050	—	($0.48	×	700	=	$336)	=	$ 714
$1.50	×	1000	=	$1500	—	($0.46	×	1000	=	$460)	=	$1040

Fig. 9-3. Beer glass comparison. Each glass holds exactly 10 oz. Libbey Glass

look at glassware first. All of the glasses pictured in FIG. 9-3 are the same size—10 ounces. A draught of beer served in each of these glasses costs about 30 cents. Served in the glass on the left, which looks like an ordinary water glass, you might charge $1.00 for it. The beer mug would cost a customer $1.75; the schooner, $2.50; the glass on the far right, a footed pilsner, $2.75. Notice how each glass appears to hold a different amount of beer. It is the same beer, just presented in a different package. It is all an illusion and a perception of value. What the different glasses and corresponding increase in prices can do for your profits is not an illusion. (See TABLES 9-3 and 9-4. and FIG. 9-4.)

What works for beer can also work wonders with wine and mixed drinks. When serving cognacs, use a large-size, 32-ounce snifter as opposed to an 8-ounce glass, and watch the difference in sales. The glass will sell the drink. The customers will think there is more liquor in it, and they are getting more for their money. As much as possible, use a different glass for wine, bottled beer, and draught beer. The more expensive the drink, the better the glass. This is a subtle form of persuasion. You are trying to move your customer up to the higher-priced and higher-profit drinks. Serve your house champagne in saucers and your fine expensive bubblies in flutes.

In addition to the glassware, the garnishing of your drinks can add tremendous eye appeal. Eye appeal is buy appeal. By adding a slice of pineapple with a cherry to a Piña Colada, a fresh strawberry to a Strawberry Daiquiri, or a fresh, crisp stalk of cucumber and a jalapeño pepper to a Bloody Mary, you give

Table 9-3. Servings per Half Barrel (keg) of Beer

TYPE OF GLASS	OZ.	1 in. HEAD	3/4 in. HEAD	1/2 in. HEAD
HOUR	10	264	248	233
	11	233	214	203
	12	209	198	189
	13	190	180	172
	15	172	159	147
FOOTED PILSNER	8	305	283	264
	10	248	233	220
	12	208	198	184
SHAM PILSNER	7	418	377	345
	8	345	317	283
	9	305	283	264
	10	264	248	233
	12	214	203	188
SHELL	7	330	317	294
	8	294	283	273
	10	250	240	226
BEER MUG	10	248	233	220
	12	195	188	180
	14	170	165	158
	16	147	141	134
SCHOONER	10	330	293	256
	12	256	214	198
	14	203	188	168
FLAIR PILSNER	12	220	208	180
PITCHER	60	41		
	40	62		

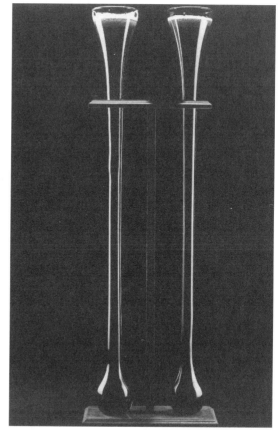

Fig. 9-4. Special yards of ale are a great tool for marketing beer. Nightwing

Table 9-4. Beer Barrel and Keg Sizes.

Container	Fluid ounces	Gallons	Liters	Net Wt/lb	Net Wt/kg
Barrel	3968	31	111.33	248	112.48
1/2 Barrel (Keg)*	1984	15.5	58.67	124	56.24
1/4 Barrel (1/2 Keg)	992	7.75	29.33	62	28.12
1/8 Barrel (1/4 Keg)	496	3.88	14.67	31	14.06

*Most popular size for bar usage.
One gallon of beer weighs 8.48 pounds and contains 128 ounces. A half barrel of beer is equal to approx. 6 3/4 cases of 12 ounce bottles.

the customer something to eat, adding taste appeal to the eye appeal.

Use your imagination when decorating your drinks and stimulate your customers' visual appetites with wild swizzle sticks, oversized straws, and funny characters that hang on the edge of a glass. The more you can add to make a simple drink appear elegant or extraordinary, the more money people will be willing to pay for it. Push food garnishes to the limit—marinated broccoli or marinated string beans for a Bloody Mary, a long (eight inches) citrus twist placed with a cognac in a snifter, or radish roses for Gin and Tonics. Any ingredient can make a drink stand out: ice cream, exotic juices, or candy-stick stir rods.

To keep costs down, always use fresh fruits and vegetables in season to add color. Add a stick of cinnamon, peppermint candy, crushed almonds, or chocolate shavings when topping off a coffee drink with whipped cream. Leave a cookie or two with each hot drink.

Along these lines, invent your own "house specialty" drinks. The Irish Coffee and the Rusty Nail were both invented by individual barkeeps, and the drinks are now known throughout the world. Price your house "signature" drink to include the glass. Customers will pay more, particularly if they feel it is a souvenir. Sometimes, all it takes is creating larger drinks in larger glasses, adding more ice and mix and not liquor, to up your price and profits.

Improving your mixes is another way to spice up sales. The easiest and most economical way to mix drinks is to purchase premixed, powered, or concentrated bar mixes. For the most part, these convenient mixes taste good, and customers are familiar with their taste. However, a few simple additions can vastly improve their taste appeal. Ideally, you would like to be able to make all of your own mixes from scratch. Some owners insist on it, even with the additional labor and materials cost.

Making your Bloody Mary mix from scratch is simple. A basic recipe (or your variation) is:

- 1 gallon of tomato juice with 1 ounce of lime juice
- 1 ounce of Worcestershire sauce
- 1 ounce of Lea & Perrins sauce

Optional ingredients to add to this or a premix are:

- fresh cracked pepper
- blend-in stewed tomatoes
- blend-in diced jalapeños

Fig. 9-5. *The Original Fish Enterprise Co.'s overhead sign in Santa Barbara, California greets patrons walking into the beer and wine bar.*

- Tabasco sauce or fresh herbs (dill or fennel seeds)

Piña Colada mixes are improved with the addition of fresh pureed pineapple and topped off with shredded coconut as a garnish. Fruit margaritas should always be made with fresh fruits in season and garnished accordingly (melon margaritas with a slice of honeydew, a strawberry with a strawberry margarita). Fresh whipping cream makes a considerable difference with hot coffee drinks. Add a hint of creme de cacao or creme de menthe to the whipping cream as you make it.

One of the best ways of communicating your unique preparation techniques is to explain your processes to your customers through a drink menu. Even if you do not have any house specialty drinks, a drink menu is a superb means of advertising what you do have for sale (see FIG. 9-5). Educate customers by listing wines top to bottom from dry to sweet. The general manager of The Original Fish Enterprise Co. called the wineries that supplied those wines shown in FIG. 9-6 and asked for a one-sentence description.

Drink menus can be printed on napkins, as table tents, or in a book format (see FIGS. 9-7 and 9-8). Descriptions should be entertaining and informative. Tell how certain alcohols are made and describe their tastes. Do the same for your drinks, wines, beers, nonalcoholic beverages, and mineral waters. Whenever possible, include the bottle labels and maps showing the place of origin for each liquor, beer, and wine.

Fads come and go in the liquor industry, as do the popularity of certain drinks. In the seventies, it was Harvey Wallbangers and Tequila Sunrises; in the eighties, it was fresh fruit daiquiris and shooters; and in the nineties, it is shooters, premium liquors, and healthy "smart" drinks (drinks that have no alcohol and include vitamins, minerals, pro-

---

BEER & WINE

Chardonnay
Santa Barbara Winery, Santa Barbara County — 17.00
Aroma of apples and spice. Well balanced with a light oak finish

Kendall Jackson, Lake County — 19.00
Flavors of tropical fruit. This is a buttery wine with a rich mouth feel

Sonoma Cutrer, Sonoma County — 18.00
Soft, round and well balanced with crisp fruit flavors of mango and tangerine

Byron, Santa Barbara County — 19.00
Soft and lush with a hint of barrel aging in the finish

Edna Valley, San Luis Obispo County   1/2 bottle 12.00   21.00
Strong flavors of tropical fruit accented with a vanilla smokiness from the oak

Qupe, Santa Barbara County — 22.00
Rich and creamy in texture. Good fruit and acidity with a hint of new oak

Sanford, Santa Barbara County   1/2 bottle 13.50   24.00
Rich and flavorful with moderate oak and a buttery character

Sauvignon Blanc
Brander, Santa Barbara County — 13.00
Medium bodied with a slightly grassy aroma and crisp acidity

Sanford, Santa Barbara County   1/2 bottle 7.50   13.00
Crisp and clean with mildly herbaceous flavors

Chenin Blanc
Santa Barbara Winery, Santa Barbara County — 11.00
This barrel fermented dry chenin blanc has flavors of citrus with a hint of oak

White Zinfandel
Santa Barbara Winery, Santa Barbara County — 11.00
Intensely fruity with flavors of raspberries and cherries

Riesling
Firestone, Santa Barbara County — 12.00
Aromas and flavors of apricots with a lovely fresh fruity quality

Cabernet Sauvignon
Meridian, San Luis Obispo County — 20.00
Rich and ripe with generous fruit flavors. Soft and supple

Hawk Crest, Napa Valley — 14.00
A lively cabernet combining flavors and aromas of cassis and berries

Sparkling Wine
Maison Deutz Brut, San Luis Obispo County — 25.00
A fresh and elegant California sparkling wine with hints of lemon, apple and pear

House Chablis
Glass 2.00   1/2 Litre 4.00   Litre 7.00

On Tap		Import	
Coors Light	1.50	Beck's	3.00
Bass Ale	2.50	Molson Golden	3.00
Heineken	2.50	Corona Extra	3.00
Domestic		Steinlager	3.00
Coors	2.00	Amstel Light	3.00
Budweiser	2.00	Samuel Smith	3.50
Budweiser Light	2.00	Samuel Adams Lager	3.50
Miller Genuine Draft	2.00	Lowenbrau Zurich	3.50
Miller Light	2.00	**Non Alcoholic**	
Bud Dry	2.00	Kaliber	2.50

Mineral Water		**Spring Water**	
Calistoga	2.00	Evian natural spring	2.50

Fig. 9-6. *A simple one-sentence description of your wine selections can help sell them.*
The Original Fish Enterprise Co.

Fig. 9-7. Table tents catch the eye with funny drawings and unusual shapes. The Elephant Bar

teins, and give you a lift—naturally). The knowledgeable operator promotes the fads and moves on when the novelty wears thin. Experimentation is good. It keeps your mind sharp and may trigger something truly unique.

Shooters gave rise to new methods of selling: the plastic test tube (see FIG. 9-9) and slammers (shots with plastic caps). Send your servers out with trays of these to sell on the spot, rather than taking orders. Shooter shot belts on a server create attention and generate sales. These merchandizing methods take the drinks to your customers and create impulse buys. Have a server walk around with a tray full of colorful daiquiris or hot coffee drinks. Or, develop a mini-bar, where a server or bartender wheels a cart around selling shots or tasters of certain wines (one to two ounces) or premium liquors (such as single malt scotches, fine cognacs, or ports) for $2 a taste, enabling a guest to sample and expand their taste buds for a modest price.

All these little extras add up to your customer experiencing something unique, whether you own a neighborhood bar or a large nightclub. Give your guests more than they expect and they will tell their friends and return. Be creative and distinct in taste and service. That's the best way to make money.

Margaritas

All margaritas made exclusively with Sauza Tequila.

Daily Special
A tangy and frosty margarita you'd cross the desert for.
$2.50

Premier
Made with Sauza Conmemorativo.
$4.50

Regular
Bigger and better.
$3.75

32 oz. Pitcher
A lot the easy way, or get a couple of glasses and share.
$6.95

Strawberry margaritas add $.25 for a glass or $1.00 for a pitcher.

Local Favorites

Kalahari Kooler..$3.75
A refreshing rum concoction with tropical juices and a shooter of Appleton Dark Jamaican Rum on the side.

Serengeti Sunrise $3.75
Our version of a sunrise made with Sauza Tequila, some great twang and a shooter of Sauza back.

"The" Long Island Iced Tea $4.50
Let the fun begin with our premier version of this old favorite.

Buana Coffee $3.50
A blend of Sabroso Coffee Liqueur, Presidente Brandy, DeKuyper Amaretto, and Creme de Banana that'll warm your toes.

Fig. 9-8. Notice the entertaining drink descriptions on this table tent. The Elephant Bar

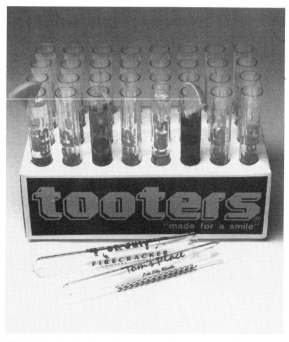

Fig. 9-9. Test-tube shots create impulse buying when a server walks around with a tray full of colorful shooters. Tooters

10

Liquor: Purchasing, storing, and inventory

Once you have determined what you need, you must decide where to buy your stock. As mentioned in Chapter 8, some states control the distribution of alcohol to the extent of a monopoly, while other states regulate by licensing wholesalers. (Refer back to TABLE 8-2.) Be aware of county and local laws that may be more restrictive than state laws. The yellow pages of the phone book will list alcoholic beverage manufacturers, distributors, and wholesalers under separate listings for liquor, beer, and wine. These sales agents can assist you in purchasing and keep you advised on quantity discounts, special sales, and promotions. There usually are regional or local trade publications that list all suppliers, their addresses, and their prices. You will be dealing with several suppliers to obtain everything you need. Check for their exclusive rights to sell certain brands and compare prices whenever possible.

In addition to lower prices, look for service from your liquor distributors. Request the names of at least three bars they currently supply. Talk to the bar owners and ask how they like the service they are receiving, then visit the distributors' warehouses to see their operations for yourself. Notice how they handle

and store their merchandise. Perishable wines and beers should be stored and refrigerated properly both at the warehouse and in transit. Corked wines and champagnes should be stored and transported on their sides. Unpasteurized beer and beer in kegs should always be refrigerated. When speaking with distributors, ask the following questions:

- How often are their stocks replenished?
- How frequently are deliveries made to retailers?
- Can you receive a short order in an emergency?
- Will a longer trip from the warehouse cost more for delivery?
- Will refrigerated items ever be shipped in unrefrigerated trucks or be left in a hot truck overnight?
- Will weather conditions cause delays in deliveries?
- Are there minimum orders for deliveries?
- Do the suppliers extend credit when permissable by law? What are their terms?

Table 10-1. Bottle and Case Size.

BOTTLE AND CASE SIZES			
Bottle Size	Fluid ounces	Units per Case	Replaces
DISTILLED SPIRITS			
500 milliliters	16.9	24	1 pint
750 milliliters	25.4	12	4/5 quart (fifth)
1 liter	33.8	12	1 quart
1.75 liters	59.2	6	1/2 gallon
WINE			
187 milliliters	6.3	48	2/5 pint
375 milliliters	12.7	24	4/5 pint
750 milliliters	25.4	12	4/5 quart (fifth)
1 liter	33.8	12	1 quart
1.5 liters	50.7	6	2/5 gallon
3 liters	101	4	4/5 gallon
4 liters	134.8	4	1 gallon
BEER			
8	8	24	
10	10	24	
12	12	24	

- Can you purchase soda mixes and other supplies from them?
- Can you participate in a pool buy if within the law?

Recommended inventory levels

After choosing your suppliers, you must decide how much to buy of any one item. That depends upon the frequency of deliveries. Usually, deliveries are made once a week. You want to have enough stock on hand so you never run out between deliveries. The recommended inventory for popular brands is at least one to two weeks' worth of stock. Slow-moving items require only a bottle or two as backup. In the beginning, as an inexperienced buyer, you will probably overstock on some beverages you thought would be popular but were not. Offer special promotions and make up unique drinks to clear your shelves of these items. You might even consider giving these bottles away as gifts to regular customers, auctioning them off to the highest bidder, or giving them as door prizes at a special promotion.

In time, you'll get to know the drinking patterns of your patrons and order your stock accordingly. You can then establish bar pars, or standard inventory levels, for each bar and your stockroom. Keep the bar par sheet posted in the bar's liquor cabinet or underneath the drawer of each cash register. This "Bar Par" sheet should indicate where each bottle of liquor belongs in the bar and the number and location of the backup bottles. It can look like a map.

By using your perpetual inventory (discussed later in this chapter), you can set minimum stock levels for each item so you'll know exactly when to reorder. Large inventories cost space for storage and represent money that could be spent in other areas, such as advertising or entertainment. The larger your inventory, the more you have to keep track of it, count it, and control it. You want the contents in your storeroom to be turning over constantly.

Liquor is commonly purchased by the case, 12 bottles to the case. The bottles are usually liters (see TABLES 10-1 and 10-2). Occasionally, you might want to buy 1.75 liter bottles for some of your call or premium brands. If you are using an automatic dispensing system, 1.75 liter bottles are not only cheaper, but require less handling. Keep in mind when buying these larger sizes that your backbar was probably designed to hold quart or liter-size bottles. Larger bottles can be used for special promotions or to stimulate conversation and sales, but they are heavy and cumbersome to use. They slow down the bartender's pouring process. For liqueurs and other slow-moving items, you can split a case by purchasing only a few bottles in a mixed case. It costs more per bottle, but is cheaper than buying a whole case of greenberry liqueur, which everyone stopped drinking long after you got such a good deal on yours.

Purchase well liquors in large quantities; they move fast. Beer should be delivered at least once a week, or daily if you have the vol-

Table 10-2. English/Metric Equivalencies

1 oz.	=	29.574 milliliters				
7 oz.	=	207.01 milliliters				
8 oz.	=	0.5 pint	=	236.59 milliliters		
¼ liter	=	8.453 oz.	=	0.06604 gallon		
10 oz.	=	295.74 milliliters				
12 oz.	=	354.88 milliliters				
14 oz.	=	414.03 milliliters				
16 oz.	=	1 pint	=	473.18 milliliters		
½ liter	=	16.907 oz.	=	0.13209 gallon		
32 oz.	=	1 quart	=	946.35 milliliters		
1 liter	=	33.814 oz.	=	0.26417 gallon		
64 oz.	=	0.5 gallon	=	1.892 liters		
128 oz.	=	1 gallon	=	3.785 liters		
992 oz.	=	7.75 gallons	=	29.337 liters	=	¼ barrel (½ keg)
1984 oz.	=	15.5 gallons	=	58.674 liters	=	½ barrel (keg)

ume, to keep it fresh. Order your house wines once a week. Purchase other wine bottles by the case once a month, and special vintages once or twice a year in large quantities if they are rare. Only purchase large quantities if you are sure you can move the brands. Buying in high volume is definitely cheaper. Liquor does not spoil, but beer and some wines can. A low price does not ensure a good buy for you and your customers.

Ordering

Once you have decided the quantities of liquor you will need, the next step is to place your order. Orders can be placed over the phone, by fax, through a salesperson visiting your bar, or, for larger operations, by purchase orders. For most bars, ordering by phone or fax is the preferred method. The only way to check orders when they are delivered is by writing them down or entering them into your computer as placed. Thus, if someone receives the shipment other than the person who ordered it, the delivery can be confirmed and accepted.

You can use a purchase order form, as in FIG. 10-1, for this purpose. You want to know what was ordered, in addition to the:

Fig. 10-1. Purchase order form.

- Person who placed the order.
- Date the order was placed.
- Seller of the goods.
- Sales agent responsible for taking your order.
- Prices quoted.
- Expected date of delivery.

You can assign a number to your order that becomes your Purchase Order number. This P.O. number is cross-referenced on the *Purveyor's Invoice*.

When the delivery arrives, the person receiving the goods must check what was shipped (the purveyor's invoice) against your purchase order. All items shipped must be the same as those ordered. If you ordered liters, don't accept 1.75 liters, and do not accept 1982 vintages if you ordered 1981. If you were quoted a price of $15.50 per bottle and the invoice reads $16.25 per bottle, do not accept those bottles.

Before signing for the goods, check for broken bottles, any stains indicating leakage or cracks, and spoilage dates for beer. Items that were ordered but not shipped should be indicated on the invoice. If any items are not acceptable at the time of delivery, have the delivery person return them to the purveyor's warehouse. Indicate on all copies of the invoice which items were returned. Both the person accepting the order and the delivery person should sign and date the invoice when anything is returned. Only when you are satisfied that all goods delivered are the ones you ordered at the prices you were quoted, should you sign the invoice, thereby transferring ownership of the goods from the seller to you.

When several bars group their orders together, it is known as *pool buying*. Pool buying in large quantities allows for discounts not possible for smaller individual bars. Pool buying is not allowed in some states. The only drawback of pool buying is that delivery is made at one location.

Proper storage

Once delivered, your liquor supply becomes potential profit and how you store it is important. Treat inventory like gold. You will need to keep track of it from the time you accept it off the delivery truck to the time it is poured into a drink and paid for. It takes very little time each day to maintain control of your inventory. By doing so, you can see exactly how much money you are earning from your liquor each day and how much you have earned to date.

Always keep liquor in a secure storage area that is wired to your security and alarm system. The individuals who have access to this room should be limited, and to protect yourself, change your locks when any key personnel changes are made. The contents of whole liquor rooms have been known to disappear overnight when proper precautions were not taken. When open for business, always keep your back door locked and never leave your liquor room open and unattended. Have a buzzer installed so delivery persons can ring a bell to your office or bar to let you know they are outside. (See FIG. 10-2.)

Proper storage of your liquor ensures that perishable items remain fresh. Rotate stock so that old supplies are used first. Anything that should be refrigerated, such as beer and wine, must be moved into locked refrigerators immediately upon delivery. Liquor bottles can be stored upright in their cases or put on shelves. Beer, wine, and champagne should be stored in a cool, dark, dry place, preferably in an area that is not subject to sudden temperature changes. The ideal temperature for wine storage is between 55 and 60 degrees Fahrenheit. Keep all beer and wine bottles away from direct sunlight and any area that may cause constant movement or vibration.

Corked bottles should be stored on their sides with the cork end lower than the bottom end of the bottle to keep the cork moist. If a cork dries out, it can shrink, allowing air to enter the bottle and spoil the wine. When the corks are facing forward in storage, any leaks

Fig. 10-2. Liquor storage room.

can be detected. Wine that has plastic corks or screw caps may be stored upright. Wine should not be refrigerated below 35 degrees Fahrenheit for any length of time or damage can result. House wine bought in bulk and table wine low in alcohol spoil quickly when opened. Refrigerate them after opening to slow down this process. (See FIG. 10-3.)

Beer must be rotated with every delivery, with older stock placed so it is used before the newly delivered cases. One way to keep track of each delivery is to write the delivery date boldly on every case. Bottled beer can be stored at temperatures between 40 and 70 degrees. At temperatures over 100 degrees, the beer will deteriorate. If the beer freezes, it will form flakes and become cloudy. After beer withstands a slight freeze, if it's clear when thawed, turn it over to remix the ingredients.

Draught beer, which is not pasteurized, must be refrigerated between 36 and 38 degrees at all times. Any temperature above 45 degrees turns the beer sour and cloudy. Draught beer should have its own refrigerator. When food is present in the same refrigerator as the kegs, odors and mildew can affect the beer's taste. Repeated opening and closing of the refrigerator can raise the temperature. Draught and package beer are best stored at 38 degrees to ensure the optimum serving temperature of 40 degrees. If served below 38 degrees, the beer loses its taste. Package beer will gush over when it is too cold. Draught beer served above 42 to 45 degrees draws wild and foamy.

***Fig. 10-3.** Backbar wine storage displays bottles for sale. Displayed products always increase sales.*
The Improv, Los Angeles, California

Serving beer properly improves sales because the beer looks and tastes good. When beer is not stored properly, it tastes bad, looks bad, and is bad for business. One way to ensure your beer-drinking customers are happy is to serve them clean glasses that have been properly chilled, not frozen. The ice particles in a frozen glass will react with the beer and cause it to foam.

The glass a beer is served in must be spotless. It should be cleaned in an odor-free detergent solution, followed by a rinse in clear water. Then the glass is rinsed again in a sanitizer and left to drain and air dry upside down on a corrugated surface. Towel drying leaves a film on the glass. Any film or fingerprints on the inside will cause the foam to break up rapidly and leave an irregular foam trail. A clean beer glass will hold its head firm and compact,

leaving foam rings down its sides. If a draught beer glass has not been properly cleaned by the time it is served to the customer, all the head will be gone and the beer will look and taste flat. Beer glasses should even be rinsed in cool water just before using to clean out any smoke or other odors that may have collected.

Proper maintenance and daily cleaning of all beer tapping lines and faucet heads will also ensure good, cold, fresh-tasting beer. Bacteria can build up in the lines and at the faucets. Any contamination will sour the beer. Draught beer is such a high profit item that it pays to spend the time to keep your system running well.

Tracking inventory

In some operations, every bottle of liquor accepted into the storeroom is stamped with an identifying mark showing this bottle is now the property of the bar. When requisitioned, it proves that it came from your liquor storeroom. If an empty bottle is returned without a stamp, you know someone is serving liquor from an unauthorized bottle.

It is possible someone forgot to stamp your bottles. It could even be that an employee has either brought in a bottle to pour from and is keeping the money for those drinks or has replaced a more expensive bottle with a cheaper brand. This situation is rare, but it does happen.

Keep your stamp under lock and key. Have only one individual responsible for its use and control. The stamp should be of a unique design that cannot be easily duplicated, and it should be changed periodically.

When all items are stored in their proper places, the quantities of each item delivered must be recorded in a Perpetual Inventory System. This can be done through a computer using an inventory control software program or by hand on an index card or notebook filing system. If done by hand, each card or page lists each type of liquor, beer, and wine in stock. (See FIG. 10-4.)

When you receive your first delivery, and for every delivery thereafter, record each bottle delivered on your Perpetual Inventory Control cards. When you stock your bars, record these movements and the date on your Perpetual Inventory Control cards. The current inventory on the card represents the number of bottles in the liquor supply room only. The total number of bottles in the entire bar is the current inventory plus the stock issued for any given day. The idea is to know where all bottles are located so they can all be accounted for. Perpetual inventory control also helps when it is time to order more liquor.

Backbar storage cabinets should be locked at the end of every business day. Some bars go to the extreme of locking up all liquor bottles,

PERPETUAL INVENTORY CONTROL CARD

NAME OF LIQUOR				
DATE	STOCK DELIVERED	STOCK ISSUED	STOCK USED	CURRENT INVENTORY

Fig. 10-4. Perpetual inventory control card can be set up on your computer accounting or inventory control program.

open or not, every night. This is only recommended in cases where the bar is exposed to people coming and going during the hours it is not open, such as a service bar in a restaurant.

No more liquor should be kept as a backup and part of the bar par than the amount used on a typical busy night. For most bottles on the backbar, only one backup is necessary. Stock two to six bottles of your well brands as backup for each station. Be careful not to overstock and lose track of the bottles hidden in the cabinets. If you don't know where all your bottles are, you can easily reorder liquor you have too much of already.

Evaluate your bar pars at the end of each month when you do your monthly inventories. Make any necessary changes and create new Bar Par sheets. It is amazing how many extra bottles you will find hidden in those cabinets. Take them out and put them back on the shelves in your liquor room and readjust your Perpetual Inventory. In order to have an accurate accounting of your business, it is absolutely essential that you be meticulous and diligent in recording and tracking your inventory. Any one bottle of liquor represents a substantial profit or loss.

Daily inventory control

As bottles are used during each shift, they need to be replaced and accounted for. Have your bartender fill out a Daily Beverage Requisition Sheet at the end of his or her shift (see FIG. 10-5). Print up a bunch of these sheets, because you'll use them every day. The bottles used are called *the break* or *breakage*.

According to your preference, you can restock and issue the new breakage at the end of each shift, or wait until the next day and issue the replacement bottles as part of the opening procedures. If you choose to double-check the movement of every bottle, you can require that all empty bottles be turned in and match them with what is on the requisition sheet. Any shortages will show up immediately.

When you have several bars in one operation, it is very common for one to borrow from another when things get hectic. If this happens, always insist that the empty bottle from one bar be left in place of the full or partial bottle borrowed; otherwise, it looks like one bar has been raided, and everyone forgets what happened to the missing bottles.

You can figure your liquor costs at the end of every day by using your Daily Beverage Requisition Sheet and extending the breakage. For example, say you used four bottles of vodka. From your liquor invoice bills, determine the cost of each bottle. It is usually printed right on the invoice. If each bottle cost you $12.00 the cost of the liquor issued is $48. At this point, if you have a computer register that inventories the sales by liquor, you can figure an individual liquor cost. Generally, you only figure the liquor cost or pouring cost (PC) on the total liquor and sales. Continue down your list of bottles and extend the costs of each. Add the totals of each column. You now have a total of $1200 for cost of issues. Take your sales total from your Daily Sales Summary record (FIG. 10-6) and enter it on your breakage sheet.

In our example, the total sales equal $6000. Divide $1200, which is the cost of the liquor inventory, by $6000, your sales, and the result is .20. Your PC for the day is 20 percent. That means that for each drink you poured, the cost of the liquor was 20 percent of the price you received for it. That does not mean that your profit was 80 percent, because you need to consider all of your other costs before you arrive at your profit margin.

Your PC is a good indicator of the amount of liquor your bartenders are pouring, however. An unusually high or low PC will indicate something is wrong (troubleshooting is discussed later in the chapter).

Transfer your daily figures from the Daily Beverage Requisition sheet to your Monthly Liquor PC sheet or enter it into your computer accounting program. Follow the form of this sheet, as in FIG. 10-7. Keep this form and each Daily Beverage Requisition Sheet in one notebook. Each day fill in your daily figures and keep running cumulative totals on costs and revenue to date.

Monthly inventory

On the last day of each month, after your business is closed and before the start of the first day of the next month, you need to make a physical count of every bottle in the house. This is called the *month-end inventory*. (See FIG. 10-8.)

Your month-end inventory figures are critical in determining your financial health. There are two ways to achieve the count. The simplest involves sighting each bottle. Start in the liquor supply room. Then go to each bar. Count all bottles, visible on shelves and in closed boxes. Count the backups in the cabinets.

For each bottle that is open, count by tenths. If the bottle is half full, record it as 0.5 on your Monthly Liquor Inventory sheet; if one-third full, record it as 0.3. Total all the

DAILY BEVERAGE REQUISITION   BAR   REG

BRAND	MAIN BAR	SERVICE	TOTAL ISSUES	SALES	COST OF ISSUES	LIQUOR COST	BRAND	STOCK REPL	STOCK USED	END INV	SALES	COST OF ISSUES	LIQUOR COST
WELL							**CORDIALS**						
Vodka							Amaretto						
Scotch							Annisette						
Gin							Bailey's Irish Cream						
Bourbon							Apricot Brandy						
Rum							Blackberry Brandy						
Tequila							Cherry Brandy						
Brandy							B & B						
Coffee Liqueur							Campari						
Triple Sec							Cherry Herring						
CALL LIQUOR							Chartreuse Green						
VODKA							Cream de Cassis						
Smirnoff							Cream de Cacao Dark						
Stolichnaya							Cream de Cacao Light						
SCOTCH							Cream de Menthe Gr						
Chivas Regal							Cream de Menthe Wh						
Cutty Sark							Cream de Banana						
Dewars (White Label)							Cream de Nova						
J & B							Drambuie						
J Walker-Black							Frangelica						
J Walker-Red							Galliano						
GIN							Grand Marnier						
Beefeaters							Kahlua						
Bombay							Midori						
Tanqueray							Ouzo						
BOURBON							Peppermint Schnapps						
Early Times							Sambuca						
Jack Daniels-Blk							Sloe Gin						
Wild Turkey 101							Strega						
Seagrams 7							Southern Comfort						
RYE							Rock & Rye						
Old Overholt							Tia Maria						
IRISH							Tuaca						
Jamison							**BEER**						
Old Bushmills							Heineken						
CANADIANS							Miller						
CC							Miller Lite						
VO							Michelob						
Crown Royal							Budweiser						
RUM							Corona						
Bacardi Amber							San Miguel						
Bacardi Silver							**WINE**						
Bacardi 151							Rose						
Meyers							Chablis						
TEQUILA							Burgundy						
Cuervo 1800													
Cuervo Gold							Dubonnet						
COGNAC							Dry Sac Sherry						
Courvoisier							Harveys Bristol Cream						
Hennessey													
Remy Martin													
Christian Brothers							Perrier						
Martell													

Fig. 10-5. Daily beverage requisition form.

DAILY SALES SUMMARY

	REGISTER 1 DAY NIGHT	REGISTER 2 DAY NIGHT	REGISTER 3 DAY NIGHT	TOTALS
BANK				
CURRENCY				
CHANGE				
PAID-OUTS				
SUBTOTAL				
– STARTING BANK				
= TOTAL CASH TO BE DEPOSITED 1				
CREDIT CARDS				
AMX				
M/C				
VISA				
OTHER				
TOTAL CHARGES 2				
– TIPS CHARGED				
AMX				
M/C				
VISA				
OTHER				
TOTAL TIPS CHARGED 3				
2 – 3 = TOTAL SALES CHARGED 4				
1 + 4 = TOTAL SALES 5				
SALES				
LIQUOR				
WINE				
BEER				
OTHER				
PROMO				
FOOD				
= TOTAL SALES 6				
– SALES TAX 7				
= ADJUSTED SALES TOTAL 8				
5 – 6 = OVER/SHORT				
PREPARED BY	DATE	DAY		

Fig. 10-6. *Daily sales summary.*

columns for each bottle of liquor, wine, and beer, including loose bottles out of their cases. Check your current Perpetual Inventory with the amounts you just totalled and see if they match. If you are off, you need to readjust your Perpetual Inventory numbers and figure out why the numbers do not coincide. Perhaps a bottle was dropped and not recorded on the break sheet. Or a bottle might have broken inside a closed case and not been accounted for. You need to stress to your employees the importance of reporting any such irregularities. The figures will also assist you in arriving at a more accurate PC. You will need these figures when you compute your monthly income statements (discussed in Chapter 16).

Knowing exactly what your inventory is at the beginning of each month is important. If your records are incomplete, you will never know exactly how much money you are making. Some owners like to take a physical inventory every week or twice a month. Once a month should be adequate, unless you notice shortages and want to try to pinpoint where they are occurring.

The second most popular method of counting your bottles involves weighing each bottle to achieve an accurate ounce count of partially emptied bottles. The Accardis Cyclops system is by far the best integrated way to track your liquor or food inventory from delivery through usage. The Cyclops is a hand-

MONTHLY LIQUOR P.C.

MONTH _____

DATE	BARTENDER	P.C. FOR NIGHT	CUMULATIVE COST TO DATE	CUMULATIVE REVENUE TO DATE	CUMULATIVE P.C. TO DATE
/1					
/2					
/3					
/4					
/5					
/6					
/7					
/8					
/9					
/10					
/11					
/12					
/13					
/14					
/15					
/16					
/17					
/18					
/19					
/20					
/21					
/22					
/23					
/24					
/25					
/26					
/27					
/28					
/29					
/30					
/31					
			LIQUOR P.C. FOR MONTH		

Fig. 10-7. *Monthly liquor P.C. form.*

MONTHLY LIQUOR INVENTORY

TOTAL LIQUOR _____ DATE _____

ITEM	SIZE	BAR 1	BAR 2	STORE ROOM	TOTAL BOTTLES	UNIT PRICE	$ TOTAL
Sauza Commerativo	L						
Sauza Gold	L						
Schnapps	L						
Seagram's 7	L						
Seagram's VO	L						
Sloe Gin	L						
Smirnoff	L						
Smirnoff Sliver	L						
Southern Comfort	L						
Stolichnaya	L						
Strega	.75L						
Tanqueray	L						
Tia Maria	L						
Tullamore Dew	L						
Triple Sec	L						
Tuaca	.75L						
Vandermint	L						
Vermouth (dry)	L						
Vermouth (sweet)	L						
Wild Turkey	L						
Windsor	L						
Wolfschmidt	L						
Yukon Jack	L						

THIS PAGE TAKEN BY: _____

Fig. 10-8. *Monthly liquor inventory form.*

held microprocessor that uses a small scanner on its end to read the Universal Pricing Code (UPC) on each bottle as a way to identify the product. The number of bottles is then manually entered by the keypad. The accompanying software automatically extends the wholesale cost and updates your perpetual inventory.

By using the optional weight scale, precision accounting is extremely fast and accurate. Place your scanned bottle on the scale. The software can calculate the remaining liquor to within 1/40th of an ounce. The program has the specific gravities of every brand of liquor and the empty bottle weight of each brand built-in. The system generates numerous reports, spreadsheets, cost percentages, and projected sales vs. actual sales.

The Cyclops is an amazing device for fast, pinpoint accuracy and inventory controls. It can interface with numerous accounting programs. One of the advantages, besides its accuracy, is its speed. Spot checks of inventory can be accomplished quickly, as the counting procedure is extremely fast. Spot checking inventory is useful when you are trying to troubleshoot inventory problems, check on a particular bartender, or determine shortages and overages in PCs. It will also assist you in tracking which brands are selling the fastest and which are not, establish minimum bar pars, and assist in daily purchases. (See FIG. 10-9.)

After your inventory count, you'll need to arrive at your monthly *cost of sales* by using the Monthly Pouring Cost form in FIG. 10-10. First, you need to locate any overages or shortages turned up by your physical inventory. Add up the cost of your opening inventory, plus the purchases for the month, then subtract the cost

Fig. 10-9. *The Accardis Cyclops is an amazing hand-held bar code scanner that can also weigh and inventory bottles to 1/40 of an ounce.* Accardis

```
┌─────────────────────────────────────────────┐
│          INVENTORY OVER OR (SHORT)          │
├─────────────────────────────────────────────┤
│                                             │
│     OPENING INVENTORY          $ _____   │
│                                             │
│  +  PURCHASES                  $ _____   │
│                                             │
│  −  COST OF REQUISITIONS       $ _____   │
│                                             │
│  =  BALANCE TO ACCOUNT FOR     $ _____   │
│                                             │
│  −  CLOSING INVENTORY          $ _____   │
│                                             │
│  =  INVENTORY OVER OR (SHORT)  $ _____   │
│                                             │
└─────────────────────────────────────────────┘
┌─────────────────────────────────────────────┐
│            MONTHLY POURING COST             │
├─────────────────────────────────────────────┤
│                                             │
│     OPENING INVENTORY          $ _____   │
│                                             │
│  +  PURCHASES                  $ _____   │
│                                             │
│  −  CLOSING INVENTORY          $ _____   │
│                                             │
│  =  COST OF SALES              $ _____   │
│                                             │
│  %  COST OF SALES          = $ _____ = PC│
│     SALES FOR MONTH                         │
│                                             │
│                       PC = _____ %       │
└─────────────────────────────────────────────┘
```

Fig. 10-10. *Inventory over or (short) and monthly pouring cost forms.*

of requisitions (from your Daily Requisition Sheets), which will give you the dollar balance to account for. Then subtract the cost of your closing inventory. You should arrive at zero. Any other figure will require a little detective work to find the discrepancy.

To determine the cost of your sales or bar cost, or PC, take the cost of your opening inventory, add all purchases, and then subtract your closing inventory (in dollar amounts) to arrive at cost of sales. This figure represents the cost of liquor sold that month. Now divide this figure by the total sales for the month and you will arrive at your true PC. These figures will be used in figuring your monthly profit and loss statement, as shown in FIG. 10-11.

Annual inventory

If you have been doing your inventory controls each day and each month, your year-end figures should be a snap to put together. At this point, you can see how a small percentage increase in your PC can affect your profit. You can also plot your sales on a month-to-month basis, which helps you to visualize your sales and compare those of past years. If you are considering a price increase to offset higher costs for supplies, you can play with your yearly figures and see how much it would affect your total sales.

Use your Perpetual Inventory Control cards or computer-generated reports to see what liquors are not turning over in your bar. Decide if they are worth storing or carrying any longer. Clear your shelves and start the new year fresh. As the years go by, you will notice patterns in your operation. During the summer, you might sell more beer, rum, and tequila, while in winter, it might be scotch and bourbon. These figures will also assist you in scheduling your employees for holidays and other occasions.

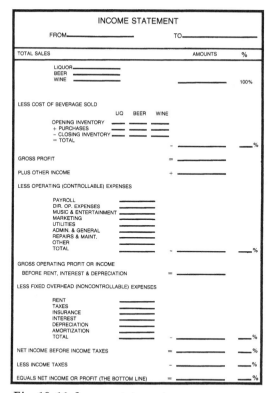

INCOME STATEMENT

FROM_____ TO_____

TOTAL SALES		AMOUNTS	%
LIQUOR_____			
BEER _____			
WINE _____		_____	100%

LESS COST OF BEVERAGE SOLD

	LIQ	BEER	WINE		
OPENING INVENTORY					
+ PURCHASES					
– CLOSING INVENTORY					
= TOTAL				– _____	___%

GROSS PROFIT = _____

PLUS OTHER INCOME + _____

LESS OPERATING (CONTROLLABLE) EXPENSES

PAYROLL	
DIR. OP. EXPENSES	
MUSIC & ENTERTAINMENT	
MARKETING	
UTILITIES	
ADMIN. & GENERAL	
REPAIRS & MAINT.	
OTHER	
TOTAL	– _____ ___%

GROSS OPERATING PROFIT OR INCOME
BEFORE RENT, INTEREST & DEPRECIATION = _____

LESS FIXED OVERHEAD (NONCONTROLLABLE) EXPENSES

RENT	
TAXES	
INSURANCE	
INTEREST	
DEPRECIATION	
AMORTIZATION	
TOTAL	– _____ ___%

NET INCOME BEFORE INCOME TAXES = _____ ___%

LESS INCOME TAXES – _____ ___%

EQUALS NET INCOME OR PROFIT (THE BOTTOM LINE) = _____ ___%

Fig. 10-11. Income statement.

Troubleshooting

Suppose you are noticing that your PC is slowly creeping higher and higher and you cannot determine why. It can happen when your liquor costs keep rising and your drink prices remain the same. One remedy is adjusting your drink prices. You must be able to cover your costs while not pricing yourself out of the marketplace. Keep constant tabs on your competition's prices, because their liquor costs are probably the same as yours.

Make sure that all bartenders are pouring correctly and according to your drink recipe guides. Perhaps a new bartender is not used to pouring the quantities you desire. Check your daily PC sheets and see if the PC is always high on the days that a particular bartender

works. Watch how he or she pours and if that is the problem, retrain the bartender. If you feel your bartenders cannot pour accurately, have them pour using a shot glass or switch to a premeasured pour spout.

An automated drink dispensing system provides the ultimate control. Due to the high cost of installation, however, these systems are only recommended for very high-volume bars. Bartenders may also be giving away drinks and not collecting for them. Bottles could be escaping from the liquor room. Because bottles do not have feet, someone who does might be assisting.

Again, be sure your liquor room is never left unattended and unlocked. Notice who goes in and out. If you allow your employees to drink on the job, maybe they are abusing the privilege. If you do not allow it, take steps to prevent or catch it.

Spotting when the shortages occur narrows down the people who may be involved. See if the cleaning crew drinks while it works. And always double check your shipments against your invoices to see that they match. Check to see if all bottles thrown in the trash are empty bottles. Sometimes full bottles are dumped, only to be picked up later.

Check to see that servers are charging the correct prices. Could a server and bartender be working together? Five drinks go out of the bar and only four are rung up and accounted for? Are guest checks being reused, voided, or blended together? Who has access to the void key? Is a bartender bringing in his or her own bottle to use? Can anyone ring up and enter another bartender's cash drawer? Who counts the money before and after each shift? Managers have been known to lift money as well as other employees. Controls and double checks along the way ensure that drinks are accounted for and the cash winds up in your bank account. The point is not to be paranoid, because trusting your employees is important; just eliminate any holes in your system.

If you think the bartenders are overpouring and continue to do so after you have talked to them about the problem, you can change from fast-pouring spouts to slower-pouring spouts or switch from free-pouring to pouring out of a shot glass. If worst comes to worst and you still cannot figure out what is going wrong, hire someone, known as a *spotter* or *shopper*, to come in and watch your operation from the customer's point of view. This person should be thoroughly trained in all aspects of your operation and be unknown to your employees. Sometimes an outsider can spot discrepancies more easily than you can.

In most cases, the discrepancies only occur when you or your manager are not around. The use of a spotting service, available for a fee through restaurant and bar management consulting firms, should only be considered as a last resort.

Any firing should be done at the beginning or end of a shift, never in the middle, unless the offense is blatant. When employees are forced to leave against their will, they will often tell you who is doing what in your operation. Never take anyone's word as positive proof that someone else is stealing until you have thoroughly investigated the situation yourself. If you catch someone in the act, terminate him or her on the spot. If the employee refuses to leave, say you will call the police and press charges of theft.

The proper care of your inventory is a vital link in your operation, one that will lead to greater profits. Make your purchases carefully, keep abreast of new product developments, know how your inventory is being handled and where it is at all times, and you'll be happier and richer for your efforts.

11

Marketing:
Successful promotions

The marketing of your bar is an integral part of your ongoing business strategy. A major component of marketing is the image you project to current and future customers. This image starts with the publicity and advertising you use to promote your business, and ends with the physical environment created as your bar.

It is a good idea to have a logo that is eye-catching and tells people what your concept is all about. This logo will be used on everything that has your name on it. (See FIG. 11-1.) Have a graphic artist design your logo. You could design it yourself using the graphics capabilities of your computer, or contact your local art school and see if you can have a student or a graphics class do it as a class project. Offer a prize for the design you like the best. Your prize could be cash or trade for a dollar amount of food and drinks at your bar.

Preopening publicity

Creating the right image for your bar before you ever open your doors is important. The best way to accomplish this is to involve yourself, as the owner, in your local community. Join the local Chamber of Commerce and ser-vice clubs, or align yourself with charitable or other public service organizations.

Plan several private parties prior to your official public opening. They should include a Purveyors' Night, when all of the suppliers and others who have helped you open come and see the finished bar. Besides the purveyors, invite your competitors, civic leaders, and business-persons in the neighborhood. Visit them personally with invitations. Letting them be the first to enjoy your place is very important. People will be asking them about your bar, so give them the opportunity to know it firsthand.

These preopening functions are intended to generate publicity. They serve the additional function of allowing your staff to get used to the way your operation is run. It is a good time to smooth out any problems before you officially open. Your parties should include food, often catered, and complimentary drinks.

Another way to spread the word about your bar is to ask people in the neighborhood if they know anything about the new place opening down the street. Then proceed to tell them what "you've heard." Or, try a teaser campaign. This is an excellent way to introduce a new place and start people talking. Two

SPORTS BAR & RIB ROOM

3243 PIERCE   346-6824   BE SAFE CLOSE COVER BEFORE STRIKING

Fig. 11-1. Examples of logos.

months before you open, introduce billboards, newspaper ads, or bumper stickers that say, "JIMMY'S IS COMING!" Then when you are sure of your opening date, add the date to your ads, "JIMMY'S IS COMING! WATCH FOR OUR GRAND OPENING MAY 1ST!"

As a further incentive for opening night, send out a unique invitation. It could be a high-ball glass with your logo and a note telling people to bring it in for a complimentary drink. It might be a coaster, or a record if you are a dance club, or a schedule of upcoming sports events for a sports bar with half of a season ticket stub

to be matched at your bar on opening night. Make it fun and people will come. Rent searchlights to attract attention. To ensure that important individuals or celebrities show up, provide them with door-to-door limousine service. Have your own photographer, as well as a videographer, on hand to record your opening. You may think documenting all of your events is a waste of time, but you never know when or who might need this documentation (good for your yearly anniversary parties).

Your opening should have a "visual" that

is interesting, shows action, and can be photographed. The fact that you are opening your doors is not in itself newsworthy, but if your interior was designed by a noted artist or architect, then it becomes exciting. Include a time capsule in a cornerstone, or have a local politician or celebrity tend bar opening night. Tie your opening with a fundraiser for a popular cause in your community, such as cleaning up the beaches or saving 100-year-old oak trees. Newspapers, magazines, radio, and TV stations are always looking for interesting stories. If your event is unique, the media will come and broadcast live.

If you are too busy to deal with the pre-opening publicity details, hire a publicity agent or firm. Their expertise will cost you; however, they should have established media contacts and a gift for creating unusual events and promotions. Private Eyes, an upscale nightclub in New York City, hired a public relations firm to publicize its opening. The club was an instant success due to two parties planned by the firm. They resulted in 22 weeks of continuous press coverage. Pictures of celebrities at Private Eyes appeared on front pages and within the society sections of many newspapers and magazines. Almost overnight, success was guaranteed, as people came to see this new place they had read about. (See FIG. 11-2.)

Media coverage

As you near your opening date, be prepared to contact the news media for the first of many times. The word must be spread to all the media at once. That is often accomplished by mailing or faxing a press release to newspaper editors and the news editors of your local radio and television stations. Follow up with phone calls. If you write your press release in the form of a newspaper article, a busy newspaper may run it as it is written.

HARVEY MANN
PUBLIC RELATIONS CONSULTANT

- FOR GENERAL RELEASE _

We are proud to introduce you to Robert Shalom's PRIVATE EYES video-nightclub, 12 West 21st Street, located just off Fifth Avenue in New York City's fashionable Chelsea neighborhood.

The Wall Street Journal says, "PRIVATE EYES isn't just drawing a lot of people - it's drawing the right people".

Since the grand opening, July 17, 1984, this innovative club, known for pristine high-tech functionalism, has become precisely what owner Robert Shalom and program relations director Steve Sukman envisioned - a place for relaxation rather than dancing (there is no dance floor, per se, although many manage to find a comfortable spot, anyway) and a club that does not cater the the needs of one specific group.

PRIVATE EYES has been described by many who have seen it as a "MINIZOETROPE STUDIO", and owner Robert Shalom says that Private Eyes "puts attention to detail and quality (of the club and videos) far beyond that of any other club in the country".

PRIVATE EYES often co-hosts promotional parties and provides assistance developing special music/video programming, room decorations and overall coordination. An event may also be promoted through a postcard mailing to appropriate portions of PRIVATE EYES 14,000+ name mailing list. A secured VIP area provides additional privacy for special events.

Celebrity-photos taken from PRIVATE EYES glittering night-life only uncover the surface of what is happening at this video-nightclub that comfortably accomodates approximately 500 people. Designed to double as a television production facility, by day, PRIVATE EYES hosts pre-recorded and live media talk shows. PRIVATE EYES sophisticated video capabilities have proven ideal for many diverse trade demonstrations. The sleek, contemporary interior has served as the ideal setting for fashion/beauty and advertising photo sessions.

By night, Robert Shalom's PRIVATE EYES is brimming with people drawn to the most elaborate video system in New York and a post-modern cocktail party and nightclub atmosphere that has become PRIVATE EYES distinctive trademark. A look at just a few of PRIVATE EYES events shows that the video-nightclub is perfectly sized and ideally equipped for success.

- LP release parties for Madonna, Culture Club, Frankie Goes to Hollywood.
- theme parties sponsored by the Jamaican Tourist Council, Delta Airlines, Perrier Joet Champagne and Crazy Eddie stores.
- post-concert parties for The Cars, Go-Go's and Missing Persons.
- software release events with RCA/Columbia and CBS/Fox Home Video.
- movie release promotions with all of the major studios.
- premier screenings of numerous new videos and artist projects.

Fig. 11-2. *Publicity release.*Private Eyes

In small towns, you can call the editor of the local newspaper, appear at the press club, or hold a breakfast for the media. In a larger city, you might have to use the "wire." This is a city news service that you call with information about your event, its time, date, and the phone number of a person to contact for additional information. This "news" is then relayed to every organization that subscribes to the service. (See FIG. 11-3.)

Be prepared to hand or mail out a "media" or "press" kit. In a folder include drawings and photographs of your bar, a few short paragraphs explaining who the owner(s) are, what is unusual about your place, your hours of operation, your prices, and a description of the event and its purpose. Be brief. Keep your press release to two pages, one page describ-

LIPPE • JACK • MEDINA

MEDIA ASSOCIATES

NEWS

FOR IMMEDIATE RELEASE — Contact: Laine Medina 714-833-7673

YOU DON'T HAVE TO BE IN HIGH SCHOOL TO GO TO THE PROM

Bobby-soxers will have the opportunity to relive the excitement of PROM NIGHT at THE HOP on June 19th. 50's formal party attire will be the dress for the evening and a real "prom" photographer will be there to take pictures of everyone in their finery. Hundreds of balloons will decorate the "high school gymnasium-style" dance floor of the Righteous Brothers' night club. The music, as always at The Hop, will be from those "crazy 50's - 60's days!"

A prom King and Queen will be chosen to reign for a year and they will receive valuable prizes. Other prizes and Hop concert tickets will be given for the most original 50's prom outfits or maybe even for "the most likely to succeed"!

The doors will open at 7:30 p.m. for the "Lovin' Feelin' Prom", with a midnite buffet to top off the evening!

For ticket information please call: 714-963-2366

P. O. Box 268 • Sunset Beach. California 90742 • 714/840-3747

Fig. 11-3. Press release. The Hop

ing your bar, and the other describing the event. Include any previous press clippings. Then hold a press conference. You will want to provide the media with this information for each event you plan.

If possible, hold morning or early afternoon functions, thereby giving the media enough time to edit coverage of your event for the evening news. Late night events may not appear until the following day and then must compete with more current news for coverage.

Many bars are hiring a sales representative, a person who exclusively markets their establishments, often by telephone. This is an additional position separate from the promotions coordinator. This telemarketer usually works for a base salary plus commissions. A sales rep will come from a similar position in a hotel or large restaurant chain. Have video tapes of your bar and your promotions for use by any person generating outside sales.

Post-opening promotions

Once you open your doors, you will be promoting your business constantly. A *promotion* is anything that excites interest in your bar, both inside and outside your doors. Its purpose is to build desire and demand for your bar.

In-house promotions consist of items that people can take home with them, anything with your name and logo on it. They include napkins, coasters, matches, lighters, pens, pencils, buttons, and even ashtrays. (see FIGS. 11-4 and 11-5). You can offer these and other items for sale: special glassware, drink recipes, mixes for special drinks, calendars, T-shirts, hats, sun visors, sunglasses, sports bottles, jackets, tennis racket covers, beach towels, etc. (see FIG. 11-6). Almost anything can become a promotional item. Pick what you think will interest your clientele. It might be a tackle box, frisbee, calculator, headband, or umbrella. Whatever the item, with your name and logo on it, it becomes an advertisement for your bar.

Promotions are an effective way of increasing and building your business. Unusual promotions create tremendous word-of-mouth advertising. Some will be expensive, others will cost you next to nothing. The objective is to stimulate interest and revenue. You'll use promotions to build business on slow nights or during slow hours, to convert daytime customers to nighttime customers, to attract new customers and keep the regulars coming back, and as a way to differentiate yourself from the competition. Offer your customers something special and they will love it.

Happy hour began as a way to increase business during the slow, after-work hours. It

Fig. 11-4. Napkin and coaster designs make great promotional items that customers can take home.

is a national phenomenon now and taken for granted by bargoers. Originally, happy hour meant reduced drink prices, then two drinks for the price of one, and with many states banning excessive happy hour drinking promotions, more and more bars are offering food

Fig. 11-5. Promotional items to give away. Arlen Advertising

Fig. 11-6. Promotional items for sale at The Hop.

and entertainment instead of lower prices. Before running any advertisements, check your laws governing what you can and cannot say. Many states do not allow you to advertise prices. (See FIG. 11-7.)

You, the owner, are the best promotion of all. You should be meeting and talking to your customers. They like knowing you; to them you are a local celebrity. Your employees can be the next best promoters of good will by providing excellent service and telling their customers about your events. Encourage them to promote your business. Have business cards printed for each employee. Encourage them to give the cards to their acquaintances. When a customer presents a card to another server or bartender, he receives a free drink or free admission. Stamp a "to be used by" date on these cards. Give your employees a percentage of the bar's gross if they book special parties. Finally, your customers

Fig. 11-7. *Fantasia happy hour promotion flyer.*

promote your business when they talk about your bar to their friends. Make their experience in your place worth a return trip.

Promote your bar as "the place" for business or club meetings. You want to expose your bar to as many people as possible. To this end, on nights that are traditionally slow, open your bar to special private parties. If an organization wants to hold an awards or annual fund raising event, let them charge an admission at the door that is theirs to keep, while you keep the money for all drinks sold. In this way, you both benefit.

Contact your local visitors' and convention bureaus and tour operators and let them know what you are willing to do to accommodate groups from out of town. You could host a "wrap" party to celebrate the finishing of a project, or a party sponsored by a business to introduce a new product. Get the word out to car rental agencies, hotel door hosts, concierges, and travel agents in your area that your bar is the place to come to have a good time or celebrate a special occasion or event. (See FIG. 11-8.) If area restaurants, bars, and ho-

---

Hi! This is Ingrid Croce. In the sixties, I was singing in a group with six guys, auditioning for a folk singing contest. And Jim Croce was the judge. He picked our group, and more importantly, he picked me. It was love at first sight. And for seven years we sang together, wrote together, argued together, and of course, dreamed together. In 1972, I had just given birth to our son A.J. when "You Don't Mess around with Jim" went gold. Our dreams came true. But the irony was that after building our lives together, it was time for Jim to do it alone. After two years on the road, Jim and I moved to San Diego. I remember that weekend, he came home insisting on a babysitter and a night on the town. I was so excited. We hardly ever went out to dinner and I really missed my best friend. Now, fifteen years later, I remember that terrific night. The warmth and the love Jim and I shared remains and when you come to Croce's Restaurant & Jazz Bar downtown you can feel it. Say I love you to the best friend you have. Bring them to Croce's.

Live tag by ANNOUNCER: For special memories. Croce's downtown. At the corner of Fifth and F Street.

Fig. 11-8. *Promoting your bar as a special place. A 60-second radio commercial for Croce's in San Diego, California.*

tels do not have the large capacity you do for corporate or banquet facilities, let them know how you will work with them on acquiring business (this could add to their sales pitch in booking hotel, meals, and other events).

Someone must be in charge of conducting your promotions. In small bars, the owner or manager can oversee each event. In larger bars, the director of entertainment and advertising will manage your promotions. Depending on your promotion schedule, this job may be full-time or part-time. If part-time, your promotions coordinator could be a server, bartender, DJ, or an exceptionally gregarious individual on your staff. This is an excellent way to advance someone within your business. If the employee works at night, then his or her days are spent working on the promotions. In addition, if the promotion calls for contests or judging of contests, someone must host or be Master of Ceremonies (MC). The MC excites the crowd, gets the audience involved, conducts the contests, lets the audience judge the contests by clapping and screaming for their favorite contestant, and hands out the prizes. MCs are often, but not always, actors, radio or TV personalities, or local celebrities. However large or small your promotion, one person needs to be in charge to oversee all the details.

Planning successful promotions

Allow plenty of time to plan your promotions. First, begin by assessing your needs and creating a realistic objective. You may wish to increase your body count on Tuesday, Wednesday, and Sunday. Perhaps you would like a shift in clientele and bring in new faces, or have your current customers come in earlier or later, or attract an older crowd. Another goal of a promotion would be to triple draft beer sales, or add another cover charge night. Determine your target clientele (review Chapter 4 on Selecting Your Clientele). Be as specific as possible. If you have been in business awhile, then evaluate your past promotions and sales. What worked before? Why have other promotions failed?

The next step is to evaluate your competition. You need to know what makes their operations work, and what their businesses are like during various times of the day and night. Notice the ages of their customers and how they dress. Ask the customers how they heard of your competitor's bar, and if they have heard of yours. Look at their entertainment. Is it a jukebox, a DJ, a live band? Does the DJ play an interesting mix of music? Does the DJ talk and involve the audience or just play music? You need to understand their entertainment format so you can position yourself accordingly. Does the DJ promote other nights of the week? Is he or she excited when they make their announcements? Do you feel like you are missing something if you do not come in on another night? Are the employees talking about the promotions, and/or wearing hats or buttons? Is the Door Host passing out flyers and talking about the promotions? Are the drinks different? How is the quality? What are the prices like? How is the service? Do you like the atmosphere? Would you return?

Whether you like what your competition is doing is irrelevant. If they are busy and you are not, there is a reason. They are filling a void in the marketplace and you are not. You need to figure out what is missing in your operation or what you can do to add additional customers.

After looking at your competition, you need to evaluate your own customers. In Chapter 4, the advantages of a marketing survey and focus groups are discussed. You may wish to have a formal focus group or an informal survey handed out to your customers as they enter your bar. You would like to know where your customers live and how far they travel to your bar. Have they been here before? How many times a month do they visit? How many times last month? What do they like most about your place? Dislike? What radio stations do they listen to and what newspapers do they read? Do they like your drinks and prices? Service? Employees? Atmosphere? Entertainment? What would you as a customer do to improve the bar? Its promotions? Its drinks? Its atmosphere?

It should be clear to you who your current customers are, so you can design your promotions towards attracting the same group or a different crowd. Knowing your competition allows you the opportunity to do something different by countering their format or improving upon it. If they play country music, you should play rock and roll or newer, more progressive music. If you both are running an upscale billiards room, and your competition charges a $5 cover, then you charge $5 or less and give each person one half off on a drink or food item or the first hour of play free. You offer more value for your guest's money.

When planning your promotions, begin by concentrating on building business one day at a time. Figure out your break even point, or at what point the promotion covers its costs and you begin to generate additional revenue.

Let's assume you would like to increase business on another night of the week. The majority of bars are busy Fridays and Saturdays, with Thursdays running third in revenue. Promoting Sundays can be tricky, as most of your customers have to be at work Monday morning. Bars in college towns and resorts are the exception. Good times know no day of the week boundaries.

Choose either Monday or Tuesday as your next day to build. If you were to promote Wednesdays, you run the risk of shifting your Thursday customers to Wednesdays, and then you have not gained any new business. Once your Mondays or Tuesdays are busy, then

move on to promoting Wednesdays. As you begin developing ideas, keep these 10 points in mind:

1. Choose a budget that will enable you to sustain the promotion for the time allowed. A successful promotion should produce a minimum of three times its cost. A promotion should begin paying for itself after three weeks.

2. Allow eight to twelve weeks for any promotion to establish itself. Do not advertise an ending date. By not having a specific end, you can continue the promotion indefinitely, or cut it short if it flops. (If you have never run a promotion that flops, consider yourself lucky. However, by following these steps, you should avoid major errors.)

3. Involve as many people as possible. Most contests, like a Male/Female Hot Body Contest (although very successful), have a handful of contestants; you want everyone to have fun.

4. Do not stop your music or dance floor to stage your promotion. When you stop the flow, the energy level drops. You can lower the sound level, but keep the beat going. The same rules apply whether you are a neighborhood bar with a tape running or a high-energy dance club. (Some dance clubs insist on stopping the music. If you absolutely have to, keep it short, no more than 15 minutes, or your dancers will become impatient.)

5. Keep your guests late. Stage your finale to occur between midnight and 12:30 AM.

6. Each promotion should have three levels of participation:

   • A drink special that benefits everyone.

- Nightly prize giveaways (10 or more).
- A grand prize where the nightly (weekly) prize winners must return at the end of the promotion.

7. Keep abreast of local and national trends in the entertainment industry. Read *Billboard*, *Cheers*, and *Night Club and Bar* magazines. New forms of technology attract attention and are great to design promotions around. Remember when VCRs were new, or compact discs? Keep informed as to what is next. A portable wrist phone?

8. Take an old successful promotion and give it a new twist. Dance marathons have been around for decades. Change it to accommodate the latest fitness movement. Guessing the number of beans in a pot for a prize can be guessing the number of computer chips, or the number of songs on all the compact discs in the jar.

9. Each promotion should include something visual. The prize(s) should be placed prominently for all to see.

10. Create tie-ins with other merchants to expand everyone's business.

Successful promotions can involve businesses other than your own. Look around for businesses that attract the same clientele as your bar. Cross-promoting generates sales in areas you may have overlooked. If your target guests are between the ages of 21–35, they go to the movies, buy cassette tapes and compact discs, rent video tapes, spend money on haircuts, go to fitness centers to work out, participate in sports, and buy cars, cameras, camcorders, shoes, and clothes. If they are 25–45, they purchase all of the above and need the services of stock brokers, attorneys, accountants, and real estate and travel agents. If you do not serve food, look to restaurants and fast food outlets for prizes. Once you begin to see the possibilities of tie-ins, it is endless.

When you approach another business for tie-ins and prizes, explain to them the benefits of cooperating. You both attract the same customers. Tell them how many people come through your doors each night, week, and month. You will mention their name in your advertising at no cost to them (occasionally a large prize item or promotion may involve shared advertising costs due to the nature of the event, such as a car giveaway). Their name will be mentioned three times an evening by your DJ or person running the event. Invite them to your bar to see how you operate and promote.

When looking for prizes, first try to have other businesses provide the items for free. Second, offer to split the cost. If either of these methods fail, then finally offer to pay for the items at cost. You should not have to pay full price. The more prizes, the more potential for new customers.

One of the ways to move your customers to their stores is to provide prizes that are discounts on services or goods. For instance, a hair salon provides you with ten prizes each week for eight weeks. These involve four $10 discounts on cuts, three free manicures, and three free bottles of shampoo with any cut. At a video rental store, the prizes may be rent one video and receive the second one free, or $5 off on any movie purchase. A clothing store's prizes might be free socks with the purchase of any pair of jeans, or half off on the purchase of shirts, or a free pair of earrings, or a free dress. Don't forget your liquor companies. They have the wealth and experience to provide tremendous support. You also have their millions of dollars of advertising to use to your advantage—and it's free.

Your tie-in businesses need to commit themselves to promoting your bar as well. Give them plenty of flyers to hand out to their

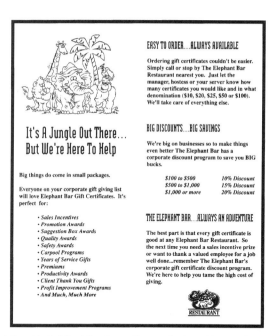

It's A Jungle Out There... But We're Here To Help

EASY TO ORDER...ALWAYS AVAILABLE

Ordering gift certificates couldn't be easier. Simply call or stop by The Elephant Bar Restaurant nearest you. Just let the manager, hostess or your server know how many certificates you would like and in what denomination ($10, $20, $25, $50 or $100). We'll take care of everything else.

Big things do come in small packages.

Everyone on your corporate gift giving list will love Elephant Bar Gift Certificates. It's perfect for:

- Sales Incentives
- Promotion Awards
- Suggestion Box Awards
- Quality Awards
- Safety Awards
- Carpool Programs
- Years of Service Gifts
- Premiums
- Productivity Awards
- Client Thank You Gifts
- Profit Improvement Programs
- And Much, Much More

BIG DISCOUNTS...BIG SAVINGS

We're big on businesses so to make things even better The Elephant Bar has a corporate discount program to save you BIG bucks.

$100 to $500	10% Discount
$500 to $1,000	15% Discount
$1,000 or more	20% Discount

THE ELEPHANT BAR...ALWAYS AN ADVENTURE

The best part is that every gift certificate is good at any Elephant Bar Restaurant. So the next time you need a sales incentive prize or want to thank a valued employee for a job well done...remember The Elephant Bar's corporate gift certificate discount program. We're here to help you tame the high cost of giving.

Fig. 11-9. The Elephant Bar took the gift certificate idea one step further for companies that want to thank their employees.

customers. You may wish to provide them with free drink or admission passes that are dated. Have the store or employee sign the back of the pass so you can measure the results. Dated passes are handed out and good for two weeks. You want to motivate new customers to act quickly. It helps to pick a specific night you are trying to promote and build, such as, "Good for Wednesdays Only," rather than having the passes good for any night.

Once you have your concept, dates lined up, and tie-in businesses, prepare and distribute a press release. Then, inform your staff and motivate them to sell the promotion. Have a meeting and explain the what, where, and when of the event. You must also tell them what is expected of them. Give them a written schedule of events that includes their responsibilities and guidelines on how to present the promotion. Staff involvement is a key element in pulling off a successful promotion.

One motivating factor for your employees is the obvious one of more patrons resulting in more tips. However, your staff can also work on their off hours to promote. A manager should accompany each employee promotion squad in its outings. When a manager is showing the way by working alongside the employees, morale is improved and results increase.

Employees can enthusiastically pass out flyers in malls, shops, and fitness centers, at the beach, on the slopes, and in office buildings. You can pay them or offer another incentive. Give them the same passes you supply to your tie-in businesses. For each pass that is returned with their name on it, they receive 25 or 50 cents. The winner receives a bonus. In this way, everyone benefits and is rewarded, just like your customers. No passes can be distributed within your bar. The contest is daily or weekly. Be sure to date your passes. The pass could be used to participate in the contest or an event, not necessarily to offer a discount or free admission.

A fun way to grab attention is to have an employee dress up as a sheriff. He or she is your Party Sheriff. Your Party Sheriff goes to areas where your target clientele congregates and the Sheriff issues party tickets (free guest passes or drink coupons) to those individuals "badly in need of a good time." Potential patrons can be cited for "looking too good," for being a "hot fashion dresser," or "creating a party atmosphere for too few people."

Within your bar, decorate several days before the time of the promotion so your customers start asking questions and begin creating word-of-mouth advertising. Every employee needs to be enthused about the event and happily telling everyone they meet. Managers need to make a point of setting examples and introducing themselves to ten new customers a shift.

If you work with a DJ, he or she should mention the promo 2–3 times an hour. Keep the message short, about 20 seconds, and never talk over the vocals in a song. Promote one event at a time. If you have a video system, then run your own commercials two times an hour.

As people exit the bar, the door host should hand each person a flyer or small wallet calendar with information on upcoming promotions. (See FIGS. 11-10 and 11-11.) Each guest should be thanked for coming, by name if possible.

After two weeks have passed, review and analyze your promotion. Is it working? Are you getting the response you expected from your advertising? Are all your plans being carried out? Are your tie-in businesses promoting? Your employees talking it up? The DJ or announcer working the crowd properly? Do your customers like the promotion? Has your competition reacted? Seek responses from employees and customers and do not hesitate to alter and improve your promotion. If this one is successful, then begin planning your next promotion, as they do not last forever.

Hot Tropical Nights: A case study

Let's examine a promotion for a bar that does not have dancing (but could easily work for a dance club), and on a typical weekday night, gathers a crowd of 200 customers, mostly aged 21–35. It snows and is cold in the winter. The management would like to increase Wednes-day night business to 300 patrons. The promotion will run from February 15th through April 15th. It will be called Hot Tropical Nights. Each week will feature a tropical drink special for $1.75, only to those persons wearing sunglasses. The passes handed out by the bar's employees and tie-in businesses will enable each guest to receive a free pair of sunglasses (donated by a local travel agent and workout center with their logos imprinted on the sides of the glasses). Prizes donated from local merchants include free hours at a tanning salon, passes to the fitness center, discounts for income tax preparation (to tie-in with April 15th), haircuts, compact discs, limousine rides, swim wear, boogie boards, and a Grand Prize trip for two to Hawaii. Planning took place in this sequence:

Eight weeks before the start date: planning sessions with key personnel to brainstorm about promotions.

Seven weeks before the start date Final promotion planned based upon previous week's suggestions.

Six to four weeks before the start date Tie-in businesses and prizes lined up. Final promotion details finished. Order decorations. Layout flyers and passes. Send out press releases to monthly publications that require advance notice.

Three weeks before the start date Passes and flyers printed and distribution begins.

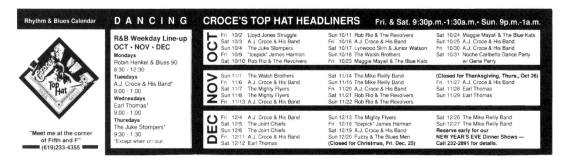

Fig. 11-10. This small wallet calendar folds up to business-card size. Croce's, San Diego, California

Fig. 11-11. An action-packed calendar that folds up to fit in a pocket and advertises drink and food specials and other events. The Elephant Bar

Two weeks before the start date Press releases sent out. Announcer (DJ) begins promoting. A mannequin dressed in swim wear, sunglasses, and holding a surfboard is placed in an eye-catching spot to generate interest.

One week before the start date Heavy distribution of passes and flyers by employee promo squads, and Announcer makes heavy selling effort as do the employees and Door Hosts.

First two weeks of event Heavy distribution and promoting continues, management and key personnel evaluate progress and results, and fine-tune if necessary. Send out thank you notes to sponsers.

After four weeks of event Management decides to slow pace of promo squads because club is filled to capacity.

After eight weeks Management and key personnel are tired of going to the bank to deposit extra funds and discuss extending or ending the promotion, and begin discussions for their next promotion.

After twelve weeks Management decides to extend this successful promotion for another four weeks. Thank you notes are sent again to all the sponsors and companies who donated prizes telling them of the success and any publicity generated.

If you have a success on your hands, it might be difficult to end it. However, you will need all the support from your tie-in businesses to continue. Your Hot Tropical Nights could become an annual event followed by Ski Down Under, where you send someone off to ski in New Zealand. In the Southern Hemisphere, winter is beginning when the Northern Hemisphere's is ending. Tie-ins could be with New Zealand Airlines and New Zealand beer and liquor companies looking to promote

Planning successful promotions **143**

their products, along with local businesses. As your promotions prove successful, it will be easier to attract tie-in companies.

100+ successful promotions

Consider the following ideas and adapt or improvise to suit your bar's particular needs. Hundreds of bars across the country have made money with these promotions.

Holidays and events

Holidays are always good for celebrations and promotions.

January New Year's Day lends itself to a Football Bowl Game Marathon, particularly if you have more than one large TV screen. Offer special high-energy or smart drinks for patrons to pick up their energy levels and start the New Year off right! Martin Luther King, Jr.'s Birthday on the 15th is often observed on the closest Monday. Super Bowl Sunday towards the end of the month is a blockbuster. When you have these national pastime events and large crowds at your bar, these are good times to advertise upcoming promotions in your bar. Take advantage of this captive audience.

February Lincoln's birthday is on the 12th, Washington's birthday is the 22nd and President's Day falls on a Monday between the two. Valentine's Day is a fabulous day for sweethearts. Your employees should wear red. Pass out free roses or chocolate roses, heart-shaped chocolates, or candies. Try a Luscious Lips Contest, where the ladies imprint their lips on white cards and votes are cast for the prettiest, sexiest, and fullest lips. Use lips in your ads. Tie-in with make-up and hair salons and even a modeling or talent agency.

March St. Patrick's Day on the 17th always brings out the Irish in everyone, so stock extra Irish whiskey. Serve green beer by adding green food coloring to your draft beer. Have live Irish music for sing-alongs. The first day of spring on the 20th can also be a day for lovers: TWOgetherness. Couples buying drinks together receive half off on both drinks.

April Start of daylight saving time on the first Sunday of the month. Easter Sunday varies as to the exact date and is a nice time to include families with a Family Picnic Outing. National Secretaries' Day is the third Wednesday of the month. Offer free drinks, flowers or prizes. The Kentucky Derby runs this month and allows opportunities for creating drinks for the favored horses (see FIG. 11-12). Earth Day falls on a Sunday and is a fantastic day to sponser a charitable cause, either local, such as

Enjoy Traditional

Maker's
(SIV) Mark

Mint Juleps

(The official 1985 Kentucky Derby Bourbon)

or

One of these Special Derby Drinks

Rosebud
Kauai King
Black Gold

(each is named in honor of a past winner of the Kentucky Derby)

AVAILABLE
ALL WEEK
APRIL 29-MAY 4

Join us to watch the Running of the Roses Saturday Afternoon May 4th

Fig. 11-12. T.J. Applebee's and Maker's Mark Kentucky Derby drink promotion.

cleaning up your community's river, or global, such as preserving our old growth forests.

May Mother's Day is usually the second Sunday of the month. When a mother is present, have a photographer take the family's portrait. Have a Give Your Mother Some Rest Day contest where the mother with the largest family in attendance wins a week at a spa. Also in May are Armed Forces Day and Memorial Day. Red, white, and blue drinks are a natural promotion.

June Flag Day arrives on the 14th followed by the first day of summer on the 20th or 21st. Summertime promotions easily attract customers. Sponsor trips to the beach, swimwear fashion shows, best tan contests, homemade swimsuit/bikini contests, and numerous outdoor sport team sponsorships. Father's Day on the third Sunday of the month could lead to a Father/Son or Father/Daughter Golf Tournament, or an Ugly Tie Contest.

July Independence Day on the 4th should inspire your bartenders to invent a special "firecracker" drink. You could rent a bus and take people to the fireworks show, and, expect a rush of people after the show is over.

Make up an Ice Cream Day with ice cream drinks for the hottest days in the middle of summer.

August It usually is so hot, have a "Christmas in August" promotion complete with artificial snow. If you are close to water, such as a lake, river, or intracoastal waterway, have a Bathtub Regatta, or a Floating Ducky Contest . . . anything to get people into the water and cool off.

September Labor Day on the first Monday of the month should be cause for an all-day celebration. Grandparent's Day comes in the middle of the month. The First Day of Autumn on the 22nd is a sure bet with an End of Summer Celebration the day before, followed by kicking off your Fall promotion schedule the next day.

October Columbus Day is observed on the Monday closest to the 12th. United Nations Day comes about two weeks later, followed by the End of Daylight Savings Time on the third Sunday of the month. The Baseball World Series is so popular that any theme concerning baseball will bring customers in. An unusual and fun twist is to set the price of beer throughout the whole baseball season contingent upon the major league baseball player with the lowest batting average. If his average is .140, then a bottle of beer costs $1.40. Customers will live and die whenever he gets a hit, as his average rises, so will the cost of their beers. Then, during the World Series, a bottle of beer will cost his ending average.

The final day of the month is Halloween, where costume parties and haunted houses are a must. Have a pumpkin carving contest for your employees to decorate your bar and also one for your customers.

November Promote civic pride on Election Day (the first Tuesday) by offering a free drink or appetizer to every customer who shows you a voting stub. Design drinks and food items after the political candidates. You could hold a victory party for the candidate of your choice. As a prelude to election day, invite the local candidates to tend bar one night and answer questions from interested customers. Veteran's Day is on the 11th. Honor them with drink and food specials. Thanksgiving Day is the third Thursday of the month. Run a special on Wild Turkey or recreate an old tradition for your bar: pass out turkeys to good customers and employees or sponsor turkey dinners for the homeless or less fortunate.

December You should be calling on businesses and private individuals promoting your bar as the only place to hold their holiday parties. But first, on December 21st, you must celebrate The First Day of Winter. Import snow, and have a snowman building contest or give away a pair of skis, a ski trip for two, or other outdoor winter sports equipment.

Christmas comes only once on the 25th and many out-of-towners need a place to eat and drink and have some fun after they have visited with their families. New Year's Eve, on the 31st, is one of the largest revenue-producing days of the year. Have plenty of party hats, confetti, horns, and champagne on hand. You can charge more for drinks, add a cover charge, or increase your cover charge on New Year's Eve. If you increase your prices in any way, be sure to give your customers something extra so they feel they are receiving more value for their money (have a live band or free champagne).

Besides these obvious holidays, your area may celebrate others. By being creative, you can make any day a special day and its annual celebration a tradition. Births and deaths of famous people, special events, and products lend themselves to such festivities. You might want to celebrate the demise of the Edsel car, the birth of the Polaroid camera, or Bach's birthday. Anyone who comes in on his/her birthday receives a free drink.

Tastings Have a White Wine Day with wine tastings, a Beer Tasting Day, and a Liqueur Tasting Day. Invite local vintners, brewmasters, and liquor representatives to lead these tastings and lend their expertise. Your tastings day could always be the first Monday of the month.

Celebrity bartender A celebrity bartender pouring on a given day is a sure way to attract a crowd of his or her fans. You cannot expect celebrities to be great bartenders, but they are there to draw a crowd. Consider donating a portion of the profits from the drinks the celebrity pours to a charity.

Buy a drink and get to know . . . Invite a well-known person to give a short 15-minute talk and answer questions from your crowd. If you want to attract an intellectual crowd, have a Best-seller Night. Successful authors or poets can give readings or sign copies of their books. A variation on this theme would be to invite a movie or TV director, actor, or professional athlete to showcase the latest movie or a montage of the season's best games.

Employee talent day Promote any special talents of your employees with publicity and newspaper articles. Perhaps you have a dancer in your group, a former child star, or an accomplished painter. Run videotapes of their performances or an exhibition of their artworks.

Remote radio broadcast Contact your local radio station and see if it will send someone to your bar to stage a Remote Radio Broadcast. The station can broadcast your band "live and in concert," or it can originate a talk show, interviewing celebrities, customers, and employees on topical issues. Sponsor a Sunday Jazz Concert, a Seminar on Investing in Stocks, or an in-depth look at World Famine. Look for the long-term benefits of such promotions when a portion of the large crowd comes back again. Repeat business is what you are trying to achieve.

Body contests Numerous bars have promoted nights with Wet T-shirt Contests, Male Exotic Dancing, and Hot Legs Contests for both men and women. Variations include Most Physically Fit Male/Female, Best Winter Tan, Best Summer Tan, and Best Handmade Bikini/Swimsuit Contest.

Ladies' night Ladies' nights are extremely popular when all women get in free and receive a complimentary drink or a rose (if you run this promotion, have a Gentlemen's Night where they come in free, as you could be setting yourself up for a gender-biased discrimination lawsuit).

Ugly tie day Clothing affords numerous opportunities. Customers wearing the designated clothing item receive a free drink. Ugly Tie Day brings out the worst or best in everyone's wardrobe. Cut those ugly things off their necks and hang them up on the rafters, but only after the crowd gets to vote for its favorite tie. You can change the theme to be Ugly Shoes Day. Ugly Hat Day is another one that works well.

Wild west days, pilgrims' day, gold diggers' day These are all fun events for your customers, especially if you are located in an area that has historical interest. Prizes can be handed out for the most authentic, most original, and funniest costume. Any nostalgia period can be celebrated: the fifties, sixties, and seventies. Play that era's music and have your employees dress up in the fashions of the day.

Look-alike contests Your customers compete to look like their favorite celebrities. Choose old stars or the current heartthrobs. It can generate a tremendous amount of publicity.

Lip sync or karaoke sing-alongs These can be part of the look-alike contests. In the Lip Sync contest, contestants sing along with recordings, trying to imitate the look of popular singers.

Shorts and shots night Every person wearing shorts gets a free shot. Variations might be a PJ Night, Lingerie Night, Bikini Night, or T-shirt Night.

Fashion auction A Fashion auction is a big crowd pleaser. Models show current designs that are then auctioned to customers. Many promotions of this type are designed for singles bars to attract women, which in turn, attracts men.

Fragrance night Have a perfume or cologne manufacturer sponsor a fragrance night where samples of the latest colognes are handed out to patrons. Males search out the females in attendance for the one woman wearing the secret scent, or females search for the male cologne-wearer. You could call this promotion Scentasional Search, Manhunter Night, or Womanhunter Night.

Armadillo bathing beauty contest The crazier the idea, the better it works. A bar in Texas held an Armadillo Beauty Bathing Contest. Local fashion designers submitted special bathing suits for the little critters. The proceeds of the event went to charity.

Animal races A beach bar in California held Tuesday night sandcrab races and turned a slow night into one with an overflow crowd. The same thing has been done with frogs, turtles, or any animal indigenous to your area.

Models/celebrity volleyball challenge If you have several model agencies in your area, they can compete and raise money for a favorite charity through a friendly competition on the volleyball court. It could be on a baseball diamond, basketball court, or soccer field. The same fundraiser could be played with actors and actresses. Members of competing baseball, basketball, or hockey teams could also participate in a Volleyball Challenge. Take people out of context and let them do something different and everyone has fun.

Monday night at the movies When a new movie is released, try Monday Night at the Movies. Hand out numbered tickets to customers as they enter, then have a drawing where the winners receive free tickets to see the movie.

Casino night Simulated gambling can be an exciting attraction. Organize a Casino Night, where customers buy chips from the bar to play blackjack, roulette, or craps. The customers do not receive anything for their efforts, as that would constitute illegal gambling. They are buying chips to experience the excitement of the games and practice their techniques. Hire experienced casino dealers to run the games.

Millionaire's night A variation on the gambling theme (in states where lotteries are legal) is to pass out free lottery tickets to anyone coming in on Lottery Night or Millionaire's Night.

Wheel of fortune Use a Wheel of Fortune to let customers spin for free or reduced drinks and prizes. The wheel can also be used to set all drink prices for a predetermined time period. Your Wheel of Fortune can be used at any time for any promotion. Customers spin for free drinks and food items, a chance to enter into a drawing for a grand prize, a chance to have their drinks cost $1 all night, or for other prizes. Your Wheel of Fortune can be your only promotion or part of a larger event.

Guess the number of beans in the jar Guessing the number of items in a jar can be tied to any event. Pack a jar with keys and key chains, with the correct guess winning a Rolls Royce or Ferrari rental for one day (Ferrari Fantasy). Load up a jar with computer discs, and the winner receives a laptop computer. Put pages of the phone book in a jar and the correct number of telephone numbers wins a cellular phone. Tie-ins with area businesses are a natural for these promotions.

Sexy lingerie and briefs night Instead of guessing the number of items in a jar, fill the jar with items that customers pick and keep. Your DJ or announcer asks for specific items, such as an out-of-state driver's license, a local workout studio's membership card, video rental card, library card, fishing license, and other fun items. The first person to come up with the item gets to reach into the jar and pick a prize. Stuff your clear glass jar with sexy lingerie and men's briefs, all imprinted with your logo. Wrapped inside each item are other prizes: cash, discounts or gift certificates from area businesses, and a Grand Prize.

Diamonds are a girl's best friend You can vary the jar game with Diamonds Are A Girl's Best Friend, stocking a huge brandy snifter with one real and a hundred fake diamonds.

Redhead night Secretary Week, Carpenter Night, Executive Night, or Redhead Night, can attract whatever type of crowd is appropriate for your bar.

Hospitality industry party night Target a particular industry to invite on a slow night. Many bars have successfully run a Hospitality Industry Party Night (HIP), where other restaurant and bar personnel, caterers, travel agents, and hotel, airline, and car rental employees are issued special HIP passes that allow them discounted admission or drinks on a Monday or Tuesday Night. (See FIG. 11-13.)

College student night You may wish to cater to 18-and-over, or keep it 21-and-over if enough students can fill your needs. A College Night can be extremely successful. Some bars have Animal House Toga Parties.

Team sponsorships A favorite promotion for many bars is the financial support they give to an amateur sports team that plays in weekly competitions. The team meets after the game at your bar. Competing teams also join your team for a few friendly rounds of drinks. You can sponsor leagues at your bar, such as darts, pool, Ping Pong, bowling, softball, soccer, even volleyball, surfing, or tennis. Many games become fads, and bars sponsor competitions to increase business. Remember backgammon, Rubik's Cube, and trivia contests? All of these attracted customers who felt they were on top of the latest fads and trends. It never hurts for you to be the first to take notice and sponsor such events.

Sports tournaments and races When sports are big with your customers, organize a tournament for them and make it an annual event. This could be a golf, bowling, tennis, volleyball, or fishing tournament, or a skiing or mountain bike race. Have an Olympic or well-known athlete officiate the final match. (See FIG. 11-14).

Event sponsorships Sponsoring events that do not take place within your bar is also a good idea. Support events you believe in. Your involvement could range from providing free soft drinks and juices for the participants in a charitable run to footing the entire bill. Your location itself may suggest other func-

PROUD MEMBER IN GOOD STANDING OF
THE PARTY CORNERS

Riddler's - SALOON -   THE **KAMAKAZE KLUB**
822-9291   822-7119

· EXTEND ALL COURTESYS ·

1854-60 WESTCHESTER AVE. · THE BRONX · N.Y.

Signature   Date
THIS CARD ENTITLES HOLDER & One Guest
· Immediate express admission to Club
· Admission to special cardholder parties
· Lowest prevailing price on public nights
· Special cardholder privileges
This card is the property of SHENANNIGANS. It cannot
be used by a non cardholder. By accepting this card,
holder agrees to abide by all rules and regulations. Card
must be surrendered upon demand.
For Private Parties Call... 312-642-6800

Fig. 11-13. Examples of plastic passes issued to your best customers to build up business.

Yoli Plastic Card Company

tions. If your bar is in an historic district, you could sponsor a walk around the neighborhood touring old houses and buildings. Consider donating some money for trees and flowers to beautify your street.

The press and people in general want to hear about those who make contributions to the community just as much as they want to hear about fires, deaths, and what the President is doing. When kids and animals are involved, you'll have a real attention-grabbing event. Donate money to the local zoo for the care and feeding of some rare animals. Drinks named after these animals can be sold, with some of the proceeds going to organizations working to save endangered species.

Club meetings Many clubs in your area need a place to meet. A travel club or a ski club will need a place to gather and show films and videos. Entice them to your bar with free munchies or free soft drinks and give them a special time or room to meet in private. Check your local newspapers under social events for

other groups that need meeting places: singles, single parents, and business and professional organizations.

Hire a bus—see a game Many bars also rent buses and drive their customers to a professional game. Purchase a block of tickets in advance, and repeat this outing throughout the season. For one price, the customer receives a ticket to the game, transportation to and from the event, and free beer on the bus. It could be A Day at the Races, A Night with the Braves, or A Night at the Courts. A variation would be to arrange a night out at a cultural affair or concert.

Drink yourself around the world Beer lends itself to many promotions. If you stock a large selection of beers, you can print up a card listing all of them and their country of origin. Sponsor a Drink Yourself Around the World Contest or a Beers of the World Club. After a customer has filled up a card by drinking 30 different beers, he receives a free beer mug with his name engraved on it. Hang these mugs over your bar.

Fig. 11-14. Legends golf tournament handbill.

After two cards you can give a T-shirt that says, "I Drank My Way Around the World" and put a photo up on the Beer Drinkers' Hall of Fame Board. Increase the value of the gifts for the number of cards filled up. The customer who drinks the most beer in a year wins a trip to a famous beer capital of the world. During October, run an Oktoberfest and have plenty of German beers on hand.

Weather games If the weather poses special problems in your area, turn this negative into a positive. Promote a Rainy Day Blues Day with jazz music, or offer free umbrellas with your logo printed on them. If it's a cold spell, plan a Winter Solstice Beach Party on December 21, complete with suntanning lamps, sunglasses, and a Best Winter Tan Contest.

Cellular phone night All portable telephone owners come in and list their numbers on a board receiving a two-digit code. Customers play telephone tag and call each other up.

CB night CB Night promotes those who ride the highways and use CB radios. They can sign in with their "handle" on a big board and receive a free drink or a T-shirt that carries the bar's handle or slogan. Spread the word over the CB about the promotion.

Name that tune Certain promotions change as the times change, but the idea is the same. You can copy some ideas from TV game shows. A popular one with customers is Name That Tune. It requires a DJ or prerecorded music. This game has been updated to Name That Video. In a few years, with advances in technology, it might be Name That Hologram!

Customer-named drink menus If your favorite customers drink something special, name the drinks after them. Create a menu of these drinks with funny descriptions of each and include photos.

Customer appreciation night Celebrate your bar's anniversaries with special promotions. Customer Appreciation Night can be at any time, or when you have your 100,000 Customer, 250,000 Customer, or your 100,000,000 Customer. Roll back prices to what they were when you first opened your doors. You are in the entertainment business, so any excuse is a good one to have a party.

Late-night happy hour If your customers tend to leave early, institute a Late-Night Happy Hour after midnight, a Late-Night Hungry Hour, or a Late-Night Breakfast Buffet. You could have an After-Hours Club, where no alcoholic drinks are served, but non-alcoholic and high-energy drinks are sold along with an all-you-can-eat breakfast buffet. After hours can start at 2:00 AM.

Beat the clock Try a Beat the Clock promotion. The earlier a person arrives, the cheaper his or her drinks will be for the entire night. Arrive between 7:00–7:30 PM and your drinks cost $1, 7:30–8:00 PM and they cost $1.50, 8:00–8:30 PM and they cost $2. Each person receives a numbered card or wrist band upon arrival with their time punched on it, the drink price, and a limit to the number of drinks purchased. The card or band is valid for one day only.

News hour Host a News Hour starting at 5:00 PM with the latest stock quotes and world news flashing on your TV screens or electronic message boards.

Twilight dancing On the other end of the time table, encourage customers to arrive earlier in the evening by starting your dancing at 4:00 PM instead of 8:00 PM.

Alternative uses for your bar During the times when your bar is empty or closed, you can lease it for other activities or explore alternative uses. Many bars are used as locations for movies and TV productions. Alert your local or state film commission. These film bureaus advise out-of-state production companies of the locations available in their area.

Sunday during the day may be slow. If you have a dance floor, tap into the teen market by allowing teens to dance during daytime hours. Invite square dancers or ballroom dancers to use your facilities. Physical fitness and exercise programs could also use your dance space. Your sound system will be an asset. Look around, someone could be using your space. This could be part of your community service program or an additional source of revenue.

T-shirt promotions T-shirts are a great way to advertise your promotions and special events. Numerous bars sell them all year long. They can be humorous or of unique design. Customers like to wear them and feel they are part of a special "club." Tourists like to buy T-shirts to show where they've traveled, so be sure to include your city and state as part of the design (The Hard Rock Cafes are masters at this technique). Use quality merchandise and hire a graphic artist or advertising agency to design the shirt for you.

Special tourist events Ongoing promotions for tourists can generate fantastic word-of-mouth advertising. If there is something unique or special about your area, take advantage of it, especially if your location attracts large numbers of tourists. Calaveras County, California, has the Annual Mark Twain Frog-Jumping Contest. In your area, it could be bronco-busting, crab cakes, chili recipes, or key lime pies. If this event or specialty can be written about in tour guide books or tours brought to your place to participate in the fun and excitement, you have a winner. Tourists love to seek out anything with "local color" or "local flavor." Tourists have time and money to spend. Go for it!

Designated driver program If bars and drunk driving have a bad image in your area, stress the positive things you will be doing to combat this problem. Send out press releases about your designated driver program in which one member of a party decides not to drink alcoholic beverages, and receives nonalcoholic drinks free for the entire night. That is a popular way to ease community and customer concerns about drunk drivers. The owners of Jukebox Saturday Night in Chicago have two tow trucks they use to tow someone home who has had too much to drink. This way, both the customer and his or her car arrive home safely.

You can contribute to endless civic and charitable causes. Being a concerned member of your community should be an on-going process. You will spread extremely valuable goodwill by extending yourself in this way. In the process, the news media will give you free publicity worth far more than any advertising you could buy.

Free drink recipes Another good way to generate publicity is to concoct both alcoholic and nonalcoholic drinks for holidays and special occasions that can be featured in the food section of your local newspaper or on a local television news show. Get to know your food editor and suggest story ideas:

- How to use fresh fruits in drinks.
- Cool, refreshing summer drinks.
- Hot drinks to take the chill off cold winter days.

- How to hold a beer-tasting party in your home.

Try to have a variety of promotions and events that will appeal to different interests. They can be educational, about serious causes, or simply fun and entertaining. Your customers will love the extra excitement and will start talking about your place to their friends. Before long, your bar will be packed all of the time, and you'll be thinking of duplicating your success by opening another, larger club. (See FIGS. 11-15 and 11-16 for more promotional ideas.)

Fig. 11-15. *J. Sloan's Sunday night promotion.*

 **presents**

AT THE NEW **RItz**

THURSDAY FEB. 20th   9PM

PERFORMING FOR THE EVENING

DIRECT FROM PUERTO RICO

GILBERTO SANTA ROSA
& HIS ORCHESTRA

FROM NYC

TITO NIEVES
& HIS ORCHESTRA

LADIES FREE UNTIL 11 PM

MEN $12 BEFORE 11PM • MEN & LADIES $15 AFTER 11PM

DRESS CODE: CLASSY, ELEGANT, YOUR BEST

AGE: 21 & OVER

WE'RE BACK EVERY THURS. AT THE RITZ

THE RITZ (formerly Studio 54) Located at 254 WEST 54th ST., NYC

(West of Bdwy) • (212) 541-8900

COMING FEB. 27th: DIRECT FROM PUERTO RICO

NINO SEGARRA

CO-PRODUCED BY VAL & ROLLO PRODUCTIONS

Fig. 11-16. A Ritz postcard promoting Thursday nights.

12

Marketing: Advertising

Most bars advertise on a regular basis or for special promotions. Some are fortunate and never have to advertise. The purpose of "advertising" is to let the public know about your past, present, and future events. People will not come to your bar or participate in your promotions if they do not know about them. Advertising should interest people and motivate them to spend their time and money at your bar.

Positioning is a concept used in advertising to distinguish one product from another, to define who will use the product, and to demonstrate the value of the product to the buyer. Remember that your location, concept, decor, employees, clientele, and promotions are all geared to reflect a certain "sense" about your place. You want your customers to have a clear image of it. This image or positioning strategy should guide all of your advertising. Once you have decided on a position, stick to it, and be consistent. If you are a friendly neighborhood bar, then stress that in your ads: "Gail's Pub—Good Drinks & Good Friends," or "Bill's Tavern—Your Neighborhood Bar and Grill." "Fantasia—The Nightclub of Tomorrow" positions itself as a futuristic club, and its decor, fixtures, and advertising carry out this theme.

You may find that you are too busy to handle your advertising needs by yourself. Producing an ad involves either artwork or a photograph, copy translated into type, and a paste-up of the finished product. Each step costs money and takes time. Depending on the amount of advertising you will use, it may be beneficial to hire a graphic artist or an ad agency to assist you or someone who works in-house using the graphics capabilities of your computer. You will need to provide a budget and some concepts that can be developed. Advertising budgets generally run between 1 and 3 percent of each month's revenue. Larger bars know the value of advertising and may even spend up to 10 percent, with proportionately larger returns for their money. An ad agency will provide creative input, produce your ads, and buy advertising space for you. You can use an agency for any or all of your needs. You may want it to come up with a concept and execute the ads, while you place them.

What makes a good advertisement?

Advertising is not an exact science. You will notice the results of your advertising efforts, however, if you aim for results-oriented ads. These are ads that seek to increase your business, as opposed to image advertising, that simply puts your name out there. Advertising has been known to decrease as well as increase business.

Effective advertising can generate tremendous returns. Increasing business from a $300 a day gross to $3000 a day, or even $6000 a day, is not difficult, provided you have the facilities to handle the volume. To be effective, you must first define your bar in simple terms. You have already done so by deciding the type of bar you want to operate. Next, accurately identify the "target audience" you wish to reach. Once you know the demographics of your clientele (information you already have from researching your location), you will be able to match your demographics with those of the medium you choose for advertising.

Next you need to crystallize your objective. Is it to increase revenue by adding entertainment, or to achieve a standing-room-only crowd? Scrutinize what the competition is doing, and evaluate its strengths and weaknesses. You want to achieve your own particular niche in the marketplace, and then advertise your strengths. Advertising stresses the differences between products and services, not the similarities. Thus, proclaim your uniqueness:

- "We Pour Only Premium Liquors from Our Well."
- "Dance on the Westside's Largest Dance Floor to Our Earthquaking Sound System."
- "We Stock more than 100 Beers—Drink Yourself around the World."
- "Good Drinks, Good Eats—Every Sandwich a Meal."

Emphasize in your ads that you have cheaper drinks, fresh squeezed juices, satellite direct TV viewing of sporting events from around the world, or dancing from 4:00 PM till 4:00 AM. These benefits will entice customers to come to your place instead of patronizing your competitors.

Setting out the above strategies and objectives should help you create ads that make viewers or listeners stop and take notice. Just being clever isn't enough. Humorous copy or a striking photograph may not move people to action. Your ad must motivate them by offering a benefit so appealing that there will be a line of people waiting outside when you open. That is the result of good advertising, and it happens all of the time. Be prepared for the additional business once an ad appears. You do not want to be overwhelmed and underprepared, thereby defeating the whole purpose of generating new business.

Getting the most from your advertising budget

In-house advertising takes place within your bar. Your customers are a captive audience. Train your staff to consider themselves part of your advertising team. Give them buttons, hats, and T-shirts to wear promoting your events. Inside, use posters, bulletin boards, and table tents to announce events and special drinks. When guests sit at a table, a table tent should explain upcoming promotions on one side and display colorful photographs advertising your drink or bar food specials on the other side. Use your drink menu to describe and cleverly sell your drinks. (See FIG. 12-1.) Often your liquor suppliers can provide you with promotional items (when permissable by law), such as table tents, buttons, T-shirts, and unique items for your backbar.

When drinks are delivered, the napkin or coaster and even the swizzle stick should be imprinted with your name. (See FIG. 12-2.) These and the matches on the table are great take-away items that people love to collect.

MARIX
tex mex restaurants

Marix "Kick Ass" Margarita
Cuervo 1800 and Cointreau

Smirnoff Madras
You'll go mad about our Madras mixed with cranberry and orange juice and the world's leading vodka…Smirnoff

Purple Hooter
You're sure to develop a crush on this purple haze of Smirnoff, Chambord and 7-Up

Wild Iced Tea
Wild Turkey, sweet & sour and cola make a Wild Iced Tea

Jungle Juice
From the depths of the jungle comes Cuervo 1800, rum, Sprite, pineapple, cranberry and orange juices

Marix "Kick Ass" Watermelon Margarita
Cuervo 1800, Cointreau and fresh watermelon

Cuervo Side-Out
You'll love the Cuervo Side-Out featuring cranberry juice, triple sec, lime juice and the true gold tequila… Cuervo Gold

Smirnoff On-Tap
Enjoy Smirnoff Vodka marinated with fresh fruits… a taste sensation

Try any 1800 Margarita served in a shaker cup for two

Fig. 12-1. Clever drink menus stimulate sales. Marix

Fig. 12-2. Coasters are an inexpensive and classic way to advertise. Leave several with each guest to take home upon paying their tab. American Coaster Company

The napkin is often forgotten as a valuable advertising tool. It can be folded in such a way as to expose printing on the inside. This could be a calendar of events, or a drink and/or food menu.

Windows (San Francisco, California) uses a small bulletin board just outside the door to announce customers' birthdays. Signs atop your building or hung from your windows can advertise your hours and special events. (See FIG. 12-3.)

If a favorable article about your bar appears in the local press, cut it out, frame it, and put it on view. Someone else praising your place is sometimes worth more than all of your paid advertising. Respected newspaper columnists or radio or TV commentators mentioning a bar can literally make it an overnight success.

A popular device that many bars use is an electronic moving message display. Messages are run along a light board. It is an excellent tool for in-house advertising. You can program it to display whatever you want. In addition, you can subscribe to news, weather, and sports services, along with local advertising from area businesses. Legends (Long Beach, California) uses a 30-foot board to display stock quotes. Place one facing the street and

Fig. 12-3. Legends' banner is so visible it is hard to miss when driving by.

one at the main bar. Customers can read it at their leisure.

Using your computer and TV, you can create countless graphics to run as ads promoting your bar within your bar. There are numerous ways to run your own commercials. The most effective is to actually shoot and produce your own and run them on your TVs. These in-house commercials can be used to promote up-coming events or on-going promotions with scenes taped from a previous week or last year's event. You can also advertise drink specials or golf tournaments by running the ad below what is being shown on the TV, simply as a moving message scroll.

If you usually have people lining up outside your club to get in, place a TV monitor so the customers waiting in line will be able to watch TV and see your commercials for drink specials and upcoming promotions. These people waiting in line are a captive audience and waiting to be sold and validated that they made the right decision to come to your place. You can run a live feed to this TV by means of a camera recording live what is going on inside your bar. The excitement of what is happening will be contagious.

Every customer walking through your doors should leave with a clear idea of what is happening at your bar and when. Give them promotional items to take home. Hand all customers a calendar of your events as they leave. These items, along with your staff's excitement and good service, should encourage them to return. And when you do have a full house as a result of a successful promotion, that is the time to promote any upcoming events.

Word-of-mouth advertising is very effective. To achieve it, make sure your promotions and your operation give customers something interesting to talk about. It could be your old ten-drawer wooden cash register, the colorful array of fresh fruit used in your daiquiris, or the fact that you grind your own coffee, brew your own beer, or exhibit artwork in your bar. The more visual and unique the imagery, the better your chances of stimulating word-of-mouth advertising. Certain bars owe their success to word-of-mouth advertising resulting from clever attention to details.

To maximize the return on your advertising dollars, use ads that produce a measurable result. That may mean limiting your advertising to one medium or including a coupon or special offer in the ad. When customers turn in their coupons or ask for the special, you have a means of measuring the effectiveness of the medium and the promotion.

Repetition is the key to any advertising campaign. It takes several impressions before a person is motivated to act. If your budget is small, concentrate your advertising dollars in one area and run the campaign properly. A great ad in the wrong place can produce no results. Match the medium to the message.

How to buy advertising space

The first step is to match your target audience with that of the various media. Each medium will provide you with the demographics of its audience. You will be working with media representatives who are extremely knowledgeable and quite helpful. They can explain the ways to use their media most effectively, any discounts, special issues, or programs coming up, and what has worked for similar ads in the past. Timing is a critical element in planning your promotions. Always take into consideration the time needed for production on your end as well as the media's end. Plan ahead. (Review the last chapter on planning promotions.)

Usually, each medium offers a kit that includes their rates, demographics, mechanical requirements for submitting ads, deadlines for committing to space, and closing dates (the deadline for your finished ad). Keep a file for each medium, and recheck its rates before you plan your budget as rates do change.

You also need to compare the effectiveness of the different media by studying the cost per thousand (CPM) of reaching your audience. Will the audience for different editions or time slots vary? Will a newspaper ad reach young, single professionals, or will radio be a better choice? The newspaper's CPM might be $25, while the radio's CPM is only $10. The radio's target audience might match yours exactly, while the newspaper will reach a much broader readership. Don't waste your money if the viewers or listeners only include a very small percentage of your targeted audience. In that case, you might want to advertise on the radio alone, but do it more frequently.

Prepare your budget and a timetable. Once you decide on the medium and how often to use it, start the production process. Keep your files current with tear sheets or samples of the ads, their placement, and the response, so you have a history to refer to when planning future campaigns.

Advantages and disadvantages of the various media

There are many different ways to reach potential customers. The following are a few alternatives with advantages and disadvantages discussed.

Direct mail

Direct mail is an extremely precise medium; its results are easily measured. Mailing lists can be bought or leased to target any audience by zip code, income, car ownership, profession, census data, or based on recent purchases, magazines subscribed to, or a wide variety of other criteria. No other medium matches its capabilities for targeting. The response time is typically two to six weeks. A 1 percent response is considered average.

Almost any type of package can be delivered to people at their business or home by mail, parcel post, or messenger. The creative possibilities in concepts and packaging are limitless: records, glasses, letters, coasters, etc. The major advantage here is that you have your potential customer all to yourself, without competing ads, distractions, or temptations to turn the page or zap to another channel. You can mail a package by itself or insert it with merchandise being shipped, insert it in bills or statements or with a group of other direct mail material.

Direct mail is the most expensive of all advertising media. Costs mount up quickly for design and printing, addressing, handling, and postage. Be sure your package shouts to be opened or it can turn out to be an expensive item that is deposited in the trash without ever being read. Address the envelope by hand so it looks like a personal letter or greeting card. Direct Mail is a specialized field of advertising, and if you plan on using a direct mail agency, request examples of their past work. You can develop your own lists by gathering business cards at your door or asking people to sign a register.

Many bars use an in-house newsletter to spread the word about upcoming promotions and events. It can carry articles about your staff and customers, photos of recent events, invitations to private functions, and offers only available to those receiving the letter. Once word travels about these offers, you will have many people wanting to be on your "preferred customer list." To reduce mailing costs, consider obtaining a bulk mailing permit. It is very inexpensive and can cut your postage bill up to 60 percent. Contact your local postmaster for details.

Newspapers

Newspapers are everywhere. People buy them to find out about news, weather, sports, entertainment, and to look at the ads. Each newspaper is usually read daily by more than one individual, and often one newspaper will serve an entire metropolitan area. You can target your market by placing your ad in certain sections geared to special interests or delivered as part of the whole paper to a separate neighborhood within a larger city. The section in which you place your ad will determine the readership. To reach the most people, put it in the general news, sports, or entertainment sections.

Newspaper advertising is quick, responses are fast, and ads can be changed daily. Your ad can be torn out and saved or read at leisure. It can be large or small and can convey a fully developed message. A sports bar would obviously place its ad in the sports or entertainment sections. A bar in the financial district would be wise to put its ad in the business section. For a general audience, the entertainment section is your best bet.

A newspaper is replaced by another each day. This temporary nature of the medium will require numerous ads to get your message across. Smaller ads must be simple and bold to command attention and there is no guarantee of selected readership. (See FIGS. 12-4, 12-5, 12-6, and 12-7.)

Newspaper ads are purchased by lines and column widths. Weekday ads are less expensive than those that run on Sunday when readership increases. If a newspaper ad proves successful, purchase a large quantity of lines for a reduced rate. You will be charged for your lines as you use them. Generally, the price

Fig. 12-4. *Different sizes of newspaper ads.*

Fig. 12-5. *Fantasia runs these ads in a line.*

per line does not vary with the section of the paper where the ad appears unless it is a special supplement such as a Sunday magazine or a travel and entertainment section. Ads can be in black-and-white, one color, or full color.

Fig. 12-6. *Pictures add visual interest to any ad.*

Magazines

After direct mail, magazines offer the next best means of reaching a targeted audience. The subject matter of the magazine attracts a consistent readership. Unlike a newspaper, which is replaced daily, a magazine is saved and read by numerous people over longer periods of time, sometimes even years. The quality of photographic reproduction is superb. Ads can be purchased in full page or in fractions of a page.

Certain ad layouts can be used to reduce the competition from other ads on the same page. One way is to purchase the bottom quarter of a double page spread, thus tying up the bottom of both pages at a fraction of the cost of buying both full pages. Editorial material will be placed on top of your ad. You can also buy the outside vertical columns of a double page spread, thereby achieving a similar effect. (See

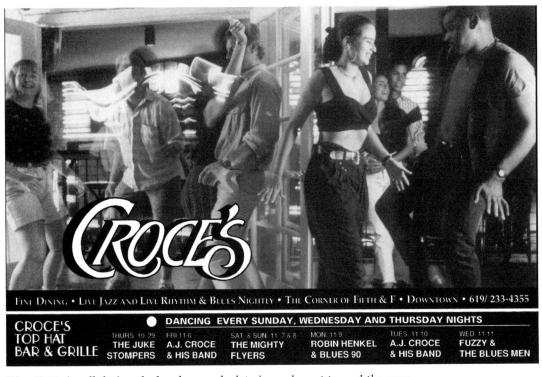

Fig. 12-7. *A well-designed ad makes you look twice and want to read the copy.* Croce's, San Diego, California

FIG. 12-8.) The CPM is high compared to a newspaper, but the target audience is extremely well-defined, which justifies the added cost.

Many national magazines have regional editions that could be a good place to advertise. The best ones for bars are city, county, and state magazines, as well as airline, hotel, nightlife, and travel and entertainment publications. The lead time for magazines is two to three months, so plan ahead.

Radio

The CPM for radio advertising is one of the lowest. Demographics are easy to match as a radio station's audience is well-defined by its programming. People listen to the radio while in their cars, especially going to and from work. The radio is on in work places and homes. It is an immediate and personal medium.

Ads can be produced without any additional expense by having the DJ read your copy live over the air. All you pay for is the air time. DJs have loyal followings, and favorable comments they make about your bar can significantly increase your business. Their enthusiastic reading of your commercial, although not a formal endorsement, definitely sounds like it.

Radio makes use of the listener's imagination to complete the audio message. Highly effective commercials can be created to excite interest and stimulate immediate action. This ability to create moods, humor, and relate a "sense" of what your bar is all about is far superior to that of any print medium.

Ads can be changed right up to the time they go on the air, allowing exceptional flexibility. You can run your ads on one station or several, and at various times of the day. You can sponsor news or special programs, or have your commercials run only at specific times of the day.

Sponsor promotions jointly with radio stations—you'll both benefit. The DJs appear at your bar, conduct interviews and contests, give away T-shirts and prizes, and hold remote broadcasts or special events of their own. In exchange, you receive free air time or greatly reduced ad rates.

Radio is probably the most effective advertising medium for a bar today. If you run your spots a few days before your promotion, you'll know when you open your doors whether or not it has been effective. The drawbacks are it requires many commercials to reach the entire audience, people must rely on their memories, and they often change stations while commercials air. Therefore, the beginning of your commercial must be an attention grabber. Sixty-second spots are ideal. Sometimes 30-sec-

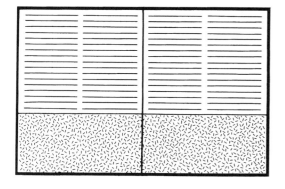

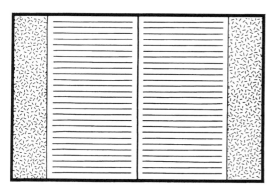

Fig. 12-8. Magazine ad layouts designed to capture two pages for the price of a ½ or ⅓ page rate.

ond spots will work, but only when your bar is well known. Twenty spots a week are recommended for a minimum of coverage. They can be placed in different time slots throughout the day, or only during certain hours if you have a specially targeted audience. (See FIG. 12-9.)

Television

TV is the ultimate medium for reaching the masses. Commercials can stimulate many of our senses with exciting visuals and sounds. They can show real people in real situations or complete fantasies. It is also very expensive to buy and produce TV commercials, though late-night spots can be more reasonable. Demographics shift from show to show. Multiple exposures are necessary, and as with radio, the ad can be zapped unless you hook people right away. Because of its expense and overly broad audience, TV is probably not the best means of advertising for a bar. However, ads placed on local cable television are a bargain and well worth the price.

Out-of-home

The out-of-home category includes billboards, transit, and other media that reach people out-side of their homes. It has the lowest CPM of any medium. The audience includes all passersby. Certain demographics can be matched by placing the ad at specific sites.

Billboards close to or en route to your bar can be very effective. A billboard should be simple, graphic, unusual, and include large type, very few words, and only three or four elements in the composition. Remember that you are exposing your message to a moving target. It must be grasped instantly. When illuminated, the board can be seen 18 or 24 hours a day. Special effects and extensions, or sections of the billboard that extend past the frame, add interest and are worth the extra expense.

You can purchase a single billboard that will be hand painted, or multiple boards that are printed and posted. A billboard takes three months of planning and a reservation of the location long before it actually goes up. The more desirable the location, the higher the fee. Boards can be rotated; that is, kept in one location for two months, then moved. Production costs are expensive, but the number of people repeatedly exposed to your message is staggering. It is a very effective means of advertising for bars. Contact the billboard companies in your area for their rates. They own the boards

---

Hi! I'm Ingrid Croce. When I left the music business and made a career change, I took my abilities as Jim's wife and A.J.'s mother to the market place. I opened Croce's Restaurant and Jazz Bar and began cooking for more than just my extended family. I found myself setting tables for a whole community. It didn't take long to realize I needed help. And that's when our Croce's staff was born. Of course, it wasn't Croce's without music. So, our family of musicians joined us too. Today, almost 10 years later, Croce's is a success. Our delicious meals and spirits, our caring staff, and of course, the best musicians in town have earned Croce's the San Diego Restaurant Association's highest award. Croce's Restaurant & Jazz Bar and Croce's Top Hat Bar & Grille have been awarded the gold medallion for the finest bars in town. Thank you San Diego, for making Croce's the most fun place to be. And remember, when you're not home, be here.

Live tag by ANNOUNCER: Croce's. The corner of Fifth and F. Downtown San Diego. See and Hear Charles McPhearson Saturday.

Fig. 12-9. When the owner does the talking, it creates a sense of intimacy and hooks the listener.
Croce's, San Diego, California

and rent you space, while also providing production assistance.

Transit advertising includes ads for the exterior and interior of buses, taxicabs, subways, commuter trains, and stations. Treat these exterior ads like billboards, as your audience is in motion. The interior ads can have longer messages, because commuters have plenty of time to read your ad. Tear-off cards can also be used for promotions. You can carefully match demographics by selecting the area through which the transportation system will travel. You will be buying numerous posters to cover an area adequately.

Other out-of-home media include site specific locations such as, benches and displays at bus stops, shopping mall displays, shopping cart ads, catering truck ads, aerial balloons, etc. One particularly effective medium is to produce your own ad or trailer to be used in movie theaters before the regular feature is shown. It can be quite effective, especially if your bar is near the theater.

Team sponsorships are another form of out-of-home advertising where your name can be visible on the playing fields, team uniforms, and depending on the sport, the equipment used. When you sponsor teams, it is a social ritual for several teams to gather at the bar after the game and relive the highlights. Any number of sports can lend themselves to a sponsorship: golf, volleyball, tennis, baseball, basketball, soccer, surfing, rugby, rowing, darts, pool, Ping-Pong, bowling, running, raquetball, and even weightlifting.

Yellow pages

Don't forget about placing a listing in the yellow pages. Newcomers to town often check these pages for places to go for entertainment. List yourself under Nightclubs and Cocktail Lounges and again under Restaurants. You can reserve a telephone number as soon as you know your location, and place an ad while you are still in construction or in the process of changing ownership. Ask the phone company for a telephone number that will be easy to remember or describes what your bar is about. Fantasia uses these phone numbers in their ads, 62-DANCE and 347-WEST, for their locations. Try for 5-DRINKS, or multiple digits such as 555-2121, to aid in remembering your number, particularly when used over the radio. Yellow page deadlines are usually six months prior to publication. You will be billed monthly once the book appears. For increased visibility in the pages, include an illustration or highlight your ad with red.

New technologies

These are electronic media that offer unique opportunities to advertisers for selective demographic targeting. Most communities have one or more subscription cable services. Ads can be in the form of live action commercials or text displayed on the screen. Similarly, video text or teletext services are displayed on TV sets or through computer terminals. Satellite communications will certainly increase in the years to come. Locations can be individually addressed and any combination of materials brought directly into that home or office.

Advertising is one of the most persuasive means of communication known today. It is a highly effective way to spread the word about your bar. You can use it to inform and entertain your audience. The right ads placed in the right medium will greatly increase your revenues.

Ten ways to increase word-of-mouth advertising

One of the most effective means of advertising is to encourage word-of-mouth advertising. It does not have to cost you anything to make favorable impressions. Here are ten ways to increase word-of-mouth advertising:

1. Find ways to reward your regular customers, either through discounts for additional drinks or food, or give them something to take home with them, such as a bottle of their special liquor with your name and theirs printed on it, or a unique glass also engraved. Make it memorable.

2. Write them a letter expressing your gratitude for their business and offer them free drink or tickets to a game or cultural event as a thank-you.

3. When a guest has had a bad experience, either with a drink or food item, correct the situation by going beyond their expectations to alleviate any bad feelings and replace it with your good intentions.

4. Give away samples of drinks and food items. Come up to a table and make a big fuss over them and tell them they are the 100th table to order drinks that night, and they will receive them free or with complimentary food items.

5. Always try for the unique. A bar in Fort Lauderdale had all the employees wearing bright red wigs. They were the talk of the town and its tourists for years.

6. Make your best customers your ambassadors. Give your regulars free drink, food, or admission passes to pass out to their friends.

7. Name drinks or food items after your customers. Place their photos on the menu or on a Hall of Fame Wall.

8. Create drinks that are oversized or come in special glasses or containers. The Red Onion in Woodland Hills, California sells a drink called The Volcano in a 24-ounce plastic sand bucket. It comes with two oversized straws and you get to keep the bucket, which has The Red Onion logo on it.

9. Find out who your first-time customers are and personally invite them back for a return visit with free drink or passes good for four people.

10. Showcase your employees' special talents, either by letting a bartender or server sing in a normally quiet atmosphere, or having a bartender make quick sketches of customers that they can take home.

13

Personnel

You should think of each employee as an investment in your business. The right staff encourages repeat business. A poorly chosen staff can create a bad impression regardless of the amount of promotion, advertising, decor, or unique services offered. Therefore, each position should be carefully filled. Remember, you can train a person to tend bar or serve cocktails, but no amount of training can teach a person honesty or dependability, or impart a happy, friendly disposition. With this in mind, let's look at the personnel needed to keep a bar operating smoothly.

Job descriptions

The following job descriptions outline each position for the purposes of training and ongoing referral. Depending on the size of your operation, certain jobs may be combined, some may not be necessary, or you may create a new position. Ideally, each employee should also be given a written copy of his own job description, and should also be required to sign it in order to ensure awareness of duties and responsibilities.

Your particular bar may call for you, the owner, to tend bar, keep the books, do the or-

dering, and just about everything else. If your operation is larger, you may be one of a group of shareholders who hires a general manager to oversee the day-to-day operations. In any case, an effort should be made to distribute the work load for maximum efficiency.

General manager

A person hired for this position is responsible for the entire operation of the establishment. The manager reports directly to the owner and carries out the owner's philosophy.

The general manager is in charge of the payroll, all purchases, equipment, maintenance, promotion, advertising, entertainment, and ultimately is responsible for profits. If there is no assistant or bar manager, the general manager also handles staffing, training, and employee relations. He institutes service standards and house policies, such as hours of operation, dress code, employee uniforms, and employee benefit programs. This individual should be knowledgeable about the competition and current trends in liquor merchandising and sufficiently experienced to handle all situations that arise in the course of running a bar.

Because he or she is a role model, the way in which a general manager deals with situations will directly influence employees, and ultimately customers. When time permits, the general manager should meet as many customers as possible and personally welcome them to the bar. The general manager is also an employee and must strive to set an example for his or her staff. In larger bars, a general manager may have an assistant.

Assistant manager

The assistant manager is an extension of the owner or the general manager and is trained accordingly. This person may work as the floor manager when the general manager is not there. Any phase of the operation may be under the control of the assistant when delegated by the general manager, such as ordering, screening job applicants, opening and closing on slow nights, or scheduling. It is not unusual for an hourly employee to be promoted to this position based on achievement and a desire to assume more responsibility. With increased knowledge and experience, the assistant manager might advance to general manager. Frequently, the assistant manager is a working bar manager.

Bar manager

The bar manager directly oversees all bar operations and personnel. The duties include hiring, training, scheduling, purchasing, inventory, and cost controls. The bar manager may work in conjunction with the general manager and owner in developing promotions, pricing, house and specialty drinks.

Often, the bar manager will work shifts behind the bar, saving the house an hourly bartender's wage. The bar manager is usually paid a salary and is further compensated by tips earned while tending bar. That also allows the bar manager to see what products are be-

ing sold and requested by the customers in order to realign and reevaluate inventory. While working behind the bar, the bar manager can improve the efficiency of the bar and remedy any problems firsthand.

The bar manager should be an experienced bartender who exhibits maturity and knowledge that enables him or her to undertake the responsibilities of management.

Bartender

The primary responsibilities of a bartender are to pour, accept payment for, and properly account for all beverages served. That includes the orders filled for the cocktail servers as well. The bartender is also responsible for all equipment, cash handling, and customer relations. Honesty and a good short-term memory are essential. The bartender oversees and controls the bar he is working as well as the servers and bar backs. When management is busy, the bartender might be called upon to make management decisions concerning problems arising in the bar.

Bartenders should be cordial, outgoing, and comfortable talking to all types of people. They must be able to handle a high-pressure environment, making drinks for the servers while also pleasing the crowd at the bar. Above all, bartenders need to be entertainers, because everyone loves to watch them work.

Bartenders should have extensive knowledge of liquors. The more skilled your bartender is at making drinks quickly and properly and at making conversation, the better off your bar will be. Many bartenders develop quite a following and can add greatly to your business.

The bartender is responsible for the bar from setup to cleanup—stocking and requisitioning all supplies. All beverages should be dispensed according to existing service standards and house policies. The bartender is accountable for any overages or shortages at the end of the shift. Before the bar is turned over to the next tender, depleted supplies should be restocked and the bar left clean. The bartender is paid either hourly or by the shift.

Service bartenders primarily make drinks for servers, and usually do not wait on customers. Because they do not have the same opportunity to make the tips other bartenders earn, they are often compensated by being paid a higher wage.

Bar back

A bar back relieves the bartender of many responsibilities, among them prepping and maintaining supplies and cleaning the bar. A bar back enables a bartender to serve drinks continuously without having to wash glasses, replenish supplies, or leave the bar for any reason. Specific duties include preparing garnishes, emptying trash, filling ice bins, unloading or stocking any merchandise received, and generally setting up the bar to ready it for customer service. Once the bar is open, the bar back should anticipate the bartender's every move and assist accordingly. When a juice bottle is almost empty, for instance, it should be quickly refilled before the bartender empties it. The bar back can also help fill drink orders by pouring beer and wine. That helps ensure the even flow of the bar operation and prompt service to customers.

A bar back can be trained to become a bartender. One way for a bar back to learn about liquor is to study and read your bar's drink manual and the labels on the liquor bottles, which contain a tremendous amount of information. As the bar back becomes more experienced, the bartender can teach him to mix drinks, greet customers, and take orders. If the bar is open after hours when it is illegal to serve alcohol, the bar back can remain behind the bar serving nonalcoholic drinks and coffee.

The bar back position does not require any previous experience, just a lot of hustle and a desire to learn about the bar business. Bar backs earn an hourly wage and are tipped by the bartenders after each shift, usually between 10 and 30 percent of the bartender's tips, and occasionally more, depending on the extent of help to the bartender.

Cocktail servers

The job of the cocktail server is to sell drinks and keep customers happy and returning. A cocktail server need not have any prior experience; the important qualifications are an outgoing personality and a sincere desire to serve the public. On-the-job training should provide an extensive knowledge of drinks and liquors.

The server is responsible for stocking and cleaning his or her work station, and collecting and paying for all drinks sold. At the end of a shift, the server tips the bartender, usually 10 to 30 percent.

An experienced server is often promoted to the position of bartender or assistant manager.

Door personnel

The main functions of the door personnel are to check IDs and to enforce any dress codes or other restrictions of the bar. They ensure no minors or undesirables enter the bar. Door personnel serve as public relations personnel, greeting customers, supplying information, and generally spreading goodwill. At the door, they can give customers news and pass out flyers about your bar's current and upcoming events.

This position requires no particular experience. Because door personnel are the first employee a customer sees even before entering, an attractive, personable individual is required.

Security

The job of security personnel is to maintain a peaceful atmosphere in your bar. Security can wear plain clothes or uniforms. Security, in order to be most effective, must be visible. It is security personnel's job to anticipate and prevent problems before they occur, usually by circulating through the bar to act as a deterrent.

If a fight does occur, security should immediately break it up and remove the parties from the premises. They should not attempt to reason or argue while still in the lounge. Neither party should ever be allowed to return to your bar. Fighting upsets your customers and ruins your business image. Ideally, you want all conflicts resolved without the use of force. If force is used, the problem was not handled correctly.

Typically, bar security personnel are athletes, body builders, former police officers, or self-defense instructors. If there is a need, armed and licensed professional security guards can be hired.

Cashier

If a bar has a cover charge, it is the cashier's job to collect it, give change, page people, and answer the phones. The cashier stamps patrons' hands with ultraviolet ink allowing them to come and go as they please throughout the evening. This ink shows up when viewed under an ultraviolet lamp. Change your stamps daily so customers cannot return the next night using the previous night's stamp. A cashier can apply wristbands to customers signalling a designated driver or legal-age drinker. In a smaller club, a doorman might double as a cashier. The cashier might also be trained as a server and should have previous experience handling money.

Checkroom

The checkroom job is usually a part-time position, often filled by a regular employee picking up an extra shift. This employee checks coats, purses, hats, and umbrellas at the entrance for the convenience of customers.

The hat check person uses two identical sets of numbers. One number is given to the customer, while the other number remains with the item checked. This individual can also sell cigarettes, candy, gum, and safe-sex items.

Floor sweeper

During peak hours of business, it is a good idea to hire someone to keep the floors clean of napkins, spilled drinks, and broken glass for the protection of your customers. The salary of a floor sweeper will be more than covered by maintaining a clean establishment. A bar back often fills this position.

Cleanup crew

A cleanup crew is hired to vacuum, empty the trash, clean windows, mirrors, restrooms, and perform general maintenance after closing or before opening for the next day's business. This crew should be reliable and trustworthy. A bar back desiring to pick up extra hours might do this work.

Parking attendants

When the parking area for your bar is limited, hire parking attendants to park customers' cars. The persons hired should be dependable and honest. Attendants should have a numbered keyboard on which to place car keys and to keep track of each car's location. A sign advertising their service should be visible. When the lot to park cars is a distance from the bar, the attendants should have two-way radios to communicate with each other. One attendant is stationed at the exit and signals the attendant at the lot to bring a specific car.

Employee benefits

A benefit is any consideration extended by the owner to the employees other than what is legally required. Some forms of benefits include insurance, paid holidays and birthdays, vacations, sick pay, and profit-sharing. The size of your operation will determine the benefits you offer. At first, you may only be able to offer benefits to management. As the business grows, management benefits may be increased, and other benefit packages may be extended to your employees on a contingency basis.

Typically, health insurance is offered after an employee has been on the job at least six months and works a minimum of 20 hours a week. Usually, the health insurance premium is split 50/50 between the bar owner and the employee. An employee can add a spouse or family to the policy by paying an additional fee. The extent of medical, dental, and eye coverage is determined by how much you and your employees decide to contribute each month to the plan.

You may extend to your employees the benefit of salary continuation. A small deduction is taken from the employee's paycheck each week to ensure the continuation of a base salary during a lengthy absence from work due to illness or accident. To be eligible, the employee must pay into this plan for a designated period, and must be out of work for a minimum amount of time. Salary continuation is usually offered in larger bars only when a majority of the employees contribute to the plan; otherwise, the plan is not cost-effective for the owner.

Another large benefit you can offer is a guaranteed salary structure with periodic written reviews. An employee is hired at a certain rate of pay and is promised a review and possible salary increase after a designated period of employment, usually three to six months.

This review by management provides employees with feedback regarding job performance. If performance, attendance, and attitude are satisfactory, they are awarded a raise.

At this time, another written review is scheduled, usually one year from the date of the raise. At this review, if management feels an employee is inadequate in a certain area, the salary increase can be withheld. Management must detail in writing exactly what the employee is failing to do, and what additional training will be offered. When this happens, a second review should be scheduled in two weeks time to see if any improvement has been made. If the improvement is slight, but not yet sufficient, you may allow a little more time. After that, if the employee is responding to the training, give him or her the salary increase. If not, you may want to try this employee in a different job within your operation, or you may have to let the person go.

In all reviews, everything agreed upon and all plans must be in writing and signed by both the employee and management. (See FIG. 13-1.) This record of counseling can protect you and your operation from paying unnecessary unemployment compensation. These records should be kept on file with duplicates given to the employee. If there is any inquiry from the labor board, your fairness in dealing with employees will be a matter of record. Also, if a future employer requests information, your records are invaluable.

Management can use the review process as a way of promoting from within whenever feasible. Employees benefit by knowing that they have the opportunity to advance. If an employee is eager to advance and management provides no opportunity, the employee may find work elsewhere. A promotion from within is proof of good work rewarded. It maintains employee unity and increases morale.

A popular way to provide a benefit for

```
EMPLOYEE REVIEW/COUNSELING FORM

NAME _____  POSITION_____

DATE HIRED_____  DATE OF LAST REVIEW_____

RATE OF PAY_____  DATE OF NEXT REVIEW_____

COMMENTS: _____
_____
_____
_____
_____

EMPLOYEE RATING:
  EXCELLENT     GOOD     AVERAGE        NEEDS IMPROVEMENT
AREAS FOR IMPROVEMENT: _____
_____

TRAINING PROGRAM:_____

FOLLOW-UP SCHEDULE: _____

INCREASE: GRANTED DENIED_____

RATE OF INCREASE_____  EFFECTIVE DATE_____

EMPLOYEE        DATE      REVIEWER           DATE
```

Fig. 13-1. Employee review/counseling form.

your employees is to allow them to frequent your bar when they are not working. As long as no one takes advantage or disturbs working employees, off-duty employees appreciate this courtesy. They may even be encouraged to bring in their friends. Some owners take the viewpoint that this nurtures comraderie and a family atmosphere. As a further benefit, you may let your employees drink at a discount.

Other forms of benefits are profit-sharing, credit unions, stock options, uniform and meal allowances, transportation and parking costs, pension plans, and employee parties.

Employee relations

If an employee does not respond to counseling or training, there may be no other recourse than to terminate. There is a right and a wrong way to do this. You never want to publicly embarrass or humiliate an individual, even if he has deliberately violated house policies.

The dismissal of an employee should be conducted as privately as possible. The end of a shift is usually a good time. Being brief and to the point is always best. Personalities should be kept out of the conversation. An employee should be told exactly why he is being terminated. If your counseling has been adequate, it should come as no surprise. He may even agree he was given more than enough opportunity to improve or change. Even though your mind is made up, listen to the employee's objections. Getting his initial feelings off his chest is important to him. His objections may not be valid and your rebuttal can convince him that you have not been unfair. By patiently listening, you are showing that you still respect his sense of dignity.

In cases where the individual has been an excellent employee, and for whatever reason you must let him go, you should try to do so with as little pain as possible. You may even wish to grant him a few weeks' pay to make his unemployment more bearable. This is known as severance pay.

Regardless of how clear-cut the decision is, firing an employee is never easy. For the good of your staff, your operation, and your own peace of mind, however, if an employee has to be terminated, do it and do it quickly. A bad situation that is allowed to go unattended will be construed as a weakness on your part by other employees. It will then be even more difficult to dismiss the next employee if there is a similar situation.

The bar business is a volatile, high-energy, emotional business. It is not uncommon occasionally to lose an employee through no fault of management. The employees who work in a bar tend, on the whole, to be more transient than those in other businesses. Generally, that is not a reflection of your operation. A job in the bar business is often one taken by students while working their way through school or as a means for others to earn a living between career changes.

If you find your staff is undergoing unusually rapid changes, there might be several reasons. As an owner, you should be concerned. Try to obtain as much feedback as possible from departing employees, getting the real reasons why they are leaving. They probably will be honest because they feel they have nothing to lose. You may learn a great deal. Perhaps the employee does not believe he has been treated fairly. In spite of all your efforts, that could be the case. It may be too late to convince this employee that you can make amends, but you can correct this problem immediately before another employee leaves.

Policies should constantly be reviewed and updated. Maybe the employee simply does not like the clientele in your bar. It is better to know this than to think it is something you have done or to try to coerce an employee to work in an environment in which he is not happy. In fact, it may be best for the employee to find a job in a different bar.

Staffing

The types of employees you hire should be consistent with your overall concept. For instance, hire a college student to tend bar in a college town or a former athlete to work in a sports bar. You probably would not hire an 80-year-old employee to work in a fast-moving, uptown singles bar; nor would you hire a shy, introverted person to be a security guard in a rowdy waterfront bar.

Advertising is the best method of recruiting the individuals who will attract, entertain, and please your customers. There are several ways to advertise for employees. The first thing you should do is put a "NOW HIRING" sign outside of your bar. Then place ads in your local newspaper. Sunday ads cost more and will bring the largest response. When placing ads, be specific about the time, date, and place to apply. Include in your ad that you will check all references.

Use advertising that speaks to the type of people you want to apply. Dull ads may not draw the right response. Try: "HELLO ALL YOU NIGHTOWLS! PARTY PEOPLE WANTED FOR HIGH-ENERGY POSITIONS IN NEW NIGHTCLUB!" Get them excited.

List your openings with student employment offices at local colleges. Check with any bartender's schools in your area. Generally, the recent graduates of these schools lack on-the-job training, but they do know how to make drinks. Also consider employment agencies that may specialize in restaurant and bar personnel. Contact radio stations that may offer free air time for employment listings as a public service.

Another method is simply word-of-mouth. Mention your needs to employees of businesses you frequent. Alert friends and neighbors. As you become familiar with other managers and owners of bars in your area, you can help each other by referring job applicants.

The hiring process

Before you begin interviewing, here are a few tips: Have on hand plenty of standard application forms that can be purchased from any stationery store. Be present when the applicants are filling out their applications in order to get a first impression. Offer the person a nonalcoholic drink while they fill out the application. Let them fill out the application in a quiet area of your bar. Do not allow them to be in an office alone, especially if cash or a safe is in the room. You leave yourself open to theft. Decide whether you will interview on the spot, or simply collect the applications, review them, and schedule interviews later. Having an initial screening process is recommended. This eliminates applicants who do not have the proper experience, appearance, and qualifications you are seeking. Matching applicants' faces with their names by taking a Polaroid picture and stapling it to each application is advisable, if legally allowed.

The interview

In reviewing an application, take note of the specific job applied for and the applicant's related experience. If there are any gaps in work history, ask about them. Life experiences other than those that are work-related may still be appropriate in dealing with the job. A person who has spent the last three years touring Europe may be an asset to a bar that caters to an international clientele. Find out if the applicant has had any prior experience in dealing with the public or creative interests. A performing arts student or budding dancer will have the right type of energy to project to the public.

Notice the manner in which the application form was filled out. A haphazard, incomplete, or sloppy application could mean the applicant does not concentrate or care enough to make a good impression, and, therefore, would not make an outstanding employee. A clean, neat, and well-organized person usually proves invaluable. At this point, you can eliminate certain applicants and schedule appointments for the ones you wish to interview further.

Where the interview takes place is important. It should be private, quiet, and free of distractions. Allow sufficient time to gather necessary details but not to socialize. As you begin, first define the job and its requirements. An applicant might decide immediately that this is not the right job for him and save everyone a lot of time. If the interview proceeds, allow the applicant to state his qualifications. That will give you a good indication of his confidence level, communication skills, and general attitude. You are looking for those qualities that make a good first impression.

Imagine you are a customer being served by this individual. Does he or she appear cordial, happy and smiling, or dark and moody? Let the applicant do most of the talking. If an applicant requests confidentiality, respect this wish, because usually, continuing current employment would be difficult if the employer knew he or she was looking for other work.

The skilled interviewer must be an excellent observer. Notice what is said as well as what is not said. Ask simple and direct questions, providing the opportunity for complete statements, rather than a yes or no answer.

- Was the bar the applicant previously worked in busy? How busy? Probe.
- How much did he sell on a crowded night? On a slow night?
- What was good and bad about his last job?
- How does this person handle intoxicated customers, people who do not tip, or patrons who complain about service?

These questions are designed to reveal the applicant's true attitude about his work. See if his responses correspond to the qualities you would like your employees to exhibit.

Find out about health, family, or other responsibilities that would interfere with the hours required to be on the job. Can he work weekends, days and nights, or split shifts? If he has children, will getting child care present a problem? There are certain questions you cannot legally ask. Check with your state labor board.

How will the applicant get to work? Does he have far to travel? Will the distance be a problem? How long has he lived in the community? Where else has he lived? Some people move around and switch jobs frequently. Did he have solid reasons for leaving his previous employment? When in doubt, ask for references and verify them. A simple phone call to a past employer could save you headaches later on. (See FIG. 13-2.)

Allow time at the end of the interview for the applicant to ask you questions. Give the applicant an idea of when he can expect you to make a decision. Assure him you will call either way. That prevents you from receiving numerous phone calls while you are trying to conduct other interviews.

If this applicant is not the right one, continue your search. You might want to file an application for later, however, should your first choices no longer be available. It is not uncommon to interview 10 or more applicants for certain positions in the bar, such as server or bartender. Take your time. Your patience will pay off later when the right individual becomes a trusted employee.

When checking references, you'll need the company's name, phone number, applicant's immediate supervisor, position held within the company, and the dates of employment. When checking the reference, start out by saying you would like to verify the employment of the applicant. Then ask:

- What were the dates of employment, positions held, and attendance record?
- Was the employer satisfied with this person's work?
- Did this person need supervision or work well alone?
- What were the person's strong and weak points?
- Did this person work well with others?
- Why did he or she leave? Would you rehire this person?

If the supervisor is not working at the company anymore, ask to speak to the personnel office or another person who worked with the applicant. If no one knows the applicant, check another reference. Check all references to make sure you are receiving consistent information about your applicant. You want the best employees. One bad employee can dam-

---

Fig. 13-2. Sample interview for a bartender.

Q: I see that you've worked for the last year at Bob's Bar, why do you want to leave?
Q: What did you like and dislike about your last job?
Q: How much business did you do on a busy night?
Q: How much did you pour?
Q: How many cocktail servers did you handle?
Q: Did you ever work with or train a barback?
Q: Are you familiar with setting up a bar, mixes and garnishes?
Q: What kind of cash register did you work with?
Q: What was your system of paying and collecting for the drinks you or your server sold?
Q: Did you free pour, use a shot glass, or a liquor gun?
Q: What was the bar pouring cost?
Q: How do you handle drunk customers?
Q: What would you do if a server wants a drink for herself while she is working?
Q: What would you do if a server asks you to give a drink to her friend?
Q: What would you do if you worked with someone you knew was stealing?
Q: Do you have any other interests or responsibilities that would interfere with the hours you will spend working?
Q: What are the most important qualities, in your opinion, that make for a good bartender?
Q: How would you handle a customer complaining about you, another employee, or the way the bar is run?
Q: Have you ever worked at night?
Q: Can you work days and nights, or split shifts?
Q: Can you work on holidays?
Q: Do you plan to continue your education, and what are your plans for the future?
Q: How far do you live from here?
Q: How will you get to work?
Q: When can you start to work if you are hired?

1. List the calling order of drinks. _____ _____

_____

_____

2. What are the abbreviations for olive, lemon twist, on the rocks, and a lime squeeze?

_____

3. List the abbreviation and ingredients for a Tequila Sunrise. _____

_____

4. In what type of glass would you serve Remy Martin? _____

5. What are the garnish and ingredients in a Tom Collins?_____

_____

6. What is the difference between Johnnie Walker Red and Johnnie Walker Black?

_____

7. What is the name of the drink made with Vodka, Kahlua, and cream?_____

_____

8. What are the ingredients of a Stinger? _____

_____

9. If you fill a nine-ounce glass about 2/3 with champagne, how many glasses will you

    need to empty a typical bottle of champagne?_____

10. What is the difference between a Martini and a Gibson?_____

Fig. 13-3. Sample test to give to servers and bartenders.

Testing

At this point, you should have in mind the type of applicants you want to hire. One way of ensuring they possess the knowledge and experience you require is to test them. (See FIG. 13-3.) Remember that each bar has its own way of preparing and garnishing certain drinks, however. The test results, in conjunction with the applicant's other qualities, should provide the basis for making a final selection.

Hiring

You may now call your final selections and give them the good news. Arrange a meeting for the people who will be working together to get acquainted. At this meeting, you will conduct introductions, tour the facilities, display uniforms, discuss scheduling, and explain all age your image. Try to eliminate these applicants during your interview and reference-checking stages.

house policies. Information should be given about parking, payroll procedures, and employee benefits, such as paid holidays, vacations, and insurance. Conclude the meeting by allowing your employees to ask any questions and offer any feedback. Then announce your training schedule.

You should have a folder for each employee, containing the original application, health forms, written evaluations, withholding certificate, and other pertinent information. Keep it up-to-date and after the employee leaves, keep the file for future reference.

Maintaining trusted, loyal, long-standing employees should be a goal of any business. The policies you implement, the quality of your management, the benefits you provide, and the salaries you offer all contribute to the longevity of your staff. To repeat, employees should be considered an investment. With proper care, this investment will mature and provide you with many rewards.

14

Operations

Before you begin operating, and before you train your employees, you must select a system for controlling the dispensing of and payment for all liquor. The system you choose determines the type of cash register you will need. When a server requests liquor from a bartender, every drink must be accounted for and paid for before the bartender releases it. In the day-to-day running of your bar, you may encounter isolated problems in the attempt to enforce these controls. The first part of this chapter presents the various systems, and the second part looks at a hypothetical day in the life of a bar owner.

The cash-and-carry system

After a server takes an order from a customer, it is repeated verbally to the bartender and paid for by the server in cash. Bartenders handle bar customer's orders the same way. There are no tickets used. Nothing need be written. The server can write orders on pieces of scratch paper if that makes them easier to remember, and can discard them after placing the order. After ringing up the sale, the bartender takes the server's cash and puts it in the register. Servers carry a cash caddy to make

change. A $20 bank can be issued from the bartender's register to the server for this purpose. It is repaid at the end of the shift.

That is the easiest and most popular way to transact business. Not using tickets is cheaper and does not require time for accounting. For the same reasons, however, there is no control other than the honesty of your employees. Although this system is perfect for a small bar, larger bars may find it impractical.

The cash-and-carry system with tickets

The cash-and-carry system with tickets is the same as the preceding system except that it uses tickets as a form of control. Numbered tickets are issued to each server at the beginning of a shift and recorded by the manager. All used and unused tickets must be returned and accounted for at the end of the shift. If a ticket is missing, the server is responsible and the manager must establish a house policy and course of action. State laws differ as to how these shortages may be collected from employees. The server uses the tickets to write the customers' orders according to the bar's calling order and presents the tickets to the bartender. That eliminates the verbal calling of drinks because the bartender only makes those drinks that are written down. The bartender draws a red line across the ticket directly underneath the drinks that have just been made. The server can reuse this ticket. If the server wishes to reorder a duplicate round all that needs to be done is to write "Repeat" or "RE." (See FIG. 14-1.) The bartender then rings each drink individually on the register.

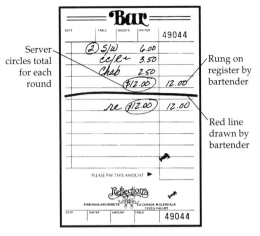

Server circles total for each round

Rung on register by bartender

Red line drawn by bartender

Fig. 14-1. How to write out a ticket.

This system requires a register that prints dollar amounts on the ticket. This amount is paid in full by the server before the drinks are taken from the bar. The bartender keeps each server's tickets separately at the bar. The tickets are not presented to the customer unless requested. The server should make a practice of recording the dollar amount offered for payment by the customer. The bartender does not have to use tickets for customers sitting or standing at the bar, because the volume of drinks poured is usually much greater than those requested by servers. Although this system provides a small amount of control and organization, it is more expensive to use and may slow service.

The ticket system

This system is identical to the cash and carry ticket system except that no money is exchanged between the server and bartender until the end of the shift. It greatly speeds service, and therefore revenue, in a high-volume bar, because no time is lost exchanging money. The server does not have to wait at the bar for each round of drinks to be made. Several orders on tickets are left with the bartender while the server goes to the tables to sell more drinks. Upon returning to the bar, the server picks up the drinks that were previously ordered. If she accumulates a large sum of money, drops can be made to the bartender or manager for safekeeping. A drop slip is filled out in duplicate and the server keeps one copy. (See FIG. 14-2.)

DROP SLIP

SERVER _____

DATE _____

TIME _____

AMOUNT $ _____

Fig. 14-2. Server drop slip to give to bartender when she is carrying around too much cash.

The best way to implement this system is with a cash register that itemizes each server's sales. At the end of each shift, the server's total is read off the register. This is the amount that must be balanced. The server uses a server checkout sheet to subtract any charges, including charge tips, from the sales total to determine the amount of cash that must be handed to the bartender. (See FIG. 14-3.) It is recommended that you use an adding machine or calculator to prevent mistakes in addition

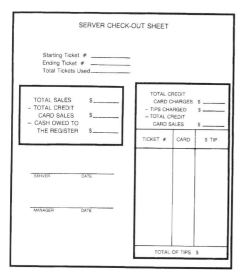

Fig. 14-3. *Server check-out sheet.*

when presenting totals to customers or when cashing out at the end of the shift. All charges must be itemized on the checkout sheet as well. The manager verifies all totals.

Running a tab

Many customers prefer to settle their account at the end of their stay rather than paying for each round or individual drink. That means a running total of the drinks ordered by an individual or group is kept by the server or bartender. House policies on this vary, but most bars have some system for keeping a tab.

One common method used in neighborhood bars is to run tabs without any collateral. A customer is extended credit by the house on the basis of good faith, knowing that he will settle the tab upon leaving. Some bars may even run weekly or monthly tabs, cash personal checks, or loan money to regular customers. These bars treat their customers like family. Because of the attitudes of the owner and the staff, these customers feel that bringing in new business is almost like entertaining in a private club or in their own home. Be care-

ful and use common sense when providing these types of services. It is wise to set a limit on house accounts and establish a regular date of payment. Unlike a bank, you do not receive interest for money or services extended.

A second method is for the customer to offer a large bill to the server or bartender to hold for payment. Again, a running total is maintained. When the total approaches the amount of the cash, the customer is notified. She can either settle the account then or advance more cash to continue running the tab.

The third method is for the house to require a customer to back a tab with a credit card. When dealing with credit cards, your staff must be trained to check that each card is valid.

A tab can be run regardless of the control system that is in use. Running a tab is a courtesy most customers appreciate. It is very rare that a tab is not paid.

Credit cards

As much as you would like payment in cash at all times, it is an absolute necessity to accept credit cards from your customers. Many people do not carry cash and prefer to charge their entertainment expenses in order to make one monthly payment. A bar that does not accept credit cards loses business. Providing these services will cost you a commission on credit card sales. Each company's commission varies from 3 to 5 percent, depending upon the volume of your credit card business. That means that for every $100 in credit card revenue, you receive only $95 to $97. Consult your bank to see which cards are used the most in your area, what percentage will be charged, the types of validation equipment available, and the procedures for depositing credit card vouchers.

Handling credit cards properly

Regardless of the control system you are using, when a credit card is offered for payment, a running total of the tab must be kept by the server. She should first check the validation and expiration dates of the card and make sure it is one your bar accepts. The card and the proper voucher are then securely placed face-up in the imprinter. An imprint is made. Next the card and voucher are removed and the imprinted voucher is checked for clarity, alignment, and quality of information. All of the digits of the credit card number, the expiration date, the card holder's name, your bar's merchant number, and the date must be clearly legible on all copies. If it is not, the information can be handwritten on the voucher or else another imprint must be made and the first voucher destroyed.

If a ticket system is in use, imprint the credit card on the back of the customer's ticket. That is just another double check for your records. Sometimes, the slip gets lost or damaged. Next, the card must be checked to see if it is over the credit limit, invalid, or stolen. The credit card companies will supply your bar with a current list of invalid cards. An authorization code should appear on all credit card vouchers. This can be obtained by calling a 24-hour, toll-free number and relaying the information to an operator. An approval or authorization code will be given and recorded on the voucher.

If your bar does a great deal of credit card business, you may wish to purchase an electronic verification terminal. The customer's identification number is retrieved through the machine's reading of the magnetic strip on the back of the card. The card's information is processed through the machine (via a telephone line hookup), and the approval or rejection, with an authorization code, appears automatically on your terminal. (See FIG. 14-4.) Certain

Fig. 14-4. Credit card authorization machine with voucher printer.

computerized cash registers have a magnetic stripe reader in the machine. Once a card is run through the reader, the correct authorization number is automatically called (through a dedicated telephone line hookup), and the authorization number is given and printed on a receipt for the cardholder to sign. This is extremely convenient and fast.

If the card is rejected or denied, an alternative form of payment must be offered by the customer. On some occasions, at the company's request, you may be instructed to confiscate the card, break it in half, and mail it to the company. Because the card is the property of the issuing company, a reward is offered to the person who turns it in. The customer must be informed and required to pay in another manner.

Always instruct your servers to keep the credit card while running a tab. If your customer objects to this practice, which is rare, just have him sign the credit card voucher and return his card.

The customer may still pay cash when the server presents the bill. If that happens, the credit card voucher is simply destroyed and discarded. When the customer does choose to pay with the credit card, the amount of the bill is transferred to the proper place on the voucher, and it is presented for signing. At this point, it is a good idea to have the card holder write his phone number beneath his signature. If the customer desires, he can include a tip on the voucher in the proper place and add it to the bill.

The server then double-checks to see that the total has been added correctly and the voucher signed. The customer's signature is mandatory to validate the card. An authorized signature should appear on the back of the credit card. If the customer's signature does not resemble the authorized one, the server should request proper identification. The card should not be accepted if the name presented as identification is different. The only excep-

tion is if the last names are the same. That could be a husband using his wife's card or vice versa or another family member. It is management's decision whether or not to accept cards under these circumstances.

If, for some reason, the customer forgets to sign the voucher, you can either turn in the voucher to the bank unsigned, or write "signature on file" in place of the signature, and hope that the bank and the customer accept it.

If everything is correct, the server should tear out the customer's copy and hand it to him. The carbons should be removed and thrown away. The other two copies must be kept, one for your records and the other to be deposited at the bank. Any tip on the charge is taken out and given to the server at the time the charge is turned in.

Computer systems

A number of computerized cash register systems are available for bars for the purposes of drink ordering, credit card authorizations, accounting, and implementing controls. These systems usually consist of a series of interconnected terminals stationed throughout the bar.

With a computer system, servers can order drinks without physically appearing at the bar. The server's drinks are prerung or ordered on one terminal and displayed on the bartender's terminal, which may be across the room. Servers have their own keys, which allows only them to order drinks or food on their tables or tickets. To enter an order, the servers press precoded keys on the register or "speed board" or enter certain codes. (See FIG. 14-5.) Servers working the system need to memorize the codes before they begin using the system, or else they will be very slow and frustrated. Once the codes are memorized, the system works extremely fast for everyone involved.

Each server is only responsible for what is

Fig. 14-5. *Speed board for ordering drinks.*

ordered on their key. On the way to pick up their drinks, servers can take several more orders and pick up dirty glasses. When the server gets to the bar, the drinks are ready. Faster and better customer service is the result.

These registers or terminals allow employees to clock in and out, thereby eliminating the need for time clocks, time cards, and manual payroll compilation. They automatically provide an accurate inventory with a complete breakdown of beverages and food sold, and they list server and bartender sales, charges, and charge tips. They can also report up-to-the-minute labor costs and provide an invaluable method of permanent record-keeping for tax and audit purposes.

Computer systems allow management to monitor all phases of a bar's operation from a master terminal. If the manager chooses, she can obtain customer counts and the current volume of business without leaving the privacy of her office. The manager holds the master key to the system. The master key is necessary to access reports or create voids when mistakes in ordering or complimentary items are ordered, but need to be taken off of a check.

Computer systems cost money and take time to learn. The company that installs the system will usually have a representative assist in the training of your employees. In the beginning, the training period can be frustrating. Once mastered, however, a computer is a very useful, efficient, and indispensable tool.

Personal and traveler's checks

Whether you will cash personal checks or allow personal checks as payment in your bar is a matter of house policy and owner preference. Most bars provide this service for known individuals, but accept only traveler's checks from strangers. Only in rare instances and as a last resort should you accept a personal check from a stranger as payment for a bill. That may occur when a credit card has been refused or the customer does not have enough cash to pay for his bill. You should first ask for the customer's driver's license. From this, obtain his current address, verify identification, and match signatures. Next, have him give you his current phone number and record it on the check. Then initial the check to verify that you accepted it. Do not write anything on the back of the check. If you do, it will become illegible, because banks stamp the back when processing checks.

With traveler's checks, the important thing is to match the signature of the person presenting the check with the signature already on the check. Bank of America Traveler's Checks provide space for countersigning the check on the back. It is placed so you can fold the check where it has already been signed and compare it with the bearer's signature. If in doubt, you can instruct your employees to ask for identification. Toll-free numbers are available for verification of all major traveler's checks in the United States. If a ticket system is in use, record the ticket number on the back of the traveler's check. The name of the employee accepting the check, the date, and time should also be recorded on the check.

Telecredit and electronic banking

Several companies offer telecredit and electronic banking services. With these, you can verify any check or credit card from any bank in the United States. The cost will vary for the use of these guarantee procedures depending on the extent of your volume. The more you

use the system, the less it costs. You can either call in the information or purchase a terminal that allows you to type the information directly, giving instant verification and an authorization number from the company.

A number of companies offer draft capture service. That means you receive instant verification of any check or credit card, and the amount is immediately deposited into your bank account. Again, the fees for this service vary with the amount of usage. The advantage of having the cash available right now, rather than waiting for checks to clear and credit card vouchers to be verified, is definitely worth the small fee.

Automated Teller Machines (ATM) that used to be available only in banks have moved into many retail operations. Their use in bars is fantastic for owners. An ATM allows your customers to perform bank withdrawals from the convenience of your business. You purchase or lease an ATM with one telephone line dedicated for its use and tied into a banking network.

The customer walks up to the machine, which has a display panel that can lead the person through the transaction. The customer swipes the card through the machine and its magnetic reader and punches in their PIN (Personal Identification Number). Your customer can request any dollar amount up to the limit you set. The ATM will verify the money in the account, deduct it, and issue a voucher, like a small credit card receipt. The customer takes the voucher to the bartender or server and the voucher is good for the amount of cash less the amount of their bill. The amount withdrawn is then automatically deposited into your account.

All withdrawals are completely guaranteed by the banking network. Some of the networks are Plus System, Cirrus, Star, Visa, and Mastercard. You receive a detailed report at the end of each day. The bonus is that you receive additional money (ten cents at time of publication) for each transaction. In a busy bar, the system begins to pay for itself immediately.

The Fair Credit Reporting Act of 1970 requires that each time you refuse a customer's check or credit card, based wholly or in part on the information received from a telecredit, consumer credit agency, or a draft capture service, the customer must be told which service you used. The customer must also be provided with the company's name, address, and telephone number.

Spotting counterfeit money

It is rare, but there are times when you or the bank discover a counterfeit bill among your receipts. Counterfeit money is easy to feel because it has a different texture from legal tender. A counterfeit bill is smoother. It does not have the bite, or tooth, that real currency has. Each genuine note has tiny red and blue fibers in the paper that can be checked under a bright light. The detail in the lines of the engravings are sharp and clear. A fake note's details will be smudgy and dark. One of the simplest ways to check the genuineness of U.S. bills is to use a counterfeit detector pen (see FIG. 14-6). It is the size of a marking pen. You place a small dot on the bill. If the bill is real, the dot stays yellow, if it is black or brown, the bill is suspect. These pens can be purchased at major stationery stores.

Proper employee training will eliminate the majority of any forgeries that you encounter. If you ever come in contact with counterfeit currency, notify the police or F.B.I. immediately. Passing bogus bills is a felony.

Daily operations

As an owner or manager, you will develop routines in implementing methods of control.

Fig. 14-6. Counterfeit detector pens can instantly detect fake bills.

The interaction between you, your customers, and your employees will create variables that change these routines and require you to adjust and improvise. The way management deals with these variables can often prevent something minor from developing into a major problem. The following is a description of a day in the life of a manager and the situations he might encounter. It is safe to say that an average day will not include all of these complications. These situations can and do occur, however, and some solutions are recommended.

A day in the life of a manager

The manager or owner is usually responsible for opening the bar. It is good practice to be on the property at least one hour before you open. This gives you ample opportunity to deal with any equipment failures, sick calls, or other extraordinary circumstances.

Develop a routine for performing your opening duties. This routine should include turning on the lights and marking the switches to day and night levels to ensure consistent lighting. Do not allow employees to adjust the lights to suit themselves. Heating or air conditioning systems should be turned on early so the bar has enough time to reach the desired temperature.

A quick walk-through of the premises will tell you how clean the bar and tables were left the previous night, and exactly what needs to be done before opening. If a workstation was not cleaned properly, check the previous night's schedule to determine which employee was responsible. Then counsel that employee.

At this time, you also want to make a visual inspection of your equipment, not only for cleanliness, but to ensure that everything is operating properly, particularly the ice machine. Once this is done, check the management logbook in your office. See if there are any important entries from the night before that require your immediate attention. The night manager or closer will have left any messages for you in this book, such as schedule changes, counseling sessions he had with an employee, shortages, ordering to be done, and general reminders.

Through the course of your shift, use this logbook to record anything you want the next shift manager to know. This log should be kept in a locked office and used by management only. While in the office, review the employee schedule and make a mental note of who is scheduled and what time they should be appearing. If you learn from the logbook that the bar needs some supplies or an employee needs a ride to work, you can call the earliest scheduled employee and ask him or her to help you. Also, by checking the schedule, you will know whether to make any last minute adjustments to cover the volume of anticipated business.

Next, count the banks that are to be issued to the bartenders, and make sure you have all the coin change you will need for the day's business. A standard opening bank for each register is $150 to $300. A typical breakdown for a $300 bank would be: $30 in tens, $100 in fives, $125 in ones, $30 in quarters, $10 in dimes, $4 in nickels, and $1 in pennies. Drink prices are usually set in 25-cent increments to eliminate the need for dimes, nickels and pennies. Your bar should carry them to make phone or other change, however.

Your safe should contain sufficient change —one and five dollar bills, nickels, dimes, and quarters—to cover any volume of business or large bills that must be changed. A standard change order should be made at your bank every day. If you know that your bank will be closed on weekends or holidays, increase your change order. You will also want to be on good terms with any surrounding businesses that can supply you with additional change in case of an emergency.

When putting the banks in the registers, double-check that each register has been cleared so all sales will start at zero. After it has been cleared, initial each register tape. That ensures that any removal or tampering with the tape cannot be done without management's knowledge.

Now take a quick inventory of supplies, and if any item is running low, make a short order to get you through until the regular weekly order is made. This type of spot ordering should not be a practice, but only a stopgap when unusual circumstances occur. If you are continually running out of inventory before your weekly ordering, you need to increase the standing order of those items. On the other hand, it is best to keep your inventory level as low as possible. Inventory represents cash, and cash should be kept in constant flow, not sitting in a storeroom.

By this time, your employees have arrived for the new day's business. Once they are on the floor setting up, you can go into the office and let them answer the phone while you review your paperwork. At this point, you can make sure the book work from yesterday's receipts has been posted, and the bar inventory updated. If you are employing a ticket system in your bar, you can issue the tickets and have them recorded and ready for the servers and the bartenders. About this time, your bartender will have a liquor requisition sheet ready. You can issue the liquor yourself or allow the bartender to fill the order.

Just before you open your doors, personally verify that any preparations needed for promotions, happy hour, or specialty drinks have been taken care of by employees. Double-check all details yourself, not because you distrust your employees, but because everything is ultimately your responsibility. Remember, anyone can make a mistake.

Now open the doors. Even if you are not 100 percent ready, it is very important to open on time. Opening on time is just one way you reinforce the daily commitment you make to your customers. Once open, there might be a slow period where you can organize additional paperwork and make phone calls.

From time to time, you might get a call from someone saying he has lost a personal item in your bar. You should have an area in a locked office where you keep all found articles. Before you admit to having an article, ask the person who lost it to describe it and its contents. If you are satisfied that he is the owner, have him come to the bar and pick it up. If the lost article is a wallet, credit card, purse, or driver's license, a customer must provide additional proof of ownership.

Suppose a bartender comes into your office to tell you that, in her opinion, a server has reported to work under the influence of alcohol. How should this situation be handled? First, thank the bartender for letting you know and tell her to go about her duties while you deal with it. Talking to the server in private is best. Do not confront the individual before you make your own observation. If, in your opinion, the server is intoxicated, do not let him work that day. If this is not the first time you have suspected him of reporting to work under the influence, it could be grounds for dismissal. If it is an unusual occurrence, however, it might be best to let the employee sit down awhile, get something to eat, and sober up.

In the meantime, call your on-call server or someone who has the day off, just in case the server cannot work. After awhile, when he is able to handle duties, let him start working. Otherwise, give him a written warning, letting him know that a repeat incident will result in dismissal, and then send him home. You might want to send him home anyway, if that is your policy. Be sure your employee is sober enough and safe to drive.

Because you are one server short, circulate through the bar. Rearrange the work stations to accommodate one less server. Your servers should be sufficiently trained and able to maintain service standards even though short-handed. See that repeat drink orders are being sold, ashtrays are cleaned, and dirty glasses are picked up. If necessary, you can pull a bar back from behind the bar and have him bus tables. That should ease things and allow you to spend at least a few moments with each employee to exchange a greeting and pleasantry. By talking to your employees while they are working, you learn things about the bar that they may not remember or share after their shifts. This is one good way to keep on top of your operation.

As you walk through the bar, introduce yourself to new customers while always acknowledging familiar faces. Show an interest in their lives and solicit their views of your operation. Regular customers like to feel welcomed at a bar by the owner and manager. They will return with their friends the next time. In general, customers need to feel they belong in your bar. Make them feel at home and encourage your employees to do the same. It is an invaluable form of goodwill. A few positive words cost you nothing. That is the key to successful bar promotion and will often make the difference between a popular place and an empty one.

You will be shaking a lot of hands and people will want you to sit down and have a drink with them. You certainly cannot accept every offer. Some managers and owners make it a policy not to drink on the job while others view it as a means of building camaraderie with their customers. If you refuse, do so politely and always thank the person and either ask for a rain check or return the offer yourself.

What if a customer you do not know overhears your offer and says he would be happy to have a free drink with some alcohol in it this time? The person could be kidding. Appease him by asking the bartender to add a little more liquor to his drink. If he is still not satisfied, then take his old drink and make a fresh drink right in front of him so he can see how much liquor is being poured. If you feel this person is just a chronic complainer, then do not accommodate him. Ask him to order and pay for a double, or an extra shot on the side. If he continues to irritate you, return his money and quietly explain that you have done the best you can for him and perhaps he would enjoy better drinks elsewhere.

Arguing over such a petty matter as one drink is demeaning. Customers gain respect for your judgment in handling even the smallest detail. A bar is a public place, and you reserve the right to refuse service to anyone as long as you do not discriminate against any particular customer.

Occasionally, you run across customers who feel you owe them a free drink just because they have walked through your door and graced the bar with their presence. When and to whom you give a complimentary drink is entirely up to you. If you feel a customer is trying to get something for nothing, without being rude, ask what line of business he is in. If he owns a gasoline station, ask how often he gives away free gallons of gas? Liquor is what you are selling. Does he offer ten gallons for the price of five? That is an easy way to end the conversation.

Other situations are not so easily resolved, such as when a customer insists he has given your bartender, Jack, a $50 bill, and Jack is certain it was a $20. Again, diplomacy is necessary. The first thing to do is ask the customer politely to check his wallet or pocket. Confess that you often find money you thought you had lost in your own pockets. Have Jack check the register to see if there is a $50 bill, and if so, ask if he could have misplaced it among the $20s? If Jack has made a mistake, apologize and return the money. If there is a $50 bill in its proper place, the customer will contend that it is his. You have no way of disproving his claim. That is always a sticky situation, but there is a way out. Never allow your employees to argue with a customer. Instruct Jack to take care of his other customers while you quickly and quietly take control of the problem at hand. Take the customer's name and phone number and tell him when the register is totaled you will return his money if there is an overage.

As a last resort, if the customer is not satisfied with being notified the next day, take an "X" reading (a subtotal) from the register and balance the register. Jack may feel you do not believe him and are not backing him up. Never embarrass any employee in front of a customer. Later, be sure to take Jack aside and discuss the situation. You want your staff to know that you trust their judgment. After all, you personally hired them to handle large sums of money daily. Explain the fact that you have a responsibility to both your employees and your customers. Show Jack how in this case the customer backed you into a corner, and you did the best you could to get to the truth of the matter. Do not let Jack misunderstand or leave the situation unresolved.

Just when you have everything under control, you shake your head in disbelief as you see Joe, one of your servers, baptize a woman, who is wearing an expensive evening dress, with a strawberry daiquiri. As much as you would like to avoid this sticky situation, it is your job to smooth it over. You are personally responsible for your employee's actions. Customers are very understanding about this sort of thing and chances are the server feels worse than they do. Try to minimize emotional displays. Immediately apologize and offer to pay the cleaning bill or reimburse the woman if the dress is beyond cleaning. Spills can often be removed quickly with a dash of soda on a clean cloth, or by rubbing salt directly on a wine spot. It might be better to let another server take this table if the first server is upset. Allowing servers to switch tables is a good policy if it provides better service or the server is being harrassed or feels uncomfortable at his or her station.

Another problem management must tackle occurs when a server informs you a customer's credit card has been refused. The best way to handle this is to ask the customer politely and privately if he has cash or another credit card. If he does not, suggest another person in his party pay the bill. At this point, if he has not offered an acceptable method of payment, your options for collecting are dwindling.

As a last resort, ask for a personal check. Perhaps he has something of value you can hold until he arranges to pay the bill. It is possible the customer made a mistake with no intent of fraud. He may offer identification and promise to make good on the tab as soon as he can. Suggest that the customer visit an ATM machine that is operable 24 hours a day and withdraw the cash for you. You always have the option of calling the police and having him arrested for fraud. However, to do that requires detaining him and may not be worth the commotion or the possibility of false arrest.

Dealing with any irate customer, no matter why he is upset, is never pleasant and always requires diplomacy. He may be raising his voice and losing control, especially after a few drinks, but that is the time to keep your cool. You must have the ability to disarm and calm people. Speak softly, extend your hand, and ask his name. Establish a personal relationship and do not let anyone else, customer or employee, intervene. Lead the customer away from the source of the problem. If necessary, tell him you are sorry for the inconvenience as you escort him out the door. Afterward, discuss with employees how the problem started and ways to prevent it from happening again.

By this time, the night shift is beginning to arrive. If it is your policy to take register readings and close out day servers and bartenders before the night crew takes over, then all outstanding tabs must be cleared. There is often some confusion when a new shift comes on. Night employees may want to visit with or get in the way of day employees. Instead, train employees to assist each other to make the transition as smooth as possible. You may now switch from day to night prices, especially if your bar has entertainment. Make it a habit to lower lighting levels at this time.

Now that the evening shift is under way, spend as much time as you can on the floor observing, because your largest flow of business occurs during this period. You need to be visible and available in case you are needed immediately. If everything is running smoothly, you may have nothing else to do except get change, talk to customers, or periodically take the large bills from the register and drop them in your safe.

Then while casually sipping coffee at the bar, you notice Alex, your bartender, making change from his tip jar. That is definitely against house policy. It may be an indication of why his sales have been lower than the other night bartenders. You have been concerned about the possibility of Alex stealing for some time. Before you accuse him, it would be best to watch him closely for a period to be certain. A good bartender works fast and it may be hard to catch him in the act. You may wish to have a trusted associate or close friend who is familiar with your operation observe him. Alex will not suspect a stranger watching him. If you have positive proof that Alex is stealing, he must be terminated. Do not press charges; it is not worth the hassle, and your other employees will resent your action.

You are interrupted in your observation of Alex by Judy, a server who has just had a party walk out without paying. You should immediately alert the door personnel and go with Judy to try and locate the party. If they cannot be found, get the particulars from Judy. "Were they intoxicated?" "Could it have been a mistake?" "Have you ever seen these customers before?" Hold the tab until the end of the night, just in case the party happens to return.

In some states, the law allows a bar to charge the server for the amount of the check in cases of gross negligence. A house policy should have already been set for handling walk-outs. If Judy was totally inattentive and careless, she should be given a written warning and charged, if the law allows. Sometimes when it happens, there is no way the server could have prevented it. If that is the case, the amount of the check can be written off as a bad debt and deducted from your taxable income.

The evening has passed and it is time to give the last call for alcohol. This is communicated to every customer in the bar and even announced over the loudspeaker if you have a disc jockey. It notifies customers that they have time to order and consume one more drink before the bar has to pick up all alcohol and close its doors. Last call should be announced at least a half hour before closing. In another 15 minutes, a warning is given that all glasses must be returned to the bar, finished or not. At this point, the lights should be turned up and all music and entertainment stopped. That is the third warning that you are ready to close. All servers and bartenders should be busy cleaning and restocking their stations with supplies. Have your door personnel circulating and ushering your guests out with polite good nights.

Unfortunately, there are always one or two troublemakers who will not obey. These persons should be informed that you are complying with a state law. However logical and reasonable that sounds, they may still be unimpressed and unwilling to give up their drinks. They also may be intoxicated and unreasonable. They may insist that because they were dancing, they did not have time to finish their drinks. It is prudent to allow a couple of extra minutes for these persons to finish their drinks and leave your premises without a disturbance.

Begin cash-out proceedings as soon as all customers have left the bar and the doors are locked. Depending on what system you have,

"X" out the registers to obtain a total to which the servers and bartenders balance. Take the money out of the registers and run your hand underneath each drawer. Check for any bills or credit card slips stuck beneath the drawer.

Have the bartenders pack the money. That means putting ones in groups of 25, fives in groups of 100, etc. Packing the money makes it easier to prepare the next bank. Always deposit the largest bills and leave the small ones as change to start the next day's bank.

Every server and bartender must present his paperwork to you for approval before you sign his time card. It will include any balance sheets, itemized charges, charge tips, and cash deposits. Encourage your employees to leave together at this late hour. Now do a "Z" (clear to zero) to be sure the register keys are reset at zero and remove the tapes. Leave the drawers of the cash registers open so that if a thief breaks in, he can see there is no money and will not break open your register to find out. Make sure the bar is clean and the breakage sheet is completed.

Before you leave, write any important messages in the log book. Turn off heating or air conditioning systems, DJ and sound equipment, and the lights. Turn on your alarm system and either make a deposit at the bank immediately or first thing in the morning. If you do make a deposit late at night, take another person with you for security. After everyone has left, relax and put your feet up. Have a drink and be proud of how you handled the day. Rest assured that tomorrow will bring a whole new set of challenges.

Ten tips for successful managing on the floor

1. Have a pre-shift meeting with your staff. Explain special drinks, promotions, and other items of interest for the shift. For those employees present who worked the previous shift, comment and compliment on jobs well done. Set sales goals for this shift.

2. Try to meet ten new customers each shift. Know their names by exchanging business cards or getting their address and phone number. Write their name in your customer mailing list book immediately. This reinforces their name in your mind.

3. Smile and greet regular customers by name. Become involved by asking meaningful questions about their lives and businesses. If you heard that Joe Patron's wife just had a baby, then send her some flowers courtesy of your bar.

4. You are the role model for your employees. How you act and react to situations will set a standard for their behaviour. Treat everyone with respect.

5. Exceed your customers' and employees' expectations. Help out when needed by taking cocktail orders, opening bottles of wine/champagne, or washing glasses behind the bar.

6. Expect excellent service from your employees. Communicate and demonstrate what superb service is. Share service tips.

7. Be positive in all your interactions with customers and employees.

8. Create an atmosphere of safety. Operate honestly and legally.

9. Think globally, act locally. Encourage recycling, waste and cost controls. Give employees bonuses for ideas that save time, money, and resources.

10. As customers leave, open the door for them and thank them for coming. Make every impression, including the last, a memorable one.

15

Management

Your bar is a business and should operate to make money. Strong and fair management is necessary to achieve this. The main function of management is to increase volume while reducing costs in order to maximize profits. All decisions should be made keeping these goals in mind. Of equal importance is the manager's role in hiring, training, and motivating employees, along with interacting with the guests.

There are many styles of management. They range from the manager or owner who works alongside employees, jumping behind the bar to lend a hand when needed, to the manager who delegates every task. The former runs the risk of being taken for granted, doing what the employees were hired to do. The latter may lose the respect of the employees if he or she does not respond to a situation where an extra hand is required. Somewhere in between is a style best suited to your personality and operation.

An important function of management is to establish training procedures and service standards for each position in the bar. The training guidelines presented in this chapter are standard procedures used throughout the country.

Training

Your bar can have the greatest location and design, ambience and entertainment, promotions and advertising available, but if your employees are improperly trained for their jobs, or if they insult your customers, your plans for success will be in vain. The customers' perceptions of your bar are directly related to the employees who serve them. An unhappy experience will probably prevent customers from returning. Proper training from the beginning is your insurance that this will not occur.

Management can correct bad work habits developed from previous jobs and retrain according to its own standards. Each employee should be trained to understand not only his or her own job, but also the overview of the operation in order to work in harmony with management and fellow employees. Extra effort spent in this invaluable training process will pay dividends later as you observe your entire operation functioning as a unit.

The size of your bar and the different types of equipment may necessitate additional training to what is presented here. You may even prepare an employee manual designed especially for your operation, including service standards, job descriptions, specific equipment, and personalized drink recipes. (See FIGS. 15-1, 15-2, and 15-3.) Allow one to three days for training. Keep in mind that the training process continues after the doors are open until everything runs smoothly. If you are just opening for the first time, you might need to fine-tune your training once you've seen your operation in action.

General training for all servers

Servers include all personnel involved in the service of beverages and food to customers,

both at the bar and at the tables. If they are available, you might want to utilize key individuals to train new employees. If you do, it is a common practice to pay the trainers more per hour than they normally receive. The trainer might also keep any tips the trainee may make, because it is the trainer's shift the trainee is working.

Servers should be instructed to introduce themselves with a smile and welcome the guest to the club. A standard greeting effective for new customers is, "Hi! My name is _____. Is this your first time here? What will you be

DRINK	GLASS GARNISH
BLOODY MARY	TALL Lime Celery
1 oz. Vodka 3 oz. Bloody Mary mix	
BRAVE BULL	ROCKS
1 oz. Tequila 1/2 oz. Kahlua	
CHI CHI	TULIP Cherry Pineapple wedge
1 oz. Vodka 4 oz. Pina Colada mix Blended	
DAIQUIRI	TULIP Lime
1 oz. Rum 4 oz. Sweet & Sour mix Blended	
DIRTY WHITE MOTHER	ROCKS
1/2 oz. Brandy 1/2 oz. Kahlua Float of Cream	
GIBSON	MARTINI Onion
1 1/2 OZ. Gin Dash of Dry Vermouth Stir over ice & strain	
GIMLET	ROCKS Lime
1 oz. Gin 1/4 oz. Lime Juice	
GODFATHER	ROCKS
1 oz. Scotch 1/2 oz. Amaretto	

DRINK	GLASS GARNISH
GODMOTHER	ROCKS
1 oz. Vodka 1/2 oz. Amaretto	
GREEN LIZARD	SHOT
1 oz. Green Chartreuse Float of 151 Rum	
HARVEY WALLBANGER	TALL Cherry Orange wedge
1 oz. Vodka 3 oz. Orange Juice Float of Galliano	
INTERNATIONAL STINGER	ROCKS
1 oz. Metaxa 1/2 oz. Galliano	
KIR	WINE Lemon twist
5 oz. White Wine Float of Creme de Cassis	
LONG ISLAND ICE TEA	CHIMNEY Lemon twist
1/2 oz. Vodka 1/2 oz. Gin 1/2 oz. Rum 1/2 oz. Tequila 1/4 oz. Triple Sec 2 oz. Sweet & Sour mix 1/2 oz. Coke	
MAI TAI	CHIMNEY Lime Cherry Pineapple wedge
1 oz. Rum 1 oz. Orange Juice 1 oz. Pineapple Juice 1/2 oz. Myers Dark Rum 1/2 oz. 151 Rum	

Fig. 15-1. Sample drink recipe manual.

PRICE SHEET

BRAND	PRICE
WELL	
Vodka	
Scotch	
Gin	
Bourbon	
Rum	
Tequila	
Brandy	
Coffee Liqueur	
Triple Sec	
CALL LIQUOR	
VODKA	
Smirnoff	
Stolichnaya	
SCOTCH	
Chivas Regal	
Cutty Sark	
Dewars (White Label)	
J & B	
J Walker-Black	
J Walker-Red	
GIN	
Beefeaters	
Bombay	
Tanqueray	
BOURBON	
Early Times	
Jack Daniels-Blk	
Wild Turkey 101	
Seagrams 7	
RYE	
Old Overholt	
IRISH	
Jamison	
Old Bushmills	
CANADIANS	
CC	
VO	
Crown Royal	
RUM	
Bacardi Amber	
Bacardi Silver	
Bacardi 151	
Meyers	
TEQUILA	
Cuervo 1800	
Cuervo Gold	
COGNAC	
Courvoisier	
Hennessey	
Remy Martin	
Christian Brothers	
Martell	

BRAND	PRICE
CORDIALS	
Amaretto	
Annisette	
Bailey's Irish Cream	
Apricot Brandy	
Blackberry Brandy	
Cherry Brandy	
B & B	
Campari	
Cherry Herring	
Chartreuse Green	
Cream de Cassis	
Cream de Cacao Dark	
Cream de Cacao Light	
Cream de Menthe Green	
Cream de Menthe White	
Cream de Banana	
Cream de Noya	
Drambuie	
Frangelica	
Galliano	
Grand Marnier	
Kahlua	
Midori	
Ouzo	
Peppermint Schnapps	
Sambuca	
Sloe Gin	
Strega	
Southern Comfort	
Rock & Rye	
Tia Maria	
Tuaca	
BEER	
Heineken	
Miller	
Miller Lite	
Michelob	
Budweiser	
Corona	
San Miguel	
HOUSE WINES	
Rose	
Chablis	
Burgundy	
WINE	
Dubonnet	
Dry Sac Sherry	
Harveys Bristol Cream	
CHAMPAGNE	
COFFEE DRINKS	
CREAM DRINKS	
EXOTICS	
SOFT DRINKS	
Perrier	

DRINK	PRICE
Bacardi Cocktail	
Black Russian	
Bloody Bull	
Bloody Mary	
Brandy Alexander	
Brave Bull	
Calypso Coffee	
Campari Cocktail	
Champagne Cocktail	
Chi Chi	
Cuba Libra	
Daiquiri	
Dirty White Mother	
Dubonnet Cocktail	
French Connection	
Gibson	
Gimlet	
Godfather	
Godmother	
Golden Cadillac	
Grasshopper	
Greyhound	
International Stinger	
Irish Coffee	
Kamakaze	
King Alfonse	
Kioki Coffee	
Kir	
Kir Royale	
Long Island Ice Tea	
Mai Tai	
Manhattan	
Margarita	
Martini	
Mexican Coffee	
Negroni	
Old-Fashioned	
Pina Colada	
Pink Squirrel	
Planter's Punch	
Presbyterian	
Ramos Fizz	
Rob Roy	
Rusty Nail	
Salty Dog	
Scorpion	
Screwdriver	
Side Car	
Singapore Sling	
Sloe Gin Fizz	
Smith & Kerns	
Snowshoe	
Stinger	
Tequila Sunrise	
Tom Collins	
Velvet Hammer	
Wallbanger	
Whiskey Sour	
Wine Cooler	
Wine Spritzer	
Zombie	

Fig. 15-2. Liquor and drink price sheet.

DRINK	ABBREV.	GARNISH	PRICE
Bourbon	B		
Scotch	S		
Vodka	V		
Gin	G		
Rum	R		
Tequila	TEQ		
Brandy	BR		
Plain Coke	PL C		
Plain Seven-Up	PL 7		
Plain Tonic	PL T		
Plain Soda	PL S		
Plain Water	PL W		
Plain Orange Juice	OJ		
Plain Grapefruit Juice	GRAPE		
Plain Pineapple Juice	PINE		
Plain Tomato Juice	TOM		
	OL	Olive	
	~	Twist	
	ON	Onion	
	X	Lime	
	CH	Cherry	
	ORANGE	Orange	
	PINE	Pineapple	
	CELERY	Celery	
On the Rocks (over ice)	/R		
Tall Glass	T/		
Straight Up, Sniftner	↑		
Bacardi Cocktail	BAC COCK .	CH	
Black Russian	BL RUSS		
Bloody Bull	BL BULL ..	CELERY	
Bloody Mary	MARY	X, CELERY	
Brandy Alexander	ALEX	Nutmeg	
Brave Bull	BRAVE BULL		
Calypso Coffee	CALYPSO		
Campari Cocktail	COMP COCK .	~	
Champagne Cocktail	CHAMP COCK	~	
Chi Chi	CHI CHI	CH,PINE	
Cuba Libre	R/C	X	
Daiquiri	DAQ	X	
Dirty White Mother	MOM		
Dry Manhattan	DRY MAN	~	
Dry Rob Roy	DRY RR	OL	
Dubonnet Cocktail	DUB COCK ..	~	
Gibson	GIB	ON	
Gimlet	GIM	X	
Godfather	GOD DAD		
Godmother	GOD MOM		
Golden Cadillac	CAD		
Grasshopper	GRASS		
Greyhound	GREY		
International Stinger	INTL STING		
Irish Coffee	IRISH COFF		
Kamakaze	KAME		
King Alfonse	KING ALF		
Kioki Coffee	KIOKI		
Kir	KIR	~	
Kir Royale	KIR ROYALE		
Long Island Ice Tea	TEA	~	
Mai Tai	MAI TAI	X,CH,PINE	
Manhattan	MAN	CH	
Martini	MART	OL	
Mexican Coffee	MEX COFF		
Negroni	NEG	~	
Old-Fashioned	OLD FASH...	CH,ORANGE	
Pina Colada	PINA	CH,PINE	
Pink Squirrel	PINK	CH	
Planter's Punch	PLANTERS ..	X,CH,PINE	
Presbyterian	PRES	~	
Ramos Fizz	RAMOS		
Rob Roy	ROB ROY	CH	
Rusty Nail	NAIL		
Salty Dog	DOG		
Scorpion	SCORP	CH,PINE	
Screwdriver	DRIVER		
Side Car	SIDE CAR		
Singapore Sling	SLING	X,CH	
Sloe Gin Fizz	SLO FIZZ		
Smith & Kerns	SMITH		
Snowshoe	SHOE		
Stinger	STINGER		
Tequila Sunrise	SUNRISE	CH,ORANGE	
Tom Collins	TOM COLLINS	X, CH	
Velvet Hammer	HAMMER		
Wallbanger	WALL	CH,ORANGE	
Whiskey Sour	SOUR	CH	
Wine Cooler	COOLER	CH,	
Wine Spritzer	SPRITZER ..	~	
Zombie	ZOMBIE	X,CH,PINE	

Fig. 15-3. Sample drink abbreviation, garnish, and price sheet.

drinking?" If the server recognizes a familiar face, he or she should acknowledge that person by name and ask how he is doing. Stress personal contact in as many ways as possible. Complaints about working conditions or a server's personal life should never be expressed to customers.

If there is any question in the server's mind as to whether the guest is of legal drinking age, a request for proper identification should be made before taking a drink order. If there are dirty glasses or ashtrays remaining from a previous customer, they should be removed. Ashtrays are changed by placing a clean one on top of the dirty one and removing it from the table. Then another clean ashtray is placed on the table with a fresh book of matches. Next, a napkin should be placed in front of each customer and drink orders taken. A dry napkin should be kept under drinks at all times. Make it a policy to suggest the house specialties. A nice touch is for servers to carry a cigarette lighter.

Servers must be trained to do more than take orders. Instruct the servers to remain attentive to their customers without being annoying. Additional drinks should be suggested before the previous round has been finished: "How about another round?" or "Would anyone like another drink?" That way, guests always have a drink in front of them, which serves several purposes:

- More liquor is sold and revenue is increased.
- It keeps customers in your bar. A customer with an empty glass may decide to leave.
- It provides better service.
- It increases tips for the servers.

Here is the way to maintain good service when two large parties arrive at the same time. First, the server places fresh napkins in front of one party, acknowledging and letting them know he will be right back. Then he takes the order from the second party and no customers have been ignored.

The method of payment is determined after the first round of drinks is served. A standard procedure for "making change" should be established if cash is offered. For instance, a customer has given the server a $20 bill for a drink order of $14.50. The server says, "That was $14.50 out of $20." The dollar amount handed to the server is always repeated. That is so the customer cannot contend he paid with a $50 bill instead of a $20 bill. If that does happen, the server should turn the situation over to management.

No employee should ever attempt to argue with customers for any reason. It is management's function to solve these situations, allowing the server to continue working. If given a large bill, the server should tell the customer to stay where he is until he can return with change. Customers must feel that their money is in good hands and is being treated carefully.

All employees should be trained to identify and deal with an intoxicated individual. The particular ramifications vary from state to state, but, in general, it is the server's responsibility to refuse service to any guest who has become inebriated. This person may be identified by any of the following: slurred speech, clumsy behavior, loud or abusive language, or falling asleep.

Do not allow this person to consume more alcohol on your premises. Offer him a nonalcoholic drink or something to eat. Again, if there is any question or the server fears there will be a problem, management should be called. An intoxicated person does no one good, least of all to the bar's reputation.

If your bar has a designated driver program (see Chapter 11, Marketing: Successful Promotions), then have the driver take the individual home or call a taxi. The situation should be handled quickly and quietly without disturbing the other guests.

Three principles that should be stressed to every server are *organization*, *preparation*, and *cleanliness*. All supplies necessary for each shift should be stocked to capacity, always prepared for the largest volume of business during that shift. A server never knows when he will be swamped by incoming customers. Advance preparation allows the server to spend more time with guests, conversing and selling liquor, instead of cutting fruit or looking for a pen.

If tables and bars are kept clean, new customers will feel they are in a healthy atmosphere. Guests will be seated more quickly, generating faster service, and a larger volume of business will result. A messy bar will lose customers. If a spill occurs, cleaning it immediately will prevent it from becoming a safety hazard while maintaining a sanitary and inviting environment.

When serving the public, sanitation cannot be overemphasized. Uniforms and hair should be neat and clean at all times, as should employees' fingernails and hands, which touch glassware. Servers should handle glassware by the stem or bottom, never putting their fingers inside or on the rim.

Servers need to be kept up-to-date on liquor laws, third-party liabilities, alcohol awareness, safety programs, new liquors, and drink recipes. One way is to subscribe to trade magazines and newspapers and keep them on hand for your employees. Distributors and purveyors can provide literature, tours of distilleries, breweries, wineries, and taste-testing sessions at little or no cost to the bar. Also keep all personnel aware of current and future promotions and any changes in house policies. Information is the tool employees use to better serve customers. A well-informed employee is the best form of advertising.

A brief discussion with employees about how to handle a hold-up might be included in your opening training session. It is not intended as a scare tactic. It is simply an attempt to prepare in order to prevent panic. It can help to eliminate the chance of someone getting hurt. Advise personnel to cooperate with the intruders and give them whatever they demand. Let employees know that the bar has insurance to cover such a situation and the employees' well-being is much more important than money lost.

Tips on tips

Here are some tips for management on how servers can increase their tips. Servers must know that owners and management take an interest in the amount of tips they make. Providing ways employees can increase their income will make for a better relationship between management and personnel. If employees see that management shows a little extra concern for them, they will do that little extra for you, which, in turn, will mean increased revenue for the bar.

Bar employees are serving in an environment where the patrons' desire is to relax, be comfortable, and be entertained. Most of all, the customers want recognition. The atmosphere created by good service is part of the total ambience. Whenever possible, greet the customer by name, especially when he or she brings in a group of new customers. The regular is then aware that friends will be treated with the same personalized service that he or she has already experienced.

Certain servers develop quite a loyal following based upon their ability to recognize, acknowledge, and sincerely personalize contact with the bar's clientele. Inquiries, such as, "How's your wife?," "Is your kid over his cold yet?," "Did you have a nice vacation?," along with a thank you, go a long way toward increasing tips. Ideally, customers should not have to ask for anything. Servers should develop a sixth sense about anticipating customers' needs.

Remember birthdays of customers with a complimentary drink or dessert. Pay attention to conversations from any customer that mentions birthdays, anniversaries, or another occasion. Make an extra effort to create a special experience for that person or couple. Mix a special drink, or upgrade their choice from a well drink to a premium.

The way a server makes change can also add to tips. A $5 bill should always be broken down into five $1 bills, and a $1 bill into four quarters. If the drinks come to $15 and the customer pays with a $20, he should be given back five $1 bills rather than a $5 bill. Most of the time, customers will ask for $5 bills to be broken down anyway. Similarly, if the drinks come to $3, and payment is a $10 bill, instead of returning change as a $5 and two $1 bills, recommend to your servers that they return a $5, a $1, and four quarters. Try it and see how it affects their tips at the end of each shift. They will be pleasantly surprised.

The way change is handed to customers is also very important. If their drinks come to $5.50, and they pay with a $20 bill, always repeat the amount due and the bill received. First place the 50 cents down on the table or bar. Next, count in this manner: "5.50 and 50 makes 6," putting the ones on top of the coins, "7, 8, 9, 10," now putting the $10 bill last, "and 10 makes 20." Any little added touch, like fanning the bills as though they were a deck of cards, shows the server cares enough to make the customer's experience special.

Suppose a guest pays for a round of drinks and has received several dollars in change. The customer takes the change and bills and puts them in his pocket, leaving only one bill on the table or bar. This was obviously left for the server. The tip should be taken right then and acknowledged with a thank-you. The next time

a round is ordered, the same thing may happen. If the server has not taken the first dollar offered, she may receive only $1 for both rounds.

There is another good reason to take tips as they are offered. A server may be busy elsewhere when customers depart. The tip left may not be there by the time the server returns. A new customer may come along and inadvertently mix his money with the tip, causing the server to lose that money.

Another service that is good for an extra dollar or two is opening a package of cigarettes for the customer. For additional flair, the first cigarette can be lit.

One last tip about tips. When a guest hands a server a $1, a $5, and a $10 bill for an $11 check, the server must immediately acknowledge the overpayment. The customer may have made a mistake, thinking the $10 was actually another $5 bill. That could just as easily happen with a $20, $50, or $100 bill, especially in a dark bar. If the extra money is intended for the server, the customer will say so.

If a guest leaves the bar and has left an amount of money that was obviously a mistake, instruct servers to put it aside. There is a pretty good chance he will either call about the money or return for it in person. Do not be greedy. Honesty will pay off. Your customer's faith in the human race will have been restored, and that usually means a tip for being so honest. At the very least, you will have gained a loyal and trusting customer.

Training a bartender

The bartender must be trained to control inventory, dispense liquor efficiently, oversee the table servers, handle large amounts of cash, maintain cleanliness procedures, and do all of these with as much speed as possible to ensure good service.

Bartenders with the best experience and most gregarious personalities should work the busiest stations, handling the largest number of customers. Bartenders with less experience should work the slower shifts or stations. Those who are quick but do not have outgoing personalities would be better suited to working the service bars, which generally take care of table servers and a minimum number of customers. A balance must be struck between making the servers' drinks and the bar customers' drinks. A bartender has to use both hands at once when making drinks. If he is not already doing so, he should be trained.

Setting up the bar

Train your bartenders to stock the bar thoroughly enough to keep it in operation for an entire shift. A quick check should be made first to ensure there is enough ice to cover the shift and that all equipment is working properly. Any irregularities should be reported to management immediately. The bartender will perform a liquor inventory and written requisition to bring the bar to par.

All refrigerated items, such as beer, including draught kegs, wine, champagne, aperitifs, and liquors should be stocked first to allow them time to chill properly. All these items, as well as everything that is stocked, should be rotated to use the oldest first.

While the remaining liquor is stocked, the sinks should be filling for glass washing. The first is filled with hot soapy water, the second with plain hot water for a rinse, and the third with hot water and a disinfectant. Next check other chilled items. That includes refilling juices or mixes, such as bloody mary and piña colada. You may prefer the bartender to squeeze fresh juices as needed.

A daily check of the soda, carbon dioxide, and nitrogen tanks is recommended. Empty tanks should be changed and marked "empty" before the shift starts. Next, a trip is made to the storage refrigerator to obtain fruit, cream, eggs, and whipped cream.

The fruit, such as limes, lemons, oranges, pineapples, and the celery, should be cut according to bar policy, and the olives, onions, and cherries stocked for the garnish trays. The paper supplies should be checked and stocked. These include napkins, coasters, straws, stir rods, plastic swords or picks, guest checks, credit card vouchers, paper clips, stapler and staples, scotch tape, rubber bands, matches, note pads, pens, and register tape.

All glassware and utensils should be cleaned and restocked, including the glasses for drinks as well as wine carafes, coffee and espresso cups, blenders and lids, mixing glasses and strainers, mixing spoons, ice picks, ice scoops, shot glasses, and ashtrays. Also at this time, check and restock supplies of sugar (loose or cubed), salt (regular and coarse, in shakers and rimmers), bitters, orange flower water, cinnamon (loose or sticks), nutmeg, shaved chocolate, and other spices. Start brewing the coffee.

Fill the ice bins and wipe the bar counter clean with bar towels. Before opening, cash banks for each register dispensed by management should be counted and initialed to verify accuracy. (See FIG. 15-4.) Make sure the register has been cleared from the previous shift. Clean ashtrays with matches should be spaced across the bar, one for every two seats. Napkins also should be arranged on the bar as well.

Pouring liquor

Some bars require bartenders to use a shot glass to measure the liquor when pouring drinks. Even though it takes more time, accurate and consistent drinks will result. A shot glass aids the house in the control of liquor as long as the bartender is using it correctly. Other bars may allow bartenders to free-pour. That means pouring straight from the liquor bottle and using a silent count or sight measure to determine quantity. The danger here is

BAR BANK VERIFICATION

Date_____Shift: DAY   NIGHT

START	BILLS	END
_____	$100	_____
_____	50	_____
_____	20	_____
_____	10	_____
_____	5	_____
_____	1	_____
	TOTAL	

CHANGE

_____	50¢	_____
_____	25¢	_____
_____	10¢	_____
_____	5¢	_____
_____	1¢	_____
	TOTAL CHANGE	
	TOTAL BILLS	
	TOTAL CASH	

_____PREPARER _____

_____VERIFIED BY_____

Fig. 15-4. Bar Bank Verification form.

in overpouring; however, it greatly increases the bartender's speed and overall service and if she is pouring properly, the profits, too.

Teaching your bartenders to free-pour accurately is not difficult. Have them fill an empty bottle with water and pour what they feel is an accurate shot, according to the specified amount of liquor in each drink. Measure this amount against a shot glass. You can also use a training device. (See FIG. 15-5.)

Your choice of pour spouts determines the amount of liquor and the speed at which it is dispensed. Pour spouts have a tendency to clog, so each time a bottle is emptied, the pour spout should be changed to a clean one or rinsed out. Customers like to see a bartender free-pouring because they think they are getting more for their money. As long as drinks are made in accordance with house policies, encourage your bartenders to develop some flair and style when pouring. Customers like the expertise and show of an experienced bartender.

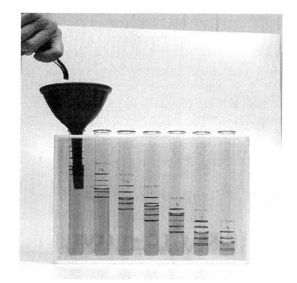

Fig. 15-5. Liquor portion control training device.
DABCO

When several drinks are ordered at once, the order in which they are made affects quality, consistency, and appearance. For example, a server orders a draught beer, two scotches on the rocks, a coke, a piña colada, and an Irish coffee. The bartender should first fill the glasses and the blender with ice, then pour the liquor for the two scotches and the piña colada, then the mix for the piña colada, then turn on the blender. While it is working, he pours the Irish whiskey and adds the coffee. Now, he pours the finished piña colada and the coke, tops the Irish coffee with whipped cream, and finally, pours the draught beer. This order prevents the coke and beer from going flat, the blended piña colada from separating, and the whipped cream on the Irish coffee from melting.

If a drink is made by mistake, instruct the bartender to strain the mistake and set it aside. The type of drink determines how long the drink can be saved. If a straight shot of brandy is mistakenly poured, it can be set aside and saved for a longer period of time than a vodka tonic, which must be used immediately or discarded as soon as the tonic goes flat. If too much of any blended drink is mixed, the extra should be placed in a separate glass and given to the person who ordered it, rather than thrown away. Customers will appreciate that.

How to speed service

When extremely busy, bartenders can speed service by telling customers the cost of their order while making the drinks. By the time the drinks are presented, the customers' money is ready. The bartender will not have to wait for customers to find wallets at the bottom of purses or inside coat pockets. The proper way to take a customer's bill is to place it on top of the register while making change, to avoid making change for the wrong bill denomination. Train the tenders to take several orders at once if possible.

Drinks can be presented to separate customers simultaneously, but one customer's money should never be used to make change for another customer without first going through the register. Bartenders should look for ways of minimizing steps and increasing their speed without jeopardizing service. It will be learned by their hands-on bar experience. Management should also observe the work habits of its staff to find other timesaving methods.

When two or more bartenders are working one bar, they must complement each other and work together. There must not be competition or an imbalance in the work load. Bartenders can help each other when one is busier by getting beer, wine, and even sharing the making of drinks to complete an order. Customers like to see a camaraderie between bartenders behind the bar.

The bartender has the responsibility of seeing that the server is ordering cocktails, handling cash, and maintaining credit cards according to existing house policy. Bartenders should also keep servers from using the station in front of them as a lounge area. That not only looks bad, but provides an unnecessary distraction to the bartender. Conversation should be kept to a minimum in this area, as mistakes can easily be made in pouring or in counting change.

Gross negligence of safety procedures is reason for dismissal, especially when it may result in injury to others. The most common example of this is when a bartender breaks a glass in the ice bin and then fails to remove all the ice and replace it with fresh ice. A small piece of glass can seriously cut or choke a person and would probably result in a lawsuit.

Cleaning

A bartender should always be busy. Cleaning shelves, wiping bottles, and wiping down the bar are just some of the things that can be done when there are no drinks to prepare. Certain maintenance and cleaning tasks can be assigned during slow shifts. Periodically soak and clean all pouring spouts to rid bottles of any sugar buildup, which attracts fruit flies, particularly for sweeter liqueurs. Refrigerators, beer boxes, liquor, and supply cabinets can also be part of a regular cleaning schedule.

At the end of every shift, all bottles in the well and the speed racks should be lifted from their holders and wiped clean. The bartenders should remove and clean the rubber or plastic boots that hold the bottles and run them through the glass washer to rid them of any sticky sugar, syrup, or soda build-up. The speed rack should be cleaned, and the pouring mats should be soaked in water with a little lime juice.

The end of the shift

If only a small amount of juice or mix is left in a container, it should be emptied, cleaned, and refilled in the morning. Unusable garnishes should be dumped and the garnish trays cleaned, with what is usable placed back in the garnish trays and refrigerated. The breakage sheet for the night should be completed, signed, and handed to the manager. Many bars restock the liquor, beer, and wine at the end of each shift or at the end of the night. Every dirty glass in the house should be washed, all ashtrays soaked, cleaned, and left drying on a towel on the sink or bar top. When the bar is wiped down, the register is cleaned and polished, the liquor and wine cabinets are locked, and all napkins, straws, and matches restocked. The bartender is finished for the shift and the next bartender can begin working immediately rather than having to start by cleaning a dirty bar.

Training a table server

At the start of each shift, the tables should be clean and set identically with ashtrays, matches, table tents, candles, and flowers. All tables and chairs should be arranged neatly. Stations should be clean and stocked with napkins, straws, extra matches, and credit card vouchers. At the end of the shift, stations are restocked, tables wiped clean, and all dirty glasses and ashtrays brought back to the bar. The server should clear any outstanding credit card vouchers, and turn in her ticket books with any cash owed the bar.

A table server should be trained to know drink abbreviations and the calling order, cocktail garnishes, how to handle cash and credit card transactions, how to be pleasant with customers, and above all, how to sell drinks.

All servers should be trained to call drinks to the bartender in a predetermined order. Regardless of how the drinks are ordered or recorded at the table, the server must rearrange and group the drinks in a preestablished order for the bartender to minimize the bartender's movements and act as a memory aid. There are two widely-used calling orders: liquor groups and glass groups.

The more popular method is grouping by liquors, with the well drinks in this order: scotch, bourbon, vodka, gin, rum, tequila, and brandy. Next come call drinks in the same order, followed by all premium drinks in the same order. While the server calls, the bartender selects the right glasses, filling them with ice and placing them on the bar in the order called.

In the second method of drink ordering, the server groups the glasses together calling: rocks, highballs, talls, buckets, chimneys, tulips, draught beer, shots, and coffee mugs. The server then must call the liquors for each glass, trying to group similar liquors together. This method is particularly useful for large orders in a noisy bar. A calling order is a practical tool that produces the best results when the server uses it properly and paces the bartender. Calling orders speeds service and thereby allows servers to spend more time with their customers. Train all servers to use the same system, whichever one you choose.

If a ticket system is in use, drink abbreviations are essential. For example, an order for an extra dry vodka martini on the rocks and two scotches and soda can be written as follows: X DRY V MART/R & 2 S/S. That speeds order-taking at the table and drink service from the bartender. How the abbreviations are derived is not important, so long as management standardizes a system and all servers use it. (Refer back to FIG. 15-3.)

In some bars, servers may be required to set up and fill glasses with ice for the bartender and even ring orders on their own registers. The server should garnish the glasses while the bartender is making the drinks. Servers should garnish drinks only with fresh fruit and according to the standard house policy. That will also help the bartender to remember the order.

Train the server to account to the bartender for every drink as soon as the order is filled. Either the order is billed to a tab or paid by cash or credit card. All servers should maintain a separate running total for each tab, so if a customer asks the amount, or thinks there is a discrepancy, the server can respond immediately with a record of what was ordered.

A server should be trained to handle a full tray of drinks and remember which customer ordered which drink. If she is overheard to say, "O.K. Who had the gin and tonic?" "Who's drinking the wine?" "How come I have an extra piña colada?" or "Oops, I'm sorry. That'll come right out with cold water," management should realize that server is in need of additional training.

Trays loaded down with drinks should be balanced to avoid any accidents. One way to accomplish this is by placing taller and stemmed glasses, and heavier items in the center of the tray, while the footed cocktail glasses are arranged along the outside. Another way is to leave the straws or stir rods out of the drinks until they are served. Many spills occur when someone reaches across a tray and knocks over a drink because of a projecting straw or stir rod.

Servers, not customers, should always unload their own trays. They should take care to maintain balance by rearranging items left on the tray. The server will learn through experience how to "feel" for the tray's balance. To help them remember people's drinks, instruct servers to take orders in a consistent manner. If they move around a table the same way each time, whether clockwise or counterclockwise, and start with the same chair at each table, they only have to remember one drink. The rest will follow in order. When picking up items from the bar that look the same, such as a rum and coke and a bourbon and coke, or a piña colada and a virgin piña colada, servers can distinguish the drinks by marking them with short straws that are removed just before serving.

The most important thing a server can do is stay on the floor selling drinks and talking to customers. Sales are not made when the server hangs out at the bar. Just the presence of a server at her tables will increase sales.

Servers generally accept that the customers in the area around the bar belong to the bartender. Bartenders and servers will usually come to a mutual agreement without diminishing customer service. If that is not the case, then management must step in and provide a solution. Servers should never take orders from customers sitting at or leaning on the bar. It is an area of potential conflict because customers often ask servers for drinks when they are at the bar. Servers should refer these customers to the bartender, or take the order and have the bartender deliver the drinks.

Security and door personnel

These personnel should be trained to be friendly and to interact with customers in a spirit of goodwill. While doing that, they will enforce the federal, state, and local regulations, dress code, and other house policies.

All customers must have proof of legal

drinking age, verified by personnel stationed at the door. One technique that is widely used to check if a license has been altered is to shine a flashlight through the birthdate to reveal if the date has been cut out and replaced. The photo on the license should match the bearer of the ID. If there is doubt, instruct these employees to request additional identification. If none is available, have the door personnel take the license and ask the bearer to recite the exact address and zip code on the license. As one final check, door employees can ask the customer to sign his name and then compare it against the signature on the license.

Security, door personnel, or the cashier may be required to place wristbands for age control on patrons as they enter your club. (See FIG. 15-6). Place these bands on persons of legal drinking age only.

In the event of potential conflict, security is trained to minimize and control the situa-tion. Usually a quiet discussion will end the problem before it gets out of control. The handling of a customer is always a delicate issue. Remember, the use of force is bad for business and should always be avoided if possible. Security and door personnel should be instructed to involve management first and not make decisions on their own unless the situation demands it. Even if the bar is justified in removing an individual, a lawsuit or threat of legal action may follow. As part of their job, security personnel should be required to fill out a daily report, with extra attention paid to any unusual circumstances. This is protection for the bar and should be filed for future reference.

In very large clubs, the security guards communicate with each other through the use of two-way radios or walkie-talkies. That allows swift handling of any disturbance. Laser penlights are effective in pointing out someone from across the room, or to get their atten-

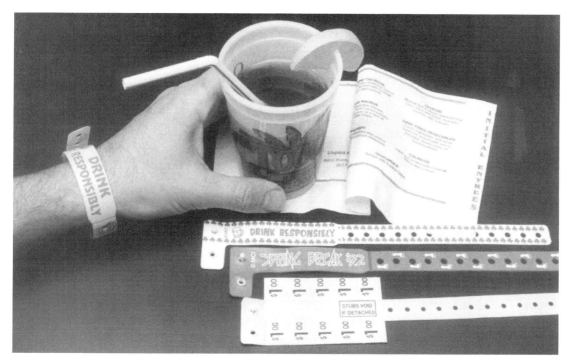

Fig. 15-6. Wristbands aid in ID controls when you have underage patrons in your bar. Secur-Ticket

tion. Care must be taken to avoid having these lights shine in someone's eyes.

Sales and motivational training

The bar business is a retail business. Your employees are your sales force. They create and influence sales. They do not take orders. They are almost like independent contractors operating within your establishment. You provide them with everything necessary to make money. Teach them to sell based on the concept that they are operating a business within your business. When this is understood, everyone will benefit and make more money.

Everyone who works for you is generating sales, by their service, by their smile, by their suggestions, by their recognition of customers. It starts with the owners and managers walking the floor, greeting people, and finding out how they like their service, drinks, food, and entertainment. On a return visit by a customer, the manager should find out more information about this customer: where she works, where she lives, what she does for a living. Show an interest. Be sincere.

Whoever greets patrons at the door is selling the night's or day's activities and future events. When someone walks in, it is not enough to say, "Hello!" Your door host should say, "Welcome! Tonight's drink specials are our frozen flavored Vodkas. At nine o'clock, check out our Magician!" And when people leave, "Thanks for coming in. Tomorrow night we start our yearly Midsummer Night's Dream Contest. You'll have a chance to win a trip to Hawaii!" Your greeter is selling, promoting, and informing.

Your servers need to upgrade drinks whenever possible and tell the guest the benefit they will achieve by upgrading. By "up-selling," they are generating more revenue for the bar and ultimately for themselves through higher check averages and tips. If 20 people per night per server switch from a well to a call or premium drink with an average increase of $1 per drink, that's $20 per night increase times five shifts per week = $100 times 50 weeks = $5000 or an average of $750 more in tips (at 15% average tip) per year. Relate this to something that has meaning in their life: a month's rent, several car payments, or two round-trip tickets to Jamaica or London.

Sales upgrading goes like this:

Customer: "I'd like a Bloody Mary."
Server: "We make a superb Bloody Peppar! It's made with Absolut Peppar, a pepper-flavored vodka, and a slice of cucumber. It's refreshing and different."

Customer: "I don't want to drink tonight. I'm thirsty, though. I think I'll have a glass of water."
Server: "We have an excellent selection of bottled waters, as well as many nonalcoholic and health drinks that look and taste great. How about a nice cold bottle of Pelligrino? (Or a Piña Colada without any alcohol? Or a fresh fruit smoothie that will give you energy?)"

Customer: "I'd like a cup of coffee."
Server: "If you like coffee, you should try our blend from the Kona coast of Hawaii. Kona coffee is one of the best in the world. It will cost you another fifty cents, but it's worth it. Better yet, have it in an Irish Coffee."

Customer: "I'm not sure what I would like."
Server: (This is a golden opportunity.) "What do you usually drink?"
Customer: "Margaritas."
Server: "We make an especially delicious fresh strawberry Margarita with Cuervo Gold and a taste of Grand Marnier."

An alternative approach for this question is to offer a drink menu that describes all your specialty drinks, alcoholic and nonalcoholic, as well as your standards. Drink menus should be on each table.

Server suggestions create better service and experiences for the customer. The customer can always say no; however, the majority of the times, they say yes. Develop a series of role-playing scenes to teach your people how to upgrade and guide customers through the decision process.

One of the best ways to generate enthusiasm and motivate your employees is to have the manager hold a short (five to ten minutes) pre-shift staff meeting. Discuss the positive points of the previous shift's successes and then the goals for this shift. You may want to explain the daily sales contest while giving an update on the weekly contest. For example, the daily contest is to see who can sell over $200 of wine, with any winner receiving a $25 cash bonus, while the weekly contest is to see who sells the most cognacs. Save your elaborate discussions for your general employee meeting.

Involve your employees in creating positive customer experiences. Reward them with praise during employee meetings. Discuss ways everyone can upgrade not only drinks, but service. Once your employees get the idea that what they create on the floor directly relates to their pocketbooks, they will take responsibility for their actions and either play in your business or move on. You want your employees to be excited about their jobs.

Your daily pep talks are crucial in motivating employees. Choose a different area of your operation to discuss each day. Generate feedback from your employees. Take their suggestions seriously and implement the ones you feel will be successful. Reward those ideas that save money or significantly improve the operation or service of your bar. Assist your employees when they need help. Having a

manager work beside them is stimulating and great for morale.

Alcohol awareness training

Problems caused by the overconsumption of alcohol are at the forefront of society's consciousness. Drinking and driving has the potential to create damage to other individuals and property. In many communities, public pressure has created stiffer and stiffer penalties on drivers who have been drinking. The legal blood alcohol levels are slowly being lowered from .10 percent to .08 percent.

Training all employees involved in the sale of alcohol to serve responsibly is critical. The majority of patrons consume their alcohol at safe levels; however, those who do not are at risk of killing or hurting innocent people. Everyone benefits through alcohol awareness training. Either develop a program you can administer yourself, or hire someone to do it. There are numerous national organizations that have programs you can purchase (see appendix for details). All employees who have participated should sign a form stating they have completed the training. Keep this form on file. In case you are involved in any type of lawsuit, your training will aid your case. Let's look at the essential elements of any training.

Educate your employees about the liquor code. Violations may result in fines, imprisonment, suspension, or termination of your license. You lose your business, they lose their jobs. There are no laws penalizing you for refusing service to a minor, someone you suspect is becoming or is intoxicated, or someone who is a known alcoholic. In some states, it is against the law to serve a known alcoholic.

Make sure everyone knows how to check IDs. Many bars institute a policy that anyone under 30 must show proper identification. Even if the ID was checked at the door, any server can request an ID if he suspects the person is underage. Check with your local police or Liquor Board to determine what constitutes proper identification. Typically, the following are valid:

- State-issued driver's license.
- State or federal government ID.
- Military ID.
- Current passport.

Always be pleasant and smile when requesting an ID. Check the photograph with the person standing in front of you. All should have a photograph. Then, take the ID out of the person's wallet or have him hand it to you. Shine a light through the back to notice any cut marks or alterations. Check to see that it is only laminated once. Feel around the edges of the photo. If it is raised, the photo has been added. If you have doubts, ask for a second ID with a photo. If you think the person is not the one represented on the card, ask him to:

- Sign his name and compare signatures.
- Tell you the zip code of where he lives.
- Repeat his social security number and date of birth.

If you think a patron is underage, refuse him entrance. If he hesitates when answering any of the preceding questions, don't let him in. If the ID appears to be a fake with obvious alterations, do not let that person in. Check with your local police department to determine if you can legally confiscate the ID. Whenever an incident occurs involving alcohol, such as false IDs, refusal of service, cutting a person off, or sending someone home in a cab, have the employee fill out an incident report immediately or at the end of her shift. Keep these on file to protect yourself.

If your bar is frequented by customers from many states, buy an ID Checking Guide and have it available for door and bar personnel. (See Appendix for suppliers.) These are small handy guides that have full-scale color reproductions of every license from every state in the United States and Canada, including government, military, naturalized citizen ID, and bank card designs. (See FIG. 15-7.)

As an owner, make a photocopy of your servers' IDs. You need a record that they are of legal age to serve alcohol. In some states, when a restaurant serves food and alcohol, the server can be 18 years old. Check to see about bar backs, buspersons, and dishwashers, who may also handle liquor in glasses.

With your employees, review recent civil cases where individuals have been served in a bar, caused an accident injuring or killing someone, and both the drunk driver and relatives of the deceased have sued and won million-dollar judgments from the bar and even from employees. The key word is negligence: negligence from stopping an intoxicated person from driving, negligence from continuation of liquor service or service to a minor or known alcoholic. Servers need to be responsible. Whenever an intoxicated person refuses to hand over his keys to you, take his license plate number and car description and notify the police immediately.

As a bar owner, you must act responsibly by providing proper employee training, including written policies on how to check IDs and how to notice if a person has had too much to drink. Maintain accurate and consistent pouring of your liquor. Be sure to have available nonalcoholic drinks and food for your patrons. Have alternative ways to get your patrons home if they cannot drive. And finally, excessive drink promotions, such as: two-for-ones, all-you-can-drink, and contests must disappear. Never allow the stacking of drinks in front of a customer.

In your training, include how alcohol affects an individual, how it is absorbed into the bloodstream, and who is at risk. Everyone

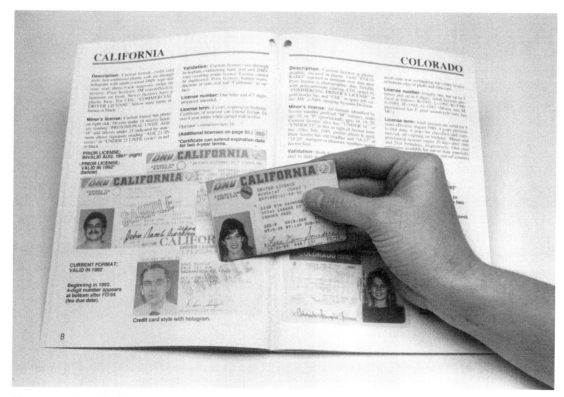

Fig. 15-7. *ID guide for every state in the United States and Canada.* Drivers License Guide Company

should know how much alcohol is present in each drink, so the number of drinks can be counted and how long it takes for a drink to be metabolized (12 oz. beer = 4 oz. wine = 1.25 oz. 80 proof liquor = 1 oz. 100 proof liquor).

Servers need to be trained to recognize the different levels of intoxication. A common way is to divide the effects into levels like a traffic signal: green, yellow, and red. A green-level person has had nothing to drink or shows no signs of intoxication. Service is quick and expedient. A yellow-level guest is showing behavorial signs due to alcohol consumption: loud talking, friendly when normally shy, and other inhibitions becoming relaxed. At this point, the server slows down service and suggests food or nonalcohol items.

When a person enters the red level, all alcohol consumption must stop. This individual's judgment becomes impaired, his eyes are blurry and cannot focus, his speech is slurred, and his physical movements are erratic. He becomes drowsy, spills drinks, stumbles, and may become antisocial. Again food and nonalcoholic drinks are offered as this person is intoxicated. Be friendly when stopping service.

Servers must be patient as they may have to repeat themselves several times to get the message across. A manager should be called as a backup or to take over. As a manager, respect the server's judgment. If you disagree, do so later, not in front of the customer. Never embarrass the customer or use physical force. Express concern for his welfare and remain calm and do not raise your voice. Do not let this person drive or leave without being in someone else's care.

A designated driver program is an excellent way to allow patrons to drink and not worry about driving. Establish a solid working relationship with a cab company so you can call on them for quick service. Some bars pay a cab to remain outside after 11 o'clock. If the guest insists on driving, tell them you are going to report them to the police and then call. Fill out an incident report.

Dealing with red-level guests is difficult and every attempt must be made to avoid patrons reaching this level. Constant employee training helps. Guests can have a great time by enjoying themselves and knowing your bar looks out not only for its guests, but for the unknowing public as well. Responsible alcohol service is a community service.

Alcohol awareness training exercises

After your employees have been trained and before they start working the floor, engage in these role-playing exercises where the employees assume the different roles. Acting out and discussing ways to handle these situations are extremely beneficial. Once the scene is played to conclusion, have suggestions on the best way to resolve these problems. These are just a few of the many typical interactions you will encounter.

Situation #1—Underage bride A close friend of the owner (who spends lots of money at the bar) has booked a large wedding reception at your place. The bride is his daughter and she is 20 years old. As the server, you observe the bride and groom drinking champagne. They have arrived in a chauffered limousine. The owner is not working at the bar today. The server does not want to offend the father of the bride. The server calls for a manager.

Solution The manager checks to see that bar policy has been followed when the recep-

tion was booked. He pulls the file and goes down the checklist noticing who booked the party and the signed statement by the father. The statement says that no underage or intoxicated individuals will be allowed to drink alcohol on your premises. The manager pulls the father aside and quietly reminds him of the statement he signed and requests that the bride please refrain from drinking. At first, the father protests, but then he realizes the entire party may be at risk, so he abides by the rules.

The manager should compliment the server on noticing the problem and calling for assistance. Exceptions are not allowed. The law does not discriminate or favor, and neither should you.

Situation #2—Intoxicated guest A party of four guests are drinking, with one person the designated driver. They have half-full drinks in front of them. One of the drinkers stands up to go to the restroom and stumbles over some chairs. This person is at the red level. The server observes what happened and as she approaches the table, a friend at another table wants to buy this group a round of drinks.

Solution The server first informs the friend that the bar's policy forbids her to stack drinks in front of its customers. The friend asks what the harm is since they have a designated driver. The server says it is against the law to serve an intoxicated individual and the law does not care if he is not driving. That individual could slip and fall upon leaving and the bar would be responsible.

Food and nonalcoholic drinks are offered to the table. The manager suggests bringing the red-level individual a complementary plain soda water. Just having a drink to hold onto, even though it is nonalcoholic, satisfies the red-level person. The manager makes sure when the party leaves that all persons are escorted to the designated driver's car.

The manager asks the server why that person was allowed to reach the red level. The server says she served him one round, and when he walked in, all appeared at the green level. Sometimes other factors affect alcohol absorption, such as stress, medication, or inexperience with drinking. The manager suggests that if the situation arises again where after one drink the person is drunk, and he has his second drink in front of him, refund his money and offer a free, nonalcoholic substitute. Arrange for alternative transportation.

Situation #3—Missing person A party of three sits at the bar. Four drinks are ordered. The bartender is informed that the fourth person is parking the car.

Solution The bartender only pours three drinks until she can ID and assess the fourth customer.

Situation #4—Guest arrives intoxicated The parking attendant notices that the arriving guest is at the yellow/red level. He has several cars waiting to be parked behind this one.

Solution The parking attendant should have a way to contact a security person, door host, or manager without leaving the parking lot (either by phone or a two-way radio). The manager or person-in-charge should invite the guest inside and serve him complementary food and nonalcoholic drinks until the level of alcohol absorption is accurately observed. Under no circumstances should this person be allowed to continue drinking at your bar. Alternative transportation should be arranged and the guest gently informed of your policies. If the guest insists on driving, inform him the police will be notified.

The parking attendant made the correct decision to alert management. If this guest was refused admission based on his intoxication level and allowed to drive away and cause an accident, in most states, the bar would be held partially responsible for the damages.

Additional training for all employees

As part of your training procedures, consider a videotape as an educational tool. On this video, employees act out typical situations that occur and the proper responses. The owner can express the bar's philosophy and goals. By showing them the tape, you can be sure that all employees have received the same information. Have the employees sign a statement that they have read or viewed and understood your training manuals, employee manuals, and/or video training tapes. Keep these signed statements as part of each employee's file.

An excellent practice is to "cross-train" your employees. For example, a cocktail server would be trained to tend bar, and a bartender would be trained to handle the floor, the door, and taught how to order liquor. When one employee is sick or quits unexpectedly, another cross-trained employee can fill that position until you hire a replacement. The added versatility gives your employees more job satisfaction and will inevitably pay off at a later date.

Cross-training also ensures that employees do their current jobs better by allowing them to see how their actions affect the performance of everyone else's job. The excellent practice of promoting from within is also facilitated by cross-training.

Scheduling

The number of employees and the hours they work are dependent upon the hours of operation, the physical layout of the bar, and, most importantly, the anticipated flow of business. Scheduling allows management to project the costs of labor against the volume of expected business. Proper scheduling ensures that desired service standards will be maintained, while at the same time minimizing costs by maximizing sales per employee work hour.

In FIG. 15-8, notice how the bar is divided into different work stations based upon expected volume. There may be natural divisions that make for easy station separations, such as a raised lounge area, a grouping of tables around a fireplace, or a separate room. If there are no natural divisions, work stations are made up by dividing the total number of seats equally. Depending upon the type of bar and the service offered, servers can usually handle between 25 and 40 seats, in addition to stand-up customers, who will mill about in the station or at stand-up drinking bars.

The number of bartenders has already been determined by the number of stations built into the bar. A second bartender or bar back may be scheduled on a busy night to ring up checks, wash glasses, or pour beer and wine.

The hours your bar is open will also determine how many shifts need scheduling. Let's assume your bar is open from 4 PM until 2 AM. You must decide whether to break the 10-hour shift into two shifts, or have one set of employees work the entire shift. If you decide on a single shift, you may be required to pay overtime. If overtime is not required, then it is cheaper to use the single shift, because there will be no time overlap of employee hours worked. The 10-hour shift becomes 10½, because one shift must take time to turn everything over to the other. On the other hand, if the 10-hour shift is split, and one employee is sick, another can usually work both shifts.

The breakdown of expected customer volume and revenue should have been completed in the budgeting phase of the business plan. Daily sales reports should be logged and will assist in scheduling once the bar has been in operation and obvious patterns emerge.

To schedule effectively, you must determine how much you are spending for labor in relation to sales. The dollar amount of labor divided by the dollar amount of daily sales gives a percentage called the *labor cost*. For example, say daily sales were $1500. The amount paid for labor that day was $300. Three hundred dollars divided by $1500 equals 20 percent. That means for every $5 in revenue, $1 pays for labor. Your labor cost should average between 12 and 20 percent of gross sales. This figure does not include the salary of management or benefits.

To use this percentage of labor cost (labor PC) as a tool in scheduling, add the hours scheduled per day and multiply that figure by the wage paid. Twenty bartender hours times $7 per hour equals $140. Forty server hours times $5 equals $200. In this simple example, the day's total scheduled labor is $340. Projected sales, based upon a labor PC of 20 percent, should be at least five times this or a minimum of $1700. Although the PC may vary greatly on a day-to-day basis, when computed monthly, it should be consistent.

The most important aspect of scheduling is ensuring excellent service to your guests. Through experience, you may find that you need fewer employees than have been scheduled. For instance, on a given shift, four servers are scheduled and sell $1500 in drinks. During several passes on the floor, management notices that although service is sufficient, the servers are not being used to full capacity.

The next week, management schedules three servers instead of four for the same shift, attempting to maximize each server's efforts. With the same customer count, sales will still be $1500 and service will not suffer. Sales per employee-hour worked actually increase because the servers will be more active on the floor selling drinks. They make more efficient use of their time because the pace is quicker and a better working rhythm develops. Also, knowing they are making more tips, they have more incentive to work harder.

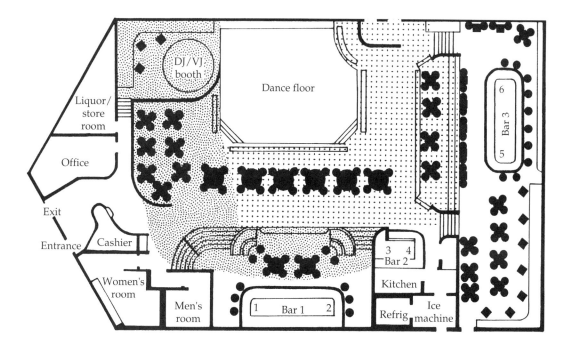

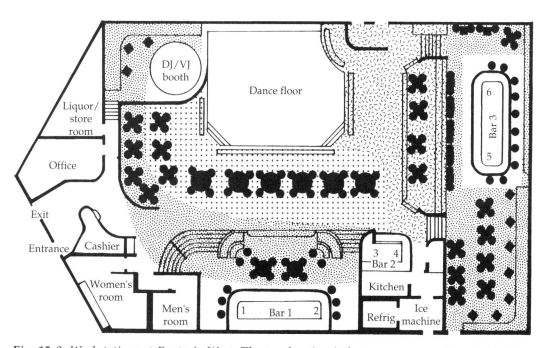

Fig. 15-8. *Workstations at Fantasia West. The top drawing is for two servers and two bartenders working out of Bar 1. The bottom drawing shows four servers working out of three bars with six bartenders.*

As a further example, if the number of servers was reduced from three to two and the same amount of sales resulted, but service standards had noticeably deteriorated, then obviously three servers for that shift is the optimum number.

Another method of reducing labor costs is to send hourly employees home during a given shift when business does not meet expectations. Do this only when you are sure that the remaining servers can provide adequate service for the balance of the shift.

One way to streamline the schedule is to stagger the times that employees arrive to begin their shifts. For example, five servers are necessary on a shift from 6 PM to 2 AM, with the peak business hours being between 8 PM and midnight. Instead of scheduling all five for the entire eight hours of the shift, amounting to 40 work-hours, costs can be cut by scheduling one server from 6 PM to midnight, two from 7 PM to midnight, and two from 8 PM to 2 AM. You still have all five servers to cover the peak business hours, and you have reduced the number of work-hours from 40 to 28, resulting in a 30 percent savings in labor costs.

In a smaller bar, patterns of the flow of business can be determined by observation over a period of time. In a larger place, more variables come into play, and you may wish to take hourly register readings and door counts to define business patterns.

Employees will appreciate a schedule posted a week or more in advance. This allows them to anticipate their days or nights off. (See FIG. 15-9.) Friday night is a good night to put up the new schedule because most of your employees will work either Friday or Saturday. This way employees will plan their outside activities around the work schedule, and not the other way around. You are also providing a courtesy that you hope will be returned when employees need days off or the bar needs extra help. Always notify an employee if there is a major change in his schedule and explain why the change is necessary. In a small bar with only a few employees, scheduling is not a big problem. In a larger place with day and night shifts, however, it can be quite complicated.

Once business patterns are established, some managers may base their scheduling on performance, others on seniority, and still others may rotate stations and schedules equally. If a problem arises with an employee, the schedule should never be used as an instrument of punishment. A more effective way of handling the situation to avoid resentment is simply a one-to-one meeting. That is the owner's most effective tool for solving any problem.

Having each employee personally responsible for his scheduled shifts is mandatory. If a conflict arises, the scheduled employee must find a suitable replacement and notify management for approval. Sick calls must be received at least two hours before the start of the scheduled shift and be made personally by the employee. You may want to schedule an on-call shift, where an employee must call in by a specified time. That way if there is an illness or an emergency, you already have someone ready to work the shift. Also, it may occur that an employee wishes to switch shifts with another employee. Management should receive these requests in writing for approval. All parties should sign the request to ensure responsibility for the shift that has been transferred.

The average work week for a full-time bar employee is four or five shifts. Some owners rotate their employees off the schedule every fourth weekend night to let them have a Friday or Saturday night free. Whenever possible, allow your employees to have their days off consecutively. Talk to them about it, and try to accommodate their wishes. Remember, showing concern for your employees and their schedules is just another way of making your bar a popular place to work. Happy employees are good for business.

WEEK OF:	SUNDAY	MONDAY	TUESDAY	WEDNESDAY	THURSDAY	FRIDAY	SATURDAY
BARTENDERS							
Rick							
Sue							
Ned							
Linda							
Craig							
Julie							
SERVERS							
Patty							
Kathy							
Dan							
Joann							
Judy							
Margaret							
BARBACKS							
Josie							
Lisa							
Dan							
DOOR							
Ricky							
John							
Tom							
SECURITY							
Sheryl							
Steve							
Jack							
Bob							

Fig. 15-9. Post a weekly work schedule on Friday nights at least a week in advance so employees have time to plan.

Employee meetings

The purposes of employee meetings are to introduce and explain new policies, iron out problems in the operation, and provide an open forum for general employee discussion. An effort should be made to create an atmosphere where your staff feels free to discuss anything. Meetings should be held at an hour convenient for everyone. If your meetings are mandatory, you must pay employees for attending. If not, attendance is optional and failure to attend cannot be held against them.

The difference between pre-shift meetings and a general employees meeting is that in your pre-shift meeting, you are trying to achieve short-term goals with that particular group of employees. Use your general meetings to talk about long-term plans and greater depth on other topics.

Keep meetings short and to the point. Do not allow discussions to deteriorate into useless ramblings. The manager conducting the meeting should control and direct discussions to ensure constructive interaction at all times. Be specific with a prepared agenda. Any new promotions or information concerning changes in operations should be clearly stated. Explain problem situations to employees. Help them to see why it is a problem and offer your solutions. If you think it would be helpful, you can ask for feedback on your solutions. As the manager, however, make a firm decision and let your employees know that this is the new policy effective immediately. After your agenda has been covered, give employees time for suggestions and complaints. Let them see you are flexible on issues they feel strongly about if they prove their motives are based on sound business reasoning. Employees are in close contact with customers and often know exactly what is needed to improve the bar's operation.

Periodically, it is a good idea to discuss emergency procedures. Have a bulletin board to post first-aid techniques and telephone numbers for fire and police departments, taxi cabs, and local emergency care centers. Directions to the nearest hospital should be posted and first aid should be taught to all employees. You may even wish to contact the American Red Cross about the availability of first aid and CPR training classes for your employees. The bulletin board should contain all schedules, memos, directives, and pertinent information, so that communication is centralized and effective. Refer employees to the bulletin board and hold them responsible for the information posted.

Employee incentives

An incentive can be defined as any motivational tool used by management to increase sales or profit margins or develop positive employee morale and camaraderie. Typical incentives take the form of sales contests, cash bonuses, and training seminars for career development. The proper way to start an incentive program is to introduce it at a general employee meeting. Explain in detail the goals and shared benefits for the bar and the employees, including prizes. Prizes may be cash or something else the employees may suggest of equal value, such as gift certificates, tickets to special events, or trips.

The most effective incentives are sales contests. They may run on a daily, weekly, or monthly basis, and the amount of the prize should vary accordingly. As further incentive, you may also wish to include a second and third prize. The contests may be for individual employees based on sales per hour or for all employees based on group sales. The important thing for an individual sales contest is that each employee is ensured a fair chance of winning. Shifts and stations must be rotated or at least taken into consideration to determine a fair winner. In a group contest, the goal set must be realistic and attainable. If the goal is not met, acknowledge the staff's effort and set a more reasonable goal.

The contest may be limited to specific items. As a promotional tool, prizes may be awarded for the most house specialty drinks sold. House wine or draught beer might be selected because of their high profitability. A sales contest may also be initiated as a way to introduce new items. As the contest progresses, post the results. That allows employees to compare their sales and serves to stimulate interest.

Varying the incentive from month-to-month, week-to-week, or day-to-day is a good idea. A little variety makes the game more attractive and keeps the interest level high. Have your employees design the contest and pick the prizes one week. You want your employees to be having fun while they work, thus making the most money for you and for themselves. Incentives will add some spark.

Some bars may reward employees with cash bonuses for exceptional work or outstanding achievement. An example of this is an employee who pulls a double shift or works two weeks straight without a day off because of another employee's illness. A cash bonus may be given to every employee who has worked on an especially hectic night or on a shift where working conditions were not up to par due to unusual repairs or equipment failures. This type of reward is usually given privately to let the employees know that their work is appreciated and never taken for granted.

In some instances, incentives other than cash may be more appropriate. Employees interested in expanding their careers may appreciate additional training provided at the bar's expense. You could arrange to enroll selected employees in classes in management, accounting, and marketing. That not only broadens an employee's knowledge, but will also be an investment for you if the employee grows with your operation. You might send an employee to a local vineyard to learn how wine is made, to a brewery or to a distillery. Upon return, that employee can share the experience and knowledge with the other employees. Wine and beer seminars can be offered to increase all employees' knowledge and interest.

Some incentives are purely spontaneous in nature. Some bar owners celebrate their employees' birthdays with bottles of champagne, food, and decorations, or give them the night off with pay. Others make it a point to treat their crew to dinner or an early morning breakfast after closing. Once you get to know your employee's interests, you will find the right incentive.

The best incentive you can offer your employees is job security. Employees need to know that they will not be dismissed for insufficient reason or unjust cause. They also need to know that they will be counseled and notified if they are falling short of management's standards. If you practice fair management, thoughtful scheduling, careful training, and efficient problem solving, your employees will want to continue working for you, and, consequently, you will have a lower turnover rate.

This works to your benefit, because you will maintain a stable operation and save money by not having to train new employees. Additional benefits occur when customers learn of your fair treatment and feel your bar is special in every way—good service, good drinks, pleasant surroundings—and you are fair to your employees.

Managing on the floor

Paperwork, phone calls, reports, and non-pressing business matters should be handled prior to opening or after peak business hours. As stated previously, the manager or owner should spend as much time as possible circulating through the bar observing and providing a visible presence. There is no substitute for first-hand knowledge of your operation, overseeing service, and spreading goodwill. Customers love to feel they have a personal relationship with the owner and manager.

A manager on the floor may not appear to be working, however, she is constantly observing every facet of the operation. Tables are checked to see if they are being kept clean and well-attended with no overflowing ashtrays or customers trying in vain to flag down a server. The bartenders should be active, pouring drinks accurately, exhibiting a friendly personality, and establishing a warm and cordial atmosphere. A manager is alert to any areas that may develop into problem situations. For instance, a spill on the floor may be hazardous if not wiped up, or a group of people at a table is drinking heavily and becoming boisterous. While these people are not yet a problem, the server for the table should be advised that they could soon get out of hand. The manager may introduce himself to these guests in order to establish a controlling presence.

From time to time, a manager should try to see the bar as a customer sees it. What are the first impressions as one walks in the door?

Do the employees appear happy? Are the other customers enjoying themselves? Is this a place where you would enjoy spending time and money? If so, chances are that all of your advanced planning is now paying off.

In spite of all of the planning in the world, though, things are bound to go wrong. That is when management's skill and judgment really come into play. As a manager on the floor, you should be familiar enough with each job, so that in case of emergency, you can cover it. Suppose your bartender has to rush home on a busy Saturday night? Have you crossed-trained another employee who can jump behind the bar and do an adequate job? Do you know enough about your own calling order, prices, and check system to assist this person? What if an important piece of equipment breaks down? You should know enough about how your equipment operates to determine what is wrong. If it is something simple, you should have an idea of how to fix it yourself. Suppose the soda guns stop working in the middle of a rush? They cannot be repaired simply. In anticipation of this event, however, you should have bottled sodas on hand.

Many other emergency situations and equipment breakdowns commonly arise and can be anticipated. Know where to get large quantities of ice if your ice machine fails on a busy night. Know how to open your cash register if the power fails and it is locked. If you do require outside help for major repairs, watch how the repairs are made. Ask questions of the repairperson. A little more knowledge of repairs or preventive maintenance may save you time, money, and headaches in the future.

Management do's and don'ts

Here are some simple do's and don'ts that can assist in a smooth bar operation:

Do's

- Instruct your staff not to give employee telephone numbers or addresses to customers without that employee's consent.
- Always be consistent and fair.
- Maintain a checklist to troubleshoot equipment failures.
- Maintain a complete and current phone list for all important numbers.
- Readily accept responsibility for every facet of your bar's operation.
- Act responsibly to your community. Think globally, act locally.

Don'ts

- Don't leave money unattended.
- Don't let your moods interfere with business.
- Don't criticize employees in front of a customer or another employee.
- Don't date employees; it only creates problems, jealousies, and accusations of favoritism.
- Don't pursue profits at the expense of another's welfare.

Management troubleshooting

The following are typical situations that can arise in the course of running a bar. These are excellent problem-solving topics for management meetings. The solutions are suggestions and are meant to stimulate your thinking into coming up with the most creative solution for your particular set of circumstances.

Situation #1—How do I change my clientele?

Solutions For various reasons, the clientele of a business is in constant flux. Maintaining and building a steady clientele of your choice is an ongoing challenge. First, you must look and see how you are meeting the expectations of your existing clientele, and what you can do to alter their expectations, and thus change your guests.

One of the easiest ways to bring in new customers is to examine where your old customers are geographically coming from. Shift your advertising from one media or radio station to another, and depending on the demographics, your clientele should change. For example, if you are currently advertising on a rock 'n roll radio station and are attracting a young crowd and you would like to attract more affluent businesspersons, then change to a jazz, news, business, or a more middle-of-the-road station. Shift newspaper ads from the entertainment section to the business or financial section.

If you have entertainment, change your format. Switch from hard rock to dance music, rock 'n roll to country, live bands to a DJ, or from a dance club to a lounge club with a cover charge and drink minimums.

Institute a dress code or a cover charge.

Raise the price of your drinks beyond the range of your existing clientele.

A more radical move would be to close down and renovate with a new name and concept.

Situation #2—My liquor costs are too high.

Solutions Check the pouring habits of your bartenders. If one is overpouring, retrain that individual. Switch from free pouring to pouring with a shot glass. Change your pour spouts from fast pourers to medium-speed pourers, or to premeasured ones. Put in a liquor gun system, or one that ties all drinks into your register.

Take inventory more frequently (if monthly, weekly or daily until you solve your problem). Check to see if the security of your bottles is tight, and check the number of persons having access to them. After closing, lock up all bottles behind the bars. Check out your cleaning crews. Mark the bottles after closing and double check upon opening.

Check to see if loopholes exist in how your money transactions take place. Change procedures or institute new systems for controls.

How are mistakes accounted for? Who has the authority to comp drinks? How are they accounted for?

Make sure your drink prices have increased according to your costs. Check your glass sizes. Maybe you need to downsize from a 10-ounce highball to a 9-ounce highball. Look at your ice cubes. If they have holes in them, switch to a solid cube or a pillow shape.

Situation #3—A competitor opened a few blocks away and half of my "loyal" customers are now drinking there.

Solutions The new place in town will always experience a tremendous amount of curiosity and take away business from everyone. You must consistently meet or exceed your customers' expectations. Make sure your service and quality of employees, drinks, entertainment, and your physical operation are running at optimum levels. You need to make sure you are giving your customers the value they seek for their money. Exceed their expectations.

Beat your competition with better and more innovative ways of promoting and doing business. Reach out to your community with sponsored events, charity events, or regularly scheduled celebrations that make your place and the event an institution.

Never speak in negative tones about your competition. Welcome them to create a better environment for your customers.

Use a focus group to establish the needs of your remaining customers and to determine how the competition's customers feel about your place.

Situation #4—My competition is cutting their drink prices and I am losing business.

Solutions If you start to cut all your prices in return, you will begin a downward price war in which you'll both be out of business. Attack their business one day at a time. Pick a day where you feel you can gain customers and go after that segment of the market. Make sure your concept is different from the competition. If they have live music and so do you, switch to a DJ. Give your customers something unique to experience so word-of-mouth advertising starts to take over.

Give your customers more entertainment for their dollars than they would expect.

If you must compete at the pricing level, lower only one segment of your drinks, such as all beers from 6–9 PM to $.99.

Situation #5—My employee turnover is increasing. How do I keep my employees longer?

Solutions Employees are a valuable resource. It is easier to keep a trained employee than to find and train a new one. Are your initial job descriptions accurate? Are you misleading new employees about the amount of tips they will earn? Are you checking their references to see if they have the experience for your positions?

Evaluate your treatment of employees. Do you empower them by allowing them to participate in decisions regarding their work and promotions in your bar? Do you allow them to grow by their mistakes? Do you lead or dictate? Do you set an excellent example? Do you provide an upgrading of their skills and a chance for advancement? Do you recognize them when they achieve goals or provide excellent service? Do they feel you sincerely care about them? Do you provide them any benefits?

Employees who feel recognized, appreciated, a part of the team, are compensated for their efforts, and have a chance for advancement, will stay.

Situation #6—My volume of business has increased over the last few years, but my net profit continues to decline.

Solutions You are not paying attention to your rising costs and have not adjusted your prices accordingly.

Check how your money is being handled. Are complementary drinks/foods being recorded properly? Pop in at closing time and see how the money is handled. Come in after closing time and see what is going on. Are employees eating and drinking after hours? Is there a chance a manager could be adjusting the sales? If there are any loopholes, then institute new controls.

Check glass sizes, ice sizes, portions, and recipes.

If you still cannot figure out what is going wrong, hire a consultant (someone unknown to your employees) and have him visit your operation and observe from a neutral vantage point. The consultant, familiar with many more bar operations than you, may be able to detect holes in your operations that you are too close to see.

Situation #7—My bar doesn't get busy until 9 or 10 PM; how do I get customers to arrive earlier and stay later?

Solutions Your customers need a reason to arrive earlier. If you offer dancing or entertainment, start the band, DJ, or show at 6 PM instead of 8 PM Lower drink prices or provide free food to entice them to come earlier. You may wish to start this on a Friday, attracting an after-work crowd by starting the entertainment as early as 5 PM

Sometimes what works is to appeal to a different crowd in the earlier part of the evening. If your regular late night crowd is the dancing and party type, then try to attract a more sedate crowd with a jazz group or soloist during happy hour. When entertainment is not the draw, but other people are, shift gears in the early hours with promotions that will appeal to after-work guests. Single out a particular profession, such as secretaries, and design activities to bring them in.

Situation #8—I am an owner/operator. At what point do I turn my business over to a general manager so I can focus on other duties?

Solutions When your business reaches the point where your time is better spent developing or running certain aspects and you do not have to be involved in the day-to-day operations, train someone to take your place gradually by slowly giving more responsibilities. You may start out by letting her open up each day, then add closing duties on several nights. Then you let her be responsible for hiring the day crew, then the night crew. You'll follow up with promotional duties, and then certain bottom line figures, such as labor and liquor costs.

Finally, see how she manages completely on her own. As you develop her confidence and you let go, notice how the net profits are going and if she is improving sales. Allow for learning mistakes and encourage successes. You want your General Manager to be as successful as you and excel in areas out of your expertise. In this way, you will both benefit from each other's experiences.

16

Maintaining records

Before going to the bank to make your first deposit, you should know how to keep track of the daily flow of money through your bar. (See FIG. 16-1.) By maintaining proper records with a procedure called accounting, financial transactions are recorded in an organized way and summarized in financial statements. These statements are essential for filling out tax-returns required by the government. Failure to do so or filing inaccurately can result in fines or imprisonment. These statements also provide information for investors, creditors, and a record of your bar's financial position when applying for loans.

The availability of computers and software makes it feasible for any bar owner to process their own records, inventory, and payroll. Even if you hire someone to do your books, you should know how these statements are derived. The analysis of these statements is a valuable tool that you or your management can use to control costs and increase profits.

Principles of accounting

The best way to maintain records in the bar business is to use a double-entry bookkeeping system. This system was developed by the merchants of Venice as a way to keep track of their trading industry and has been working successfully for centuries. The strength of this system lies in its use of *debits* and *credits*. The terms debits and credits are used to indicate increases and decreases in account transactions. They are understood as positive or negative depending upon the type of account. Each transaction that is made is recorded or posted twice; once as a debit and once as a credit. To understand this better, think of a scale. If something is taken off or added to one side, it affects the other side. For instance, you purchase an order of liquor for $1000. While you have $1000 less in your checking account, you have gained $1000 in inventory or assets. The balance is maintained.

Each of the bar's transactions is recorded in an appropriate account. *Accounts* can be general categories or subdivisions of the general category. An example of a general category is a Direct Operating Expenses account. A subdivision of this category is bar supplies. Your bar can be categorized and subdivided any way you choose with no limitations. The $1000 in liquor previously mentioned would be credited to the liquor account. The liquor account is a subdivision of the beverage ac-

DAILY SALES SUMMARY				
	REGISTER 1 DAY NIGHT	REGISTER 2 DAY NIGHT	REGISTER 3 DAY NIGHT	TOTALS
BANK				
CURRENCY				
CHANGE				
PAID-OUTS				
SUBTOTAL				
– STARTING BANK				
= TOTAL CASH TO BE DEPOSITED 1				
CREDIT CARDS				
AMX				
M/C				
VISA				
OTHER				
TOTAL CHARGES 2				
– TIPS CHARGED				
AMX				
M/C				
VISA				
OTHER				
TOTAL TIPS CHARGED 3				
2 – 3 = TOTAL SALES CHARGED 4				
1 + 4 = TOTAL SALES 5				
SALES				
LIQUOR				
WINE				
BEER				
OTHER				
PROMO				
FOOD				
= TOTAL SALES 6				
– SALES TAX 7				
= ADJUSTED SALES TOTAL 8				
5 – 6 = OVER/SHORT				
PREPARED BY		DATE	DAY	

Fig. 16-1. Daily sales summary.

count, which is a subdivision of the inventory account, which is a subdivision of the general category of assets.

Accounts should be numbered for notations on checks, ease of filing, and as an index to the journals. The traditional order of accounts is current assets, fixed assets, current liabilities, long-term liabilities, capital or equity, revenue, and expense accounts. A Chart of Accounts is an example of a typical account breakdown for a bar. (See TABLE 16-1.)

Accounts are set up to itemize the business' assets, liabilities, expenses, and capital or equity. Whenever an asset, expense, or withdrawal account increases, or a liability, revenue and capital (equity) account decreases, a debit is recorded to that account. An account is credited when assets, expenses, or a withdrawal account decreases, or a liability, revenue, and capital account increases. Debits are always posted in the left-hand column, while credits are always posted in the right-hand column. For instance, as an owner, you spend $50,000 to help open your bar; this amount is credited to your Capital account. Then, the $50,000 is debited to your checking or cash account because this asset account has now increased. When you pay a check to the power company, the check is credited to your checking account and debited to your utilities account because this is an expense. Every transaction has an effect on your assets, liabilities, capital or equity, and ultimately your net worth. Your net worth is figured by adding all

Table 16-1.

Acct. No.	Acct. Name
100	**ASSETS**
101	CASH
102	Change Funds
103	Cash on Deposit
110	ACCOUNTS RECEIVABLE
111	Customers
112	Credit Card Accounts
113	Other
114	Employee Loans and Advances
120	INVENTORY
121	BEVERAGES
122	Liquor
123	Beer
124	Wine
125	Other
126	FOOD
127	SUPPLIES
128	OTHER
130	PREPAID EXPENSES
131	Insurance
132	Deposits
133	Taxes
134	Licenses and Permits
140	FIXED ASSETS
141	Land
142	Building
143	Accumulated Depreciation
144	Leasehold Improvements
145	Amortization of Improvements
146	Fixtures, Equipment, Furniture
147	Accumulated Depreciation
148	Automobiles
149	Operating Equipment (Other)
150	DEFERRED CHARGES
151	Pre-opening Expenses
152	Other
200	**LIABILITIES**
201	PAYABLES
202	Notes Payable
203	Accounts Payable
210	TAXES WITHHELD AND ACCRUED
211	Income Tax
212	FICA
213	FUTA
214	State Unemployment Tax
215	Sales Tax
216	Employer's Share of Payroll Taxes
217	Other
220	ACCRUED EXPENSES
221	Rent
222	Payroll

Acct. No.	Acct. Name
223	Interest
224	Water
225	Gas
226	Electricity
227	Personal Property Taxes
228	Other
230	LONG-TERM DEBT
300	**CAPITAL OR EQUITY**
301	COMMON STOCK (CAPITAL)
302	RETAINED EARNINGS
303	WITHDRAWALS
400	**REVENUE**
401	BEVERAGES
402	Liquor
403	Beer
404	Wine
405	Other
406	FOOD
407	OTHER
500	**COST OF SALES**
501	BEVERAGES
502	Liquor
503	Beer
504	Wine
505	Other
506	FOOD
507	OTHER
600	**OTHER INCOME**
601	COVER CHARGES
602	GAMES AND COMMISSIONS
603	CASH DISCOUNTS
604	OTHER
700	**CONTROLLABLE EXPENSES**
701	SALARIES AND WAGES
702	Management
703	Employees
704	Other
710	EMPLOYEE BENEFITS
711	FICA
712	FUTA
713	State Unemployment Tax
714	Workers Compensation
715	Health Insurance
716	Other
720	DIRECT OPERATING EXPENSES

Table 16-1 Continued.

Acct. No.	Acct. Name	Acct. No.	Acct. Name
721	Glassware	784	Insurance—General
722	Cleaning	785	Commission on Credit Card Charges
723	Decorations	786	Cash Overages or Shortages
724	Bar Supplies	787	Security and Bank Pick-up Services
725	Guest Supplies	788	Bank Charges
726	Auto Expenses	789	Other
727	Licenses and Permits	790	REPAIRS AND MAINTENANCE
728	Other	791	Furniture and Fixtures
730	MUSIC AND ENTERTAINMENT	792	Equipment
731	Videos, Films, Tapes, Records	793	Refrigeration
732	Equipment Rentals	794	Heating and Air-conditioning
733	Royalties to ASCAP, BMI, SESAC	795	Electrical and Plumbing
734	Agents' Fees	796	Surface Treatments (walls, floors, etc.)
735	Other	797	Building and Grounds
740	MARKETING	798	Maintenance Contract Services (signs, elevators, etc.)
741	PROMOTION		
742	Travel Expenses	799	Auto
743	Entertainment Costs (Including free drinks to customers)		
744	Postage	800	**RENT AND OTHER OCCUPATION COSTS, INTEREST, AND DEPRECIATION**
745	Other		
750	ADVERTISING	801	RENT AND OTHER OCCUPATION COSTS
751	Newspapers	802	Rent—minimum or fixed
752	Magazines	803	Percentage of Rent
753	Direct Mail	804	Ground Rental
754	Outdoor	805	Equipment Rental
755	Radio and TV	806	Real Estate Taxes
756	Other	807	Personal Property Taxes
757	Preparation Costs	808	Other Taxes
758	Ad Agency Fees	809	Franchise Tax
759	Franchise Fees	810	Partnership or Corporation License Fees
760	PUBLIC RELATIONS	811	Insurance on Building and Contents
761	Community Projects	820	INTEREST
762	Donations	821	Notes Payable
765	RESEARCH	822	Long-term Debt
766	Travel Expenses	823	Other
767	Other Expenses	830	DEPRECIATION
770	UTILITIES	831	Buildings
771	Electrical	832	Amortization of Leasehold
772	Gas	833	Amortization of Leasehold Improvements
773	Water	834	Fixtures, Equipment and Furniture
774	Other Fuel		
775	Waste Removal	900	**INCOME TAXES**
780	ADMINISTRATION AND GENERAL EXPENSES		
781	Stationery and Office Supplies	901	FEDERAL
782	Postage	902	STATE
783	Telephone	903	LOCAL

of your assets and then subtracting all of your liabilities.

Journals are set up once the accounts are decided. Journals record similar transactions and group them together on a daily basis. In other words, a journal entitled "Purchases" would include separate transactions to buy liquor and glassware. This grouping makes it easier to see where money is spent. Each journal page is filled with entries of debits and credits and must be totaled. (See FIG. 16-2.) Pages will balance when all debits equal all credits posted. You should maintain the following journals:

- Cash receipts or sales
- Cash disbursements
- Purchases
- Sales tax
- Payroll

A General Journal should also be maintained to make adjustments on all the other journals. At the end of the month, all journal accounts are totaled and entered to the General Ledger, which serves as a summary of all accounts. Financial statements are then prepared from the General Ledger Accounts. The two most important financial statements are the income statement and the balance sheet. These will be discussed later in this chapter.

The best system of accounting for bars is called the *accrual method*. This provides for an immediate balance between income and expenses so as not to distort month-end figures. For example, accounts with most purveyors are usually billed in 30 days. If you buy $500 in liquor from a wholesaler on January 1st, you will not receive a bill until February 1st. If you make out an immediate check, your records would show a payment to the purveyor of $500 on February 1st. When using the accrual method in figuring month-end statements for January, however, the $500 would be counted as part of January's expenses because you derived income from this liquor in January. The same holds true for income that is delayed, such as credit card sales or house tabs. The income, for purposes of accrual accounting, is figured into profit statements in the month of the sale rather

ENTRY #	DATE	CHECK #	BEVERAGES				FOOD	BAR SUPPLIES	GLASSWARE	CLEANING SUPPLIES	DECORATIONS	GUEST SUPPLIES
			LIQ	BEER	WINE	OTHER						
1.												
2.												
3.												
4.												

(CONT'D)	ENTERTAINMENT				ADVERTISING				UTILITIES		
	MUSIC	FILM	VIDEO	EQUIP. RENTALS	NEWSP.	RADIO	TV	OUTDOOR	WATER	GAS	POWER
1.											
2.											
3.											
4.											

(CONT'D)	REPAIRS & MAINT.					
	FURNITURE	FIXTURES	REFRIG.	HEAT	AIR	EQUIP.
1.						
2.						
3.						
4.						

Fig. 16-2. *Purchase journal.*

than the month the payment for the credit card or house tab was actually received.

One rule of accrual accounting is that all income earned in a given year be included with that year's income account, even though payment could take place in the following year. Similarly, all expenses are deducted in the year you become liable, regardless of when you actually pay for them. The advantage of the accrual method is the costs of earning income are directly matched to the income earned in the year in which they take place. Your method of accounting and treatment of income and expenses should remain consistent year after year. The tax year or accounting period must also be the same. The IRS becomes suspicious when businesses change their accounting methods every year.

Daily records

Cash banks are prepared for each register. Each register should have a number (Register 1, Register 2, etc.) and a correspondingly numbered bag to be used only for that register. These bags can be obtained from your bank. Included in the register bag is a slip that verifies the starting amount of the bank. (Refer to FIG. 15-4.) At the end of the night, the bank is counted. The starting amount is then sub-tracted from the total of all the cash, vouchers, and checks. This is the amount of the cash deposit. Final sales totals are obtained from the registers.

Shortages or overages can be discovered by going through all the tickets—if you use a ticket system. You can verify that all tickets were rung properly. If there are no tickets, any overage in cash should be deposited and shortages noted in the effort to notice a pattern.

A Daily Sales Summary is then filled out as in FIG. 16-1. By using the Daily Sales Summary you have a one-page record of each day's sales and a running total of month and year-to-date figures. You will then enter the day's figures in the Cash Receipts Journal under their appropriate accounts. (See FIG. 16-3.)

When starting your business, open a separate bank account for the bar. Any monies paid out should be by means of a check written against this account with an accompanying receipt, invoice, or statement kept on file. Deposit all money and charge receipts into this account. A Cash Disbursements Journal is where all checks and purchases are recorded. (See FIG. 16-4.) When writing checks, be sure to note on the check and the stub the proper account number from your Chart of Accounts. Later, you will be able to make these entries in the Cash Disbursements Journal.

ENTRY #	DATE	CASH Dr	CREDIT CARD/Dr				ACCTS REC Dr	SALES/Cr					PROMO Cr	OVER/SHORTS Cr	ACCTS REC Cr
			AMX	M/C	VISA	OTHER		LIQ	BEER	WINE	OTHER	FOOD			
1.															
2.															
3.															
4.															

(CONT'D)	CREDIT CARDS/Cr			
	AMX	M/C	VISA	OTHER
1.				
2.				
3.				
4.				

Fig. 16-3. Cash receipts journal.

ENTRY #	DATE	PAYEE	CHECK #	AMOUNT	ACCT #	PURCHASES		DISCOUNTS	PAYROLL EXPENSE	W/HOLD TAXES	FICA	FICA TIPS	SWT	SDI	LOCAL TAXES	EMP. BENEFITS
						BEV.	FOOD									
1.																
2.																
3.																
4.																

(CONT'D)	DIRECT OP. EXP.	MUSIC & ENTERTAINMENT	UTILITIES	ADMIN. & GENERAL	REPAIRS & MAINT.	RENT & OCC. COSTS	GENERAL LEDGER
1.							
2.							
3.							
4.							

Fig. 16-4. Cash disbursements journal.

An accountant's column pad can be purchased at any office or stationery store. On this pad, label the columns with each of your accounts. When using a computer software accounting program each journal and its columns become a spreadsheet file. The information is the same, except when input into the computer, your data is stored on a disk rather than on a pad of paper. Using a computer speeds up the time required to gather reports, as the software programs record double entries for you, which enables you to have daily and cumulative reports.

Each check should be recorded in numerical order daily. If you must pay by cash, keep a receipt with an explanation to verify and describe the nature of the expense. Small amounts of cash for emergency purchases, such as ice or cream, should be taken from the cash register and the receipt or a petty cash voucher left in its place.

Don't comingle your personal funds with your business funds. Do not write any checks to cash; there will be no account to credit or debit. When making a personal withdrawal, write the check to yourself rather than to cash.

The purpose of any recordkeeping is to substantiate your income and losses. Government agencies examine your records and insist on accurate and complete documentation to support your tax returns. Keep your receipts, cancelled checks, invoices, bank deposit slips and other records in a safe place. Although certain records can be destroyed when the statute of limitations runs out, those that pertain to your tax returns can be called up at any time.

As previously discussed in Chapter 10, you must keep an accurate liquor inventory. This becomes critical at month-end when you determine costs and profits. It is also necessary to keep a separate Sales Tax Journal for all sales tax owed by recording the amounts collected daily with year-to-date totals. A journal of all house and credit card charges should be maintained by posting the dates charged and the dates the accounts were paid.

Payroll

Each employee must fill out and each employer keep on file an IRS W-4 form stating marital status and the number of exemptions claimed by the employee for tax withholding purposes. If a new employee does not have a social security number, request that he or she apply for one by filling out Form SS-5, available at any IRS or Social Security Administration office. The Employee Record is a form that capsulizes an employee's work and pay history. (See FIG. 16-5.)

Name ———————————— Social Security # ————————————

Address ————————————————————————————

Telephone ———————— Date of Birth ————————————

Employee I.D. # ———————— Position ————————————

1st Day of Employment ———————— Last Day Employed ————————

Reason for Leaving ————————————————————————

Number of Income Tax Exemptions ————————

In Case of Emergency Contact:

Name ———————————— Telephone ————————————

Address ————————————————————————————

WORK PERIOD		RATE OF PAY		HOURS WORKED		GROSS TOTAL PAY	TIPS REPORTED	WITHHOLDING					OTHER	TOTAL DEDUCTIONS	NET PAY
								FEDERAL		STATE		LOCAL			
BEGIN	END	REG	O.T.	REG	O.T.			FWT	FICA	SWT	SDI				

Fig. 16-5. Employee record.

By January 31 of each year or when employment ends, you are required to furnish each employee with a W-2 form. This form provides the totals of wages and salaries paid, tips reported, and total deductions withheld from wages for the previous year. This includes Federal Income Tax Withheld (FWT), Social Security Withheld (FICA), and where applicable, state income tax, disability or unemployment insurance, and local income taxes.

Each employer must file quarterly and yearly reports with payments to the Federal Internal Revenue Service and State Tax Boards. In addition, the social security taxes withheld from your employee's paychecks are matched by equal contributions that you as an employer pay. This is the Federal Unemployment Tax (FUT). These taxes finance the Social Security system. All payroll data is recorded in a Payroll Journal. (See FIG. 16-6.)

The IRS publishes an annual Employer's Tax Guide, Publication 15, which provides the formulas and tables for figuring taxes for both employees and employers. The guide also provides information concerning methods of payment by employers and highlights changes in any tax laws. All forms should be filed with the IRS unless otherwise stated. Important dates to remember are:

- January 31 or when employment ends—provide each employee with a

| ENTRY # | DATE | EMPLOYEE | FEDERAL | | | STATE | | LOCAL | FUTA | EMPLOYEE BENEFITS | OTHER |
			FICA	FWT	S.S.	SWT	SDI				

Fig. 16-6. *Payroll journal.*

W-2, Wage and Tax Statement. You must make a reasonable effort to deliver W-2 forms to persons no longer in your employ. You must keep any W-2 forms that cannot be delivered for four years. You should also file Form 940.

- February 28—file Form W-3, (Income Tax Withholding) Transmittal of Income and Tax Statements, with the Social Security Administration and include Copy A of all W-2 forms given to each employee. File Form 8027, Employer's Information Return of Tip Income and Allocated Tips.

- By April 30, July 31, October 31, and January 31—deposit Federal Unemployment Tax due if it is over $100. File Form 941, Employer's Quarterly Federal Tax Return or Form 941E, Quarterly Return of Withheld Federal Income Tax to pay any undeposited income and social security taxes.

An accurate system of payroll recordkeeping for each employee's hours should be established before training begins. There are no laws concerning how work hours are to be recorded. The use of a time clock and time cards, a sign-in sheet, or a computer register are the best ways.

If you use a time clock, the punch-in time is subtracted from the punch-out time. If meal breaks of at least a half hour are provided, the employee should go off and then back on the clock. A sign-in sheet should record all hours worked and breaks taken. Some computer registers have programs that allow employees to clock in and out right on the machine. These registers eliminate the need for manual payroll compilation and provide an instant readout of payroll costs.

Regardless of the method used, a manager should verify all hours recorded on a daily basis. These hour totals should then be transferred and recorded separately on a Weekly Payroll Summary and maintained as a permanent record. (See FIG. 16-7.)

If you detect inaccuracies with employees recording their work hours, hold a meeting. Perhaps your scheduling or the location of the time clock is the problem. Payroll records are examined by the Labor Department through a random audit or an employee complaint. If

POSITION	NAME	RATE	SUN	MON	TUE	WED	THU	FRI	SAT	HRS X RATE
BARTENDER										
SERVER										
DAILY TOTAL OF HOURS										WEEKLY TOTAL OF PAY
(WEEKLY TOTAL OF HOURS)										
WEEKLY TOTAL OF PAY ÷ WEEKLY TOTAL OF HOURS = AVERAGE HOURLY RATE OF PAY										

Fig. 16-7. *Weekly payroll summary.*

FROM ___ TO ___							
EMPLOYEE	POSITION	RATE OF PAY	HRS. WORKED	HRS. WORKED YTD	GROSS PAY	GROSS PAY YTD	
		REG / O.T.	REG / O.T.	REG / O.T.			
ALL EXPLOYEES TOTALS							
SALES THIS PERIOD ___ SALES YTD ___							
RATIO TO SALES THIS PERIOD ___ %		RATIO TO SALES YTD ___ %					

Fig. 16-8. Payroll costs.

PAYROLL COSTS

FROM ___ TO ___

SALES THIS PERIOD ___

	BUDGETED		SCHEDULED		ACTUAL	
	HRS.	X AVG. RATE	HRS.	AMOUNT	HRS.	AMOUNT
ADMINISTRATION						
MANAGERS						
ACCOUNTING						
BAR						
BARTENDERS						
SERVERS						
BAR BACKS						
CLEANERS						
DOOR						
CASHIER						
DOOR						
SECURITY						
FOOD						
PREP						
COOKS						
DISHWASHER						
TOTALS						
RATIO TO SALES		%		%		%

Fig. 16-9. Payroll costs.

they are deemed inaccurate, you have to reimburse all employees for back wages. This could run into thousands and thousands of dollars. Protect your business by maintaining accurate records.

The controlling of payroll expenses is a way to lower operating costs. Use Payroll Costs forms to compare budgeted costs against scheduled and actual costs. (See FIGS. 16-8 and 16-9.) The amount of payroll for budgeting and scheduling is obtained by averaging the hourly rate of pay for each employee in a department and multiplying this times the amount of hours. All dollar amounts are then divided by the sales figures, budgeted (calculated quarterly), scheduled (anticipated), and actual to obtain a percentage of payroll costs. These costs are used in monthly statements and as a basis for the next year's forecasts and budgets.

Payroll accounting is not a major problem for small bars with only a few employees. It can be quite time-consuming, however, when your bar grows. Many banks can compile all payroll records and issue employees' checks for a fee, of course. An account is established with this bank only for your payroll.

Tip reporting

In 1982, Congress required all bar and restaurant operators to provide information about their employees' tip income. Your employees must report all tips received to you by the 10th of the month for the previous month's tips. When their tips are less than $20 for the month, no tip reporting is required. Employees should report their tips on Form 4070, Employee's Report of Tips to Employer, or a similar form. This form should include the employee's name, address, Social Security number, period the tips reported cover, and the total amount of tips received. As an employer, you are required to collect income and social security taxes on all tips reported.

If you employ 10 or more employees on a typical business day, you might have to allocate tips at the end of the year. If the employees as a group do not report tips totaling 8 percent of the gross receipts of your operation, then you must allocate to tipped employees the difference between 8 percent of the gross receipts and the total of tips the employees reported. You can base your allocation on hours worked, on individual gross receipts, or any method based on a good-faith agreement between you and your employees. Do not withhold any taxes on allocated tips.

If your employees feel tips in the bar average less than 8 percent of the gross sales, you as a manager or owner, should consider making a request from the Internal Revenue Service that the rate be lowered. This rate can be reduced by the Internal Revenue Service District Director to best reflect the tipping percentage of your area. The rate will not go below 5 percent, however. If the reported gross sales of your bar do not coincide with reported tips by your employees, be prepared for an audit by the IRS.

Financial statements

If you have been keeping proper records on a daily basis, the month-end, quarterly, or year-end statements should be very easy to prepare. Whenever you close an accounting period, you will use the General Journal to make any adjustments or corrections. (See FIG. 16-10.) The General Journal is where changes in the price of liquors or supplies should be noted. Certain items paid or prepaid annually, such as insurance, taxes, licenses, and fees, can be distributed for the monthly or quarterly accounting period. Depreciation or amortization of equipment and property should be applied to the proper accounts. This provides a more accurate reflection of your true operating expenses.

ENTRY #		ACCOUNT #	MONTH	
			Dr	Cr
1.	Cost of Beverage Inventory To Reverse Last Month's Entry			
2.	Beverage Inventory Cost of Beverage To Reflect Current Inventory			
3.	Direct Expenses – Glassware Provision for Replacement To Charge Expenses for Use During this Period			
4.	Depreciation Accumulated Depreciation To Adjust Portion of Cost for Bldg. or Equip., etc., for this Month			
5.	Accrued Salaries + Wages Management Bar To Reverse Entry for Prior Month			

Fig. 16-10. Sample general journal.

The *income* or *profit and loss* (P&L) statement is a summary of revenue and expenses for any accounting period as derived from your journals. (See FIG. 16-11.) This summary is used to arrive at a figure called net income or profit. To determine this, the total cost of goods and services provided is subtracted from total revenue to determine gross profit. Your operating expenses, which consist of controllable expenses (payroll, utilities, advertising, maintenance, etc.), is then subtracted from gross profit to obtain a figure called *gross operating profit*. From this, subtract fixed expenses (rent, property taxes, insurance, etc.), interest, and depreciation. The figure arrived at is your net profit before deducting income taxes.

To determine your income taxes on a period basis, project the sales for a year and then look up your tax in a federal and state income tax booklet. Subtract income taxes and this bottom line figure is either your *net profit* or *loss*. If you are unhappy with the bottom line, some changes in your operation are in order. Maybe you feel that increased advertising or entertainment will generate business or that the prices of your drinks are too low. Perhaps you see where expenses can be reduced. It may take some experimentation to increase profits. Be patient and ask employees for their input.

INCOME STATEMENT			
FROM ________ TO ________			
TOTAL SALES		AMOUNTS	%
LIQUOR ________			
BEER ________			
WINE ________		________	100%
LESS COST OF BEVERAGE SOLD			
	LIQ BEER WINE		
OPENING INVENTORY	___ ___ ___		
+ PURCHASES	___ ___ ___		
− CLOSING INVENTORY	___ ___ ___		
= TOTAL		− ________	___%
GROSS PROFIT		= ________	
PLUS OTHER INCOME		+ ________	
LESS OPERATING (CONTROLLABLE) EXPENSES			
PAYROLL	________		
DIR. OP. EXPENSES	________		
MUSIC & ENTERTAINMENT	________		
MARKETING	________		
UTILITIES	________		
ADMIN. & GENERAL	________		
REPAIRS & MAINT.	________		
OTHER	________		
TOTAL	________	− ________	___%
GROSS OPERATING PROFIT OR INCOME BEFORE RENT, INTEREST & DEPRECIATION		= ________	
LESS FIXED OVERHEAD (NONCONTROLLABLE) EXPENSES			
RENT	________		
TAXES	________		
INSURANCE	________		
INTEREST	________		
DEPRECIATION	________		
AMORTIZATION	________		
TOTAL	________	− ________	___%
NET INCOME BEFORE INCOME TAXES		= ________	___%
LESS INCOME TAXES		− ________	___%
EQUALS NET INCOME OR PROFIT (THE BOTTOM LINE)		= ________	___%

Fig. 16-11. *Income statement.*

CURRENT ASSETS		CURRENT LIABILITIES	
CASH	________	ACCOUNTS PAYABLE	________
ACCOUNTS RECEIVABLE	________	NOTES PAYABLE	________
DEPOSITS & PREPAID EXPENSES	________	PAYROLL PAYABLE	________
INVENTORY	________	TAXES PAYABLE	________
TOTAL CURRENT ASSETS	________	TOTAL CURRENT LIABILITIES	________
FIXED ASSETS		LONG-TERM LIABILITIES	
LAND	________	LONG-TERM NOTES PAYABLE	________
BUILDING	________	TOTAL LIABILITIES	________
LEASEHOLD & IMPROVEMENTS LESS AMORTIZATION	________	EQUITY OR NET WORTH	
EQUIPMENT	________	PARTNER A	________
FIXTURES & FURNITURE LESS DEPRECIATION	________	PARTNER B	________
TOTAL FIXED ASSETS	________	RETAINED EARNINGS	________
DEFERRED EXPENSES		TOTAL EQUITY	________
PRE-OPENING	________	TOTAL LIABILITIES + EQUITY	________
IMPROVEMENTS IN PROGRESS	________		
TOTAL	________		
OTHER ASSETS			
AMOUNT PAID FOR GOODWILL	________		
COST OF BAR LICENSE	________		
DEPOSIT ON FRANCHISE CONTRACT	________		
TOTAL	________		
TOTAL ASSETS	________		

Fig. 16-12. *Balance sheet.*

The final financial statement necessary for your business is a Balance Sheet, which is prepared monthly, quarterly, and annually. (See FIG. 16-12.) The total amount of assets (what is owned) must equal all liabilities (what is owed) plus the equity and retained earnings of the business. This statement reflects the current financial status of your business. Your current assets include cash on hand and in the bank, your inventory, and any deposits and prepaid expenses. Fixed assets are the land and buildings the bar owns, leases and improvements, all equipment, fixtures, and furniture, less any depreciation. Your current liabilities are your accounts, taxes and wages payable, outstanding loans, rent, utilities, and any long-term debts. An owner's equity is the original capital contribution to start the business. Retained earnings represent profits that are kept in the business and have not been withdrawn or distributed to shareholders or owners.

The balance sheet is vital if you ever want to expand your bar, sell it, or borrow money against it. In order to obtain a loan, the bank takes into consideration what it calls the current ratio or the liquidity ratio. What the bank needs to know is if you sold everything you have, would it pay all your bills? To arrive at this ratio, divide current assets by current liabilities. When the ratio is high, the business is believed to be in a strong position to meet its current payments.

Depending upon the amount of time required to maintain your records, you might want to hire a part-time bookkeeper or a full-time accountant. If you do choose to have someone assist in the preparation of your records, periodically have your books audited by an outside accounting firm. This provides a check to ensure against fraud or embezzlement.

17
Entertainment

When you open a bar, you are selling not only liquor, but also a form of entertainment and recreation. People come to your place because they like the environment, the staff, and the drinks. When you add entertainment, you are providing an additional attraction to enlarge your clientele and your profits. Many types of entertainment have remained popular over the years. Clubs still offer games, dancing, and live acts. Technology has created new forms of entertainment, such as video games and music videos. It pays to utilize the latest forms of entertainment when they are appropriate to your concept.

Games

The oldest and cheapest form of entertainment is games. Games provide a fun way to bring people together and have them interact. Any size bar, from the corner pub to the large capacity nightclub, can benefit from the addition of games. Some bars have pool tables and dart boards, others have coin-operated games like pinball or simulated golf. You can develop leagues and sponsor competitions for any game. Your business will definitely increase because you provide a reason for people to stay longer and a reason for new patrons to come. You can charge for the use of game equipment or provide it free. (See FIGS. 17-1 and 17-2.)

Many standard board games such as backgammon and chess experience periodic rises and falls in popularity. Just be aware that any surge in popularity (often due to a movie glamourizing a game) comes with a rapid waning of interest. However, this renewed interest can give a whole new aura to a game. The movie, *The Color of Money* in the late 1980s created posh cocktail and pool bars by eliminating an old stereotype and bringing it to the attention of more upscale customers.

Coin-operated equipment, whether they are jukeboxes, pinball machines, video games, basketball, or pool, earn more money the closer they are to your bar or the pathway with the most traffic. Putting games in a dark corner or unused room means money lost. Games don't have to block traffic, just be highly visible and accessible.

New technology has replaced yesterday's pinball machines with today's video games and their pop, sizzle, and special effects. Video games are becoming more sophisticated every day. Video games are coin-operated and come

Fig. 17-1. *The pool and Ping-Pong tables at Mays' Sports Pub in Tarzana, California.*

Fig. 17-2. *Dart boards receive a lot of play, particularly during tournaments.* The Wild Bull, Northridge, California

in stand-up or tabletop models. Although video machines can be purchased, leasing is advisable. When you lease a machine, the profits are shared with the leasing company, which will also service your machines. You might have a lease that permits the exchange of machines every six months, so you always have the latest games. The typical split between the bar operator and vendor of these games is 50/50. Sometimes, it is better to take a lower cut, such as 40/60 or develop a sliding scale based on revenue earned, to enable your vendor to provide you with the latest games more frequently.

Promoting coin-op games can be fun, exciting, and drive your business to higher profits. A good way to start and to generate interest is to run a tournament within your bar for your patrons. As you become more familiar with the process, you can expand the excitement by forming leagues to play other bars. You can then create an Olympic Decathalon or Ironman/Ironwoman competition.

You can also stage contests. If you have 10 different types of games (all pinball, or a combination of pinball, pool, darts, basketball, foosball, etc.), then your contestants play each game. The highest scoring individual wins a grand prize, with smaller prizes for second and third places.

Staging a contest of this nature encourages players to practice games they do not ordinarily play. Contestants will often bring their friends to watch as they compete. You can then vary the contest for team plays, leagues, men's, women's, and co-ed teams. Be sure to make it clear to all contestants that they pay for their games in both practice and competition. You can also charge a $5 or $10 entry fee to help cover the cost of the prizes. Donate part of the money to a charity or cause for added publicity. Work with your vendor to share costs in this promotion.

Many of the participatory games, such as free-throw basketball toss, video golf, or football, can be used for halftime or commercial break competitions during televised games. The prize can be a pair of tickets to the next professional team's home game.

Indoor golf simulators are money-makers. The technology has improved so that the most famous courses in the world can be seen and played from the confines of your bar. The simulator consists of a large rectangular padded playing area with a large screen at the enclosed end. A single player or foursome can play, with a full round of golf taking about an hour to play. You charge playing customers by the hour. The advantage of this game is that weather is never a problem.

One of the fastest-growing areas of coin-op games is video poker games, such as blackjack and keno. As more states look to increase their budgets, many states have legalized video gambling. Gambling games are extremely profitable. The states exercise strict controls over their usage, and often limit the number of games per establishment to 20. These are called mini-casinos. All games are monitored and tied together by a central computer at the state level. A percentage of the revenue goes to the state, usually to support its educational programs.

Many bars have other gambling games and tables installed. Typically, blackjack tables are set up on certain nights of the week as an ongoing promotion. Dealers encourage play where players buy script or chips and play for fun and practice. Practice as entertainment is not illegal. These tables are great conversation pieces and encourage social interaction and drinking.

Television and video

In the fifties, television was a new medium, and many people were introduced to it at their neighborhood bar. Before everyone could afford a set, bars made a lot of money attracting customers to watch their TVs. Today, a color set is a standard fixture in bars.

In the seventies, large-screen TVs made their debut. The TV's electronic image is projected onto a special screen similar to a movie screen. The projector can be a mobile floor model or mounted to the ceiling for permanency. The screen can also be purchased in a collapsible floor model or installed permanently on the wall with a remote-controlled motor that moves it up and down. Many bars that bought these projectors still attract standing-room-only crowds, particularly for sporting events.

In the eighties, satellite dishes began appearing on the tops of buildings housing bars (FIGS. 12-3 and 4-2.) A satellite earth station (a dish and an amplifier) allows you to tune into the numerous international communication satellites in stationary orbit above the earth. There are hundreds of channels to choose from, including all the cable and television networks and the "feeds" beamed to their local affiliates.

Sporting events that are blacked out on local television channels can be received by satellite earth stations, along with favorite TV shows, long before they are rebroadcast on local stations. Legends (Long Beach, California), a sports-oriented bar, has four large screens linked to four dishes, each showing a different sporting event from around the world. From the tiniest neighborhood bar to the fanciest nightclub, satellite dishes have opened up a whole new world of instant global communications.

In the nineties, sophisticated interactive sports and other games are played internationally through satellite channels. Players in bars across several nations compete for prizes and measure their skills in games ranging from trivia to sports. Bars sign up for these subscription satellite services.

The NTN Network provides portable handheld devices that allow bar players to compete against 20,000 other players in bars across the United States, Canada, and Europe.

(See FIG. 17-3.) Two TVs are required, one to broadcast the sports game live, and the other to carry the questions and answers.

In addition, NTN helps you produce spots with your bar's logo to be aired. You can also sell spots to local advertisers that will be shown only in your bar. Patrons become hooked on this game, spending more time and dollars on drinks and food.

Many worldwide sporting events can still be picked up directly from satellites. However, as the satellite industry has matured, many of these major events occurring within the United States are being scrambled, requiring pay-per-view hookups that decode and unscramble the signal. Bar owners now have a choice of several networks that can feed them the channels they desire. From professional sports, movies, and concerts, the choice of satellite programming is varied, offering alternatives your patrons can't see at home. Some of these services offer ambient video that can be played during various dayparts. During lunch, for example, you show video clips of the season's highlights as teasers for an upcoming game, along with bloopers, news, and interactive bar games.

Unlike TV sets that have tuners and antennas to pick up outside signals, video monitors only receive direct signals from a player or a camera. Both TV sets and video monitors can be used to show prerecorded tapes and discs. However, the resolution of a video monitor is superior because the signal is direct rather than secondhand, and the manufacturers maintain higher standards. You might want to have one TV and several video monitors.

A wide array of television programs, motion pictures, and music videos is available on videocassettes and laser discs. They can be purchased or inexpensively rented at record and video stores everywhere. Be aware that licensing fees might be necessary. Just as you need to pay music licensing fees to ASCAP or

Fig. 17-3. *QB1 players interact with a live televised football game. Players are ranked locally and nationally and winners receive awards.* NTN Network

BMI to play music, television and motion picture companies are protecting their copyrighted material.

The owners of Private Eyes (New York) designed their club just for video, with 34 monitors, each showing something different. Their library of material is programmed by a video jockey (VJ), which is similar to a DJ. In addition, they have a complete recording studio in which to create original tapes. (See FIG. 17-4.)

One of the inherent qualities of television is that it still mesmerizes its audience. A single monitor in a bar provides a focal point of interest. When many sets are used, they are spaced every 20 to 30 degrees around the room, providing everyone with a view of a monitor. With several monitors, one video does not have to be played through them all. Each monitor can display a separate image. Images can be programmed to move from one monitor to the next. This breaks up the mesmerizing effect. Singles bars place monitors opposite each other to stimulate interaction among the clientele.

You can place several cameras throughout your bar or dance floor and play these live

Fig. 17-4. Custom-designed video control booth overlooks the club and has eight video decks and full audio/video mixing for optimum sound quality for dancing. Private Eyes

over your TV and video monitors. For added excitement, have a roving camera/sound team. Interview customers waiting outside, as well as those inside and on the dance floor. Have your employees generate energy with their live interviews. Save the best of your live recordings to be played back at a later date to promote your bar or special nights.

Sound and video systems

Sound systems are used to amplify the signals from commercial radio stations and prerecorded material, and also for announcers, paging, and live acts. Music can be background or foreground.

Background music is played softly so people can converse. When the music is intended to dominate the environment, it is considered foreground music, and a different sound system is needed.

A background music system can simply be a stereo tuner, an amplifier, and speakers. The music usually comes from a local radio station. A tape deck can be added, providing the option of playing prerecorded tapes or discs. Continuous play tapes require special tape decks, which can be leased from background music companies. These companies also package tapes with music individually programmed to your specifications. You can request, for example, that the music be mellow during the early morning and afternoon hours, with the tempo increasing during the late afternoon and evening.

New tapes can be leased for a minimal fee

each month. When you rent tapes from background music companies, the rental fee includes payment of copyright royalties. Federal copyright law protects the rights of music composers and publishers by requiring royalty payments every time their music is played in a "public performance for profit." Playing background music without paying that fee is considered an infringement on the copyright law, because patrons pay for their drinks and for the environment, which includes the music.

Any time copyrighted music is performed by a live act or prerecorded material is played by a DJ, royalty payments must be made. The rights to most recorded music in the United States are owned by three associations, The American Society of Composers, Authors, and Publishers (ASCAP), Broadcast Music Incorporated (BMI), and the Society of European Stage Authors and Composers (SESAC).

There are two exceptions to the copyright law. If you rent a coin-operated jukebox and do not charge an admission or cover fee to enter your establishment, you are exempt. Or, if you are a small bar and broadcast music received on a "home" quality radio set and speakers, you are exempt. The moment you use commercial receivers or other apparatus normally found in a commercial sound system, you are liable for royalty payments to ASCAP, BMI, and SESAC. Payments are minimal, however, and you should make them willingly.

Foreground music systems can be quite sophisticated. Live entertainment such as bands, shows, and revues require a Public Address (PA) system with different qualities from one that plays back prerecorded albums and videos. A dance music system emphasizes the deep bass frequencies; the dialogue between the drum beat and the bass guitar. Dancers key into the "down beat." The high treble ranges that give music its sizzle and liveness are also important to a dance music system. Both the deep bass and high treble responses

are absent in PA systems. When the sound system is right, no one can resist moving to the music and getting out on the dance floor. That is what you want to achieve with a dance club.

The components of each system must be individually matched to the cubic footage of the dance floor to attain undistorted high-quality sound at the volume level used. Power is not everything. Clean sound is comfortable, while distorted sound rings and causes ear fatigue. A poorly designed system is quickly noticed by patrons. The design and installation of sound, lighting, and video equipment is best left to professionals who specialize in nightclub, stage and concert systems. (See FIG. 17-5.)

Regardless of the quality of the system installed, the DJ/VJ makes the entertainment happen. The wrong DJ/VJ is no more than a talking jukebox. The "programming" of any music must appeal to your clientele. Some owners prefer to give their DJ/VJ a playlist, thereby tightly controlling the music selections. Eight fast songs followed by one slow song or only fast songs is one way to keep the energy level high. This way, owners can distinguish their music from that of other clubs, just as radio stations try to have a sound or musical format that is different from their competitors'.

The intention is to play only music that appeals to the targeted audience. Other owners allow the DJ/VJ to mix the music to suit each crowd. Some owners want the DJ/VJ to talk to the crowd between songs, while others would rather have one long uninterrupted musical beat.

When video is used, two types of images can be put on the screen: background visuals and foreground visuals. Background visuals, similar to background music, are meant to provide an unrelated visual accompaniment to a record being played. The visuals come from your library of tapes. When visuals are used in this manner, they are often called *wallpaper* or

Fig. 17-5. Simple truss lighting system hangs over the dance floor and is used for cocktail service during happy hour. Baxter's, Manhattan Beach, California

ambient video. Foreground visuals, typically music videos of entertainers performing, are made to be played while people watch or dance to the music. The latest trends in music and the hottest hits can be determined by listening to radio stations and by reading the music industry trade magazines. *Billboard* magazine is the best for records and videos.

Services specializing in assembling compilation videotapes for dance clubs can compile tapes to suit your specific needs. The sound on these tapes has been enhanced so the quality matches that of the commercial equipment it will be played on.

Dance clubs particularly like using closed circuit remote-controlled color cameras. With these cameras controlled by the VJ, shots of the crowd on the dance floor can be displayed on the screens. The audience becomes part of the show. Close-ups can key in on contestants, members of live bands, and MCs, and the system also doubles as a security system.

How to hire and work with a DJ

When you are new to the dance club business, hiring a DJ can be intimidating. The easy way out is to lure a successful DJ with a following from his or her existing job with equal or higher pay. Watching a DJ work is the best way to "interview." Invite the DJ to demonstrate one night with pay so you receive feedback from your patrons in your club. Listen to a tape if you have no alternative.

Notice how the DJ handles the crowd. Your DJ should be able to move the crowd on and off the dance floor with his or her choice of music. Also notice how the DJ interacts with the crowd. Does she talk to the crowd, against it, or not at all? When she makes a promotional announcement, it should be simple, short, and to the point (no more than 30 seconds), speaking over the instrumental portion of the song rather than the vocals, and speaking at an understandable rate. What a DJ has to say can stimulate your customers to action.

The DJ is an integral part of your dance bar's atmosphere and promotional efforts; therefore, your DJ should be excellent at plugging your drink specials and promotions. Your DJ will motivate your crowd to buy drinks and come back tomorrow night and next week.

Find out about your DJ's background. Often, he or she is a musician, singer, or dancer and has been a mobile DJ or broadcast announcer before working in nightclubs. Qualifications that are highly desirable are experience in advertising, sales, marketing, and promotions.

DJs are constantly updating their music collections. They should be reading *Billboard* magazine weekly to keep abreast of top-selling songs, and the latest trends in all music formats: country, rock, soul, jazz, and Latin. Music videos are also charted.

Typically, DJs bring their own music collection into your club to play on your equipment. In some clubs, the owners purchase the recordings or give their DJs a monthly budget for new music.

An excellent way to see how your DJ performs is to spend a night in the DJ booth observing how he mixes music, interacts with customer requests, and works the crowd. Keeping your sound equipment in top repair and having standby equipment in case of a breakdown can save you thousands of dollars in lost income if your system goes down. The extra equipment is insurance against such failures.

Include your DJ in your advertising and promotion meetings for their valuable input and ideas. Your DJ will be actively involved so it is important to make him feel a part of the planning process from the beginning. It is also a good way to let him in on the strategy behind your promotions so he can do his part effectively.

The mixing of music and songs is an art. It should be done with grace, no harsh changes, and the transition should be seamless. The technique of mixing songs by beats, one song blending with another, happens when the DJ mixes the two together using a BPM (beats per minute) measure. The steady rise in energy and pace on your dance floor comes from slowly increasing the BPM.

The choice of music is determined more by what your crowd desires than your own personal taste. If you do not give your dance crowd the music they want to hear, they will find a place that does. Thus, keeping current with entertainment and new music trends is imperative in the dance club business. Above all, you must remember you are in the entertainment business, which is constantly changing. Be adaptable.

Lighting systems

Bars with entertainment require special lighting systems. They can be anything from a simple spotlight at the back of the bar focused on the entertainer, to a bank of colored lights suspended above a stage, to sophisticated lighting and special effects over a dance floor. Your lighting should match your concept.

A small bar with a single entertainer does not need a complicated system. Dance clubs, however, may need all of the special effects money can buy. Often in dance clubs, the dollar amount spent for a sound system is at least doubled for the lighting system. The trend in dance clubs is always towards the latest in technological effects, which is part of their appeal. A lighting operator is required to manipulate all of the effects in time to the music being played. Both the DJ/VJ and the lightman can operate out of one booth. (See FIG. 17-6.) Special neon, laser, and aurora lights can be used. Fog and confetti machines also add to the lighting person's arsenal of special effects. Lights can be placed on the ceiling, walls, within the dance floor, and suspended out in the room for a total environmental effect. Special effects are not limited to the eye-popping, but also can be soft, subtle, and romantic. Lighting in combination with music, can create an infinite variety of moods and emotions.

Fantasia West's DJ/VJ booth rises and lowers beneath a stage for live acts or additional seating with tables. When lowered, closed-circuit TVs with cameras on the dance floor let the DJ watch and interact with the crowd (FIG. 17-7).

Fig. 17-6. Fantasia DJ booth is inside the spaceship and overlooks the dance floor.

Fig. 17-7. Fantasia West's DJ/VJ booth has closed-circuit TVs with cameras.

Live entertainment

Your entertainment could be a singer in the corner or a live band that has its own stage and dressing rooms. Your acts might never change, or they could change every night of the week. The concept and clientele of your bar will dictate the type of entertainment that will work best (see FIG. 17-8). In a show lounge, a group can play for periods of up to two hours at a time. In a cabaret lounge with numerous groups going on stage, each act might have only 15 minutes to play.

Generally, your entertainment will play for 45 minutes and then take a 15-minute break. That is called a set. Usually, a group will play three or four sets a night. The method of payment varies. If your act is always the same, it might be on salary. In some cases, the group receives a percentage of or all of the door charges in lieu of a set fee. The group

Fig. 17-8. Small stage and dance area at a brewpub. During the day, the large-screen TV is on for patrons enjoyment of sporting games and news.

The Brewhouse Grill, Santa Barbara, California

could also receive a percentage of bar sales. With the proper promotion and advertising, allow at least one month—preferably three—to see if your entertainment pays for itself in increased sales. (See FIG. 17-9A and B.)

The more elaborate your entertainment, the more facilities you need. Large floor shows, revues, and concert lounges need stages, dressing rooms, and separate restrooms for the entertainers. Consider having a ticket booth for advance sales (see FIG. 17-10). You will also need a backstage area for delivery of equipment and coordination of sets, lighting, and sound booths.

Your entertainment does not have to be limited to nighttime shows. Many bars start their entertainment in the early afternoon with dancing, a piano bar, or a jazz group. As the crowd changes, the entertainment can change to stand-up comedians or magic acts. In fact, you might not need a separate entertainment area at all. A small bar could have a magician, astrologer, or palmist travel from table-to-table demonstrating her talents.

There are certain restrictions on the age of entertainers. If they are under the legal drinking age but over eighteen, depending on local ordinances, they might be able to play, provided no alcohol is served in the area they are using, such as the stage.

A hybrid of live entertainment and video exists in karaoke video sing-alongs. *Karaoke* means empty orchestra in Japanese, where karaoke bars originated in the 1970s. Through a laser video disc, one of your customers chooses a song and then sings along while viewing a music video. The video features on-screen lyrics with visuals while supplying the background vocals and sound tracks. The lead vocal is missing, being supplied by the customer singing. A karaoke jockey or KJ gets the crowd involved and sings a few tunes him-or herself to show your crowd how it is done.

All types of music are represented on karaoke discs. Its appeal is widespread and attracts a diverse age group from 21 to 60. Everyone loves to sing, whether good or bad. Either charge at the door or charge a nominal fee of $1 or $2 a song. You can create audio- and videotapes of each performance and sell them to the singers. It is a fun-filled time for everyone involved.

When hiring live talent, view the band, trio, or single performer yourself. Never take someone else's word that the talent is great. See for yourself. If that is not possible, ask for a videotape to judge their performance and crowd response. An audiotape is useful to determine if their music format is something you would like to investigate further. Judging talent solely on an audiotape can be dangerous. The tape was probably made in a recording studio under

Fig. 17-9A & B. Comparison of a bar without entertainment and a bar with
entertainment.

The Sail Loft, Laguna Beach, California

Fig. 17-10. *Ticket booth for advanced sales at The Hop.*

ideal conditions using extra singers and musicians. The sound of the tape versus a live performance could be totally different.

When booking entertainment through a talent agent, the agent receives a commission from the entertainers' fee. You have the final decision on who will play in your bar, not an agent. Write up a contract specifying price, the number of performers to appear (specify those you viewed at a performance date or in a video), the time the band or performer will play, the type of music to be played, the length of a set, the length of breaks, and terms to cancel the contract.

Ask a band how much it will cost first, rather than revealing your budget (which becomes the price you will pay). Often, a band without an agent will cost less because it is not paying an agent's fee. Another source for entertainment is your local musicians' union. Sometimes, it is advantageous to allow the

band to advertise and collect the cover charges in lieu of paying it a fee. Your club then becomes a showcase for bands, each developing its own loyal followings.

One trend is for bar owners to turn over a slow night of the week to a local promoter. The promoter has an extremely large mailing list and loyal crowd. The promoter advertises and collects the door charges, with the bar making its money on liquor sales. A successful promoter might also want a percentage of bar sales.

The advantage to a bar owner of using a promoter is that it will cost you nothing to try. The promoter will bring in his or her own DJ or group of DJs, often mixed with live bands, each playing music that is not heard in the typical club atmosphere. The promoter will attract a particular type of clientele who would normally not come to your bar. The excitement for this crowd is the newness of the music and the different places they go to hear it and dance. These customers of the promoter are hard-core dancers. Outside promoters can revitalize slow nights.

Many bars have turned their business completely around by adding entertainment. Your choice of entertainment can also change your clientele. The key to entertainment is not the expense or the amount of space you can devote to it, however, but whether it enhances your concept and your profits.

18

Food service

Food has been served in taverns for hundreds of years. Today, the majority of bars serve food to attract customers at lunch and during the early evening. Snacks can be offered free or for sale. Food also buffers the effects of drinking too much alcohol and is often promoted as the Happy Hour special instead of reduced drink prices. Your customers will drink for longer periods of time when food is available. You may find it profitable to serve food throughout the day.

Seriously consider all the reasons why you should serve food and what you will gain before you make your first purchases. Food can be used to supplement your bar sales. It can be a profit center, or an inexpensive addition to round out what you have to offer your clientele. Food can be served only during private parties and special occasions. Food can also be a way to expand your customer base by letting your customers have lunch, dinner, happy hour, and late-night bites. Your food service should be consistent with your overall concept. If your place is fun and offbeat, then your food choices should be the same.

If you have food for sale, let your customers know. Menus should be given to each customer as they are seated or when a server

approaches. In a less formal atmosphere, it is important to have menus at each table, on table tents, on blackboards, and do not forget your drink napkins. (See FIG. 18-1.) Additional ways to promote your food are signs, neon blackboards, and announcements by your DJ, over your music system through prerecorded commercials, and over your TV monitors through commercials or moving messages running along the bottom of the screen. Impress upon your staff the need to sell food as well as drinks by suggesting appetizers. Appetizer sales can increase as much as 25–40 percent when drink napkins are used. (See FIG. 18-2.)

Offer special prices by combining food items with drinks. A glass of wine, beer, or a well drink can be combined with a small pizza, zucchini strips, or a cheese and fruit platter for a price less than paying for the two separately. Beer and more sour-tasting drinks go well with spicy foods, pizzas, pastas, and fried cheeses and vegetables. Wines complement cheeses, fruits, and certain desserts. Sweet drinks seek out lighter salads and sandwiches. Servers need to be trained to suggest appropriate food items with drinks.

An excellent way to introduce your cus-

Fig. 18-1. Sloan's funny and entertaining food menu includes some items named after local businesses and customers.

I N I T I A L   E N T R E E S

SUNDAY BUFFET

9:00am - 2:00pm

(all you can eat)

Options

Corner Coors & Corrales Rd.
897-2656

Liquid Assets

6910 Montgomery NE
881-6476

SHRIMP COCKTAIL
4 Large Shrimp cooked in Spices
and Beer. Served with Cocktail
Sauce and Lemon.

SUPER NACHOS
Chile, Jalapenos, Cheese,
Guacamole, Sour Cream,Lettuce,
and Tomatoes on a bed of
Tortilla Chips.

NACHOS
Tortilla Chips covered with melted
Jack Cheese and sliced Jalapenos.

CEVICHE
Shrimp and Scallops marinated in
Lime Juice with Chile, Avacado,
Cilantro, and Tomato.

DEEP FRIED VEGETABLES
Fresh Vegetables, delicately
battered, served with sauce.
Zucchini, Mushrooms, or
Combinations.

CALAMARI
Fried and served with Cocktail
Sauce and Lemon.

GUACAMOLE
Served with Tortilla Chips.

I N I T I A L   E N T R E E S

Fig. 18-2. Print your bar appetizer menu on drink napkins.

tomers to your food items is to pass out samples. You could surprise a table by bringing them an appetizer with their first round of drinks, or walk through the bar with several food choices giving them away as samples. Displaying your food items works particularly well with a raw seafood bar. Place your shellfish, shrimp, and oysters on ice. If you serve a Happy Hour buffet, include your bar menu foods from time-to-time as a way for your cus-

tomers to sample these items. Label them as available appetizers or menu items. Eye-appealing photographs on table tents can add to your sales. Promoting food sales is not any different than promoting drinks, and the cumulative effect of all your efforts will add up.

Your menu needs to be creative and fun. Look at the descriptions of J. Sloan's food menu (see FIG. 18-3). It's wacky, interesting, entertaining, and makes you want to try a bite. You also

Elephant Bar Nachos

As part of our Fajitas Fest we're serving up the best nachos you've ever tasted...probably better than you've ever imagined!

Melted Jack and cheddar cheese, tomatoes, black olives, jalapeños, guacamole, sour cream and salsa.

Enough for the whole herd.

Only $4.95

Save $1

Fig. 18-3. *Part of The Elephant Bar's table tent that uses amusing artwork and words to help sell appetizers.*

get the impression that the portions are large and priced within reason. Menus can be printed on oars, balls, buckets, bags, cups, paper napkins, and even employee's shirts! Be creative.

Based upon its purpose, your menu can be planned to keep the types of food consistent with your overall theme. Serving champagne and caviar may not be appropriate in a beer bar, but sausage sandwiches and barbequed chicken and ribs are. In a brewpub, wood-fired pizzas and specialty items such as fresh-ground top sirloin hamburgers and armadillo eggs (jalapenos stuffed with cheese and deep-fried) (see FIG. 18-4) would make sense to a clientele looking for unique and unusual items.

The amount of equipment and space required to prepare food increases with the complexity of the food served. The Health Department must issue a permit before any food can be served. Health inspectors examine food preparation, display, and storage areas to ensure codes for cleanliness and safety are being followed. All equipment, available through restaurant suppliers, should be commercial quality.

The preparation of all food must be consistent to ensure quality and fulfill your customers' expectations of receiving the same product one day, one month, or one year later. Use the same brands, cuts, sizes and degree of freshness for every purchase. Prepare a recipe card that includes:

- Menu name of item.
- List of ingredients to be purchased.
- Where and how they are stored (in the walk-in refrigerator, dry goods shelf, freezer).
- How item is prepared and steps involved (thaw, then cut to size and grill, etc.).
- How long to cook.
- Method of cooking or preparation.
- Seasoning and garnishes.
- A photograph of how the item should look on the plate.

Enforce consistency for quality, and periodically review your menu to ensure items are selling. Delete as necessary and add new items based on customer requests.

Packaged snacks

Peanuts, popcorn, pretzels, chips, and crackers are popular munchies. Make sure they are fresh and crunchy. They can be served in

MANHATTAN BEACH BREWING COMPANY

Appetizers

-Armadillo Eggs-
Mild jalapenos stuffed with cheddar cheese, breaded, and deep fried. Served with our ranch dressing. $3.95

-Buffalo Wings-
Large drumettes deep fried and smothered in a Louisiana hot sauce. Served with a side of ranch dressing and celery sticks. $4.45

-Zucchini Strips-
Fresh Zucchini dipped in batter and deep fried. Served with our ranch dressing. $3.95

-Seasoned Curly Fries-
Basket of seasoned fries. $2.45

-Onion Rings-
Sweet onion rings dipped in beer batter and deep fried. $2.95

-Garlic Bread-
Made with pizza dough, olive oil, butter, fresh garlic, and shredded parmesan cheese. $2.45

Wood-Fired Pizzas

-Traditional Cheese-
Homemade tomato sauce, sliced tomatoes, mozzarella cheese, and fresh garlic and basil. $5.95

-Barbeque Chicken-
Barbequed chicken, sliced red onion, mozzarella & smoked gouda cheeses, and fresh cilantro. $7.50

-Two Sausage-
Mild and spicy Italian sausage, homemade tomato sauce, red and yellow peppers, sliced sweet white onions, and fresh oregano. $7.50

-Vegetarian-
Mozzarella and fontina cheeses, artichoke hearts, mushrooms, yellow bell peppers, sliced red onions, diced tomatoes, and fresh basil and garlic. $6.95

-Thai Chicken-
Spicy homemade Thai sauce, chicken, cilantro, green onions, shredded carrots, bean sprouts, and chopped peanuts. $7.50

-Three Cheese-
Homemade pesto sauce, roma tomatoes, mozzarella, fontina, and parmesan cheeses, and sage. $6.95

-Pepperoni-
Homemade tomato sauce, mozzarella cheese, pepperoni, and fresh oregano. $7.50

-Hawaiian-
Homemade tomato sauce, mozzarella cheese, Canadian bacon, and pineapple chunks. $7.50

-Sausage, Mushroom, & Black Olive-
Homemade tomato sauce, mozzarella cheese, sausage, mushrooms, black olives, and sweet white onions. $7.50

Fig. 18-4. Appetizer and wood-fired pizza menu from a storefront brewpub. Manhattan Beach Brewing Company, California

individual packages or bought in bulk from restaurant food suppliers. An attractive serving bowl, basket, or wine carafe adds to their appeal. A bowl of free snacks brought to the table by a server is a nice greeting for customers. Make sure the snack bowls are always kept full.

Packaged snacks are the simplest and cheapest foods to serve. They require no preparation or special handling. Store the boxes of snacks on shelves, not on the floor, where they could get wet.

Light bites

Light bites are finger foods requiring minimum preparation. A refrigerator or freezer will be necessary for storage, and a warming dish for presentation. You can pro-mote a "Healthy Hour" with low and non-alcoholic drinks and light foods, such as raw vegetables served with a tasty dressing, precooked shrimp in a cocktail sauce, or a cheese with fresh fruit and crackers. Hard-boiled eggs keep well and are old favorites. (See FIG. 18-5.)

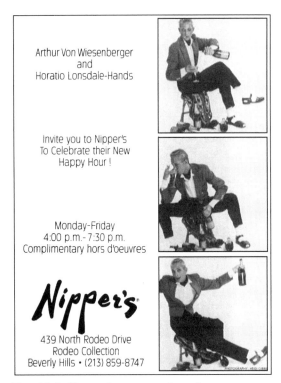

Fig. 18-5. *Happy hour magazine ad.* Nipper's, Beverly Hills, California

Nothing is as enticing as the aroma of freshly popped popcorn. Serve it hot by renting a popcorn popper. Little hot dogs, sausages, chicken wings, meatballs, mini pizzas, egg rolls, quiches, and precooked burritos can all be heated in a microwave oven or by using forced hot air ovens. The advantage of using a microwave or forced hot air oven is that no vents, hoods, special wiring, fire insurance, grease or oil are required. Hors d'oeuvres can be kept hot on a buffet table in chafing dishes. Tacos, enchiladas, and quesadillas can be prepared with a minimum of equipment. Simple sauces complement these dishes. Use paper plates for easy cleanup.

Because these items require some preparation, a bar back or another employee should be responsible for overseeing the hors d'oeuvre service. The bartender should concentrate on selling drinks and not be required to prepare food, unless the size and volume of your operation is small enough to provide the bartender with the time required. It is important to maintain a clean and appetizing serving area. This can be part of the bar, a table, a buffet, or a movable cart. Sneeze guards are required by most health departments.

Catered food

One way to serve food if you do not have the facilities is to have the food catered. If this approach works out, then you might consider spending the money to buy your own food preparation equipment. Work with local restaurants and caterers to develop special Happy Hour dishes. Talk to local pizza restaurants, delicatessens, and bakeries. You can pay for the food and then offer it free, or charge a small amount. If you would rather not worry about food service, allow your caterer to take responsibility and keep all profits.

The raw seafood bar

Fresh fish served raw or cooked is an excellent attraction, and when done correctly, an excellent profit center. A fresh fish bar involves substantial investment and commitment not only in space and equipment, but also day-to-day as the shelf life of raw goods is limited to one to seven days. Oysters, shrimp, crab, clams, and smoked fish can be sold by the piece or the plate. Work with a quality supplier and visit the aquaculture regions where your shellfish are grown.

Generally, seafood raised in farms are cleaner and do not contain the contaminants that fish caught in the open sea might have. Certain states require strict labeling of the source of shellstock to ensure it comes from safe waters. Do your research. Contact your local seafood supplier for shellstock and aquaculture suppliers and organizations. Speak with other area operators about their experiences with these suppliers.

A raw bar requires careful planning for refrigerators, water, and trash cans. When set up as an "exhibition kitchen," the shucking operation adds color and excitement. (See FIGS. 18-6 and 18-7.) A steamer, broiler, and salamander can turn cold items into hot ones. Garlic toast and clam chowders are popular menu items. Your soups can be displayed in kettles. Fish looks attractive in bowls sunk in ice.

A fish bar must have a preparation area, someone to prep the items, and someone to shuck and cook the fish at the bar. Keep raw food preparation and handling away from cooked foods. Certain raw seafoods contain bacteria that can be killed with heat. The preparation of sauces and some of the dishes can be accomplished at the raw bar or in a separate kitchen.

Keep in mind that you'll need someone to accept the delivery of the fish, usually early in the morning when the bar might be closed. You'll also need additional refrigerator and freezer storage space. This can be a freestanding refrigerator/freezer or a walk-in unit. Remember to keep food in a separate refrigerator from draft kegs. Beer in kegs can pick up odors from their surroundings.

The most popular items served in a raw bar are oysters, clams, and shrimp. Depending on your area, crab, lobster, crawfish, mussels, or other locally grown shellfish would add to the regional flavor of your bar. Oysters are raised and farmed along the Eastern and Western coasts, primarily the Pacific Northwest and Maine. There are nearly 50 different

Fig. 18-6. Close-up of The Sail Loft's oyster bar and grill. The Sail Loft, Laguna Beach, California

Fig. 18-7. *The beer and wine bar with seafood grill is part of the bar space.* The Original Enterprise Fish Co., Santa Barbara, California

varieties, typically sold in the shell by the pound or shucked by the number per gallon. You will serve them shucked. The most common are:

- Olympia
- Pacific
- Atlantic bluepoint
- Belon or European flat

Clams are grown on both coasts, although the majority of those eaten come from the Eastern seaboard. Some are eaten raw; however, most are cooked for soups or breaded and fried for appetizers and sandwiches. The most common are:

- Little neck
- Quahog

- Razor
- King
- Cherrystone

Shrimp come from all over the world in a wide variety of sizes and are sold by the pound. An 8/10 count means 8 to 10 per pound. Almost all shrimp are sold frozen. Some come in the shells; others, peeled and deveined, butterflied, or breaded. Serve with cocktail and garlic butter sauces for dipping, on sandwiches, or as a main course.

To test the waters for the popularity of a raw bar, experiment with a seasonal raw bar for special occasions. For a Mardi Gras celebration, import fresh oysters and crawfish from New Orleans. Sell them cheap and watch the crowds enjoy the shuckers working. Have a local brewery brew a special beer to complement your raw bar. The Middleton Tavern in Annapolis had the Wild Goose Brewery come up with Samuel Middleton Pale Ale to drink with the local sea and shellfish catches from Chesapeake Bay. It is now their top-selling beer.

A raw bar can be an excellent addition to your bar. Customers like the choices. The foods can be small portions for appetizers or complete meals. The raw bar is a delightful and colorful way to serve food.

The bar and grill

Should you decide to move out of the finger food category by offering sandwiches, soups, stews, salads, and grilled items, such as hamburgers and omelettes, you become a bar and grill. Deep-fried foods can round out your menu. The emphasis is still on light meals. When full-service dining is your goal, then food, rather than liquor, plays the major role in your operation, and you become a restaurant first and a bar second.

A bar and grill can be quite simple, with a small grill and sandwich board as part of the backbar. In this case, the bartender might be able to handle food preparation and also pour drinks. As the menu becomes more elaborate, however, a separate kitchen and food staff are advisable.

Beer bars often serve hot dogs and chili. These are purchased in bulk. The hot dogs can be boiled, steamed, or cooked on a small rotisserie. The chili is kept warm in an electric cooking pot or in a soup kettle on a hot plate.

Cold sandwiches can be made quickly by using presliced meat, cheese, bread, and rolls. If you add a slicer, meat and cheese can be purchased in bulk, reducing your costs. Corned beef, roast beef, chicken, ham, and turkey with cheese are popular sandwiches.

The Chestnut Street Grill (San Francisco, California) named its sandwiches after the regular customers who created them (see FIG. 18-8). Include a small side serving of potato or pasta salad and a little fresh fruit as a garnish. As with drinks, the garnishing and presentation of a plate of food make it more attractive; as a result, you can charge more.

THE CHESTNUT STREET GRILL

THE BIG BOPPER (Chantilly lace and a pretty face)
Three grilled Italian pork sausages, melted Provolone
cheese, hot sauce and crushed cherry peppers on sourdough roll.. $4.25

THE RICH CITARRELLA (Everybody needs a nautilus machine)
Three grilled Italian pork sausages, melted Swiss
cheese, raw onions and tomato on sourdough roll............... 4.25

THE JOY CUNNINGHAM (Help, nurse!)
Roast beef with lettuce, tomato and soaked with blue
cheese dressing.. 3.15

THE GARY HARBISON (Please, no more calendars)
Ham, turkey, shrimp salad, avocado, lettuce and tomato........ 4.15

THE WILHELM (Much easier than Pelham Clinton
        Wilmerding, Jr.)
Knockwurst, melted American cheese, Russian dressing,
tomatoes and raw onions on French roll....................... 3.85

THE HEADACHE EXCUSE (I promise I won't touch your head)
Shrimp salad, lettuce, tomato and mayo with roast pork........ 3.95

THE FRED ECKERT (Rochester to Fiji to Rochester?)
Roast beef, raw onions, cheddar cheese and horseradish, mayo.... 3.95

THE SAL LECESSE   (But Sal, the convention is next week)
Three grilled Italian sausages, melted cheddar cheese,
hot crushed cherry peppers, raw onions smothered in baked
beans on sourdough roll...................................... 4.25

THE BILL LACEY (This guy is a real mover)
Shrimp salad, avocado, ham, lettuce and tomato................ 3.85

THE DAN EVANS (Cable car project finished in spite of his assistance)
Chopped chicken liver, 49'er maiden sauce, corned
beef, tomato and mayo.. 3.65

THE MARCI VANWART (You wouldn't want to get involved
        in her cultures)
Two Bockwurst, melted Provolone cheese, hot crushed
cherry peppers with garlic mayo on French roll................ 3.85

THE CLAUDE COOPER (Writ writer of righteous rhetoric)
Two Bockwurst, fried onions and green peppers
smothered in baked beans on a French roll..................... 3.75

THE KATIE TOWE (Just a frustrated salmon fisherman)
Shrimp salad, ham, 49'er maiden sauce, Swiss cheese,
lettuce and tomatoes... 4.25

THE LAUREL WELLINGTON (Whad'dya mean last call?)
Chopped chicken liver, cole slaw, tomato & blue cheese
dressing.. 3.45

Fig. 18-8. Chestnut Street Grill menu where regular customers gain fame by having sandwiches named after them.

The simplest way to prepare hot sandwiches is to heat them in a microwave oven. If your menu includes several items that must be prepared ahead of time, consider buying an oven, a vapor oven, or a steam table. Once the items are cooked, they can be held at a constant temperature.

The vapor oven is a portable unit ideal for unskilled cooks. It can warm or cook vegetables, chicken, hot dogs, soup, stews, and roasts. When cooked, most foods have a high moisture content. The vapor oven prevents evaporation of moisture from foods by controlling the environment within the oven. This environment can be changed for different foods, including a drier vapor that keeps crisp fried foods from becoming soggy.

Steam tables are powered by gas or electricity. Cooked foods in covered stainless steel pans sit in larger pans filled with heated water. The steam keeps the food hot.

A great alternative to serving food when your floor space is limited and you do not want to tie up valuable space with a grill or kitchen is a cart that can be rolled into position for serving and put away when not in use. A portable deli cart can be rolled out to the bar during lunch and happy hour. It can include hot and cold items assembled by a deli chef. Roast beef carved from a tray on the cart is popular (see FIG. 18-9). The cart can also be set up as a pizza cart. Late at night, the cart can display cakes and desserts or even be used as a portable service bar for shots, beer, or margaritas.

Your kitchen can include several cooking appliances: a griddle, grill, burners, broiler, charbroiler, or oven. Commercial units can be purchased individually as tabletop or range models. A four-burner range with a griddle and oven should satisfy the needs of a small kitchen. Soup can be simmering on the back burners, while burgers and omelettes are cooking on the griddle. Sizzling in separate pans on the front burners are butterflied

Fig. 18-9. Portable deli cart. Shaker Mountain Inn, Glendale, California

shrimp in garlic sauce and a peppered steak. In the oven, you can be baking lasagna, chicken, and quiches, while browning stuffed potato skins in the broiler.

Next to the range, you might have a deep fryer. Numerous frozen and fresh foods can be dipped in batter and deep fried: chicken, shrimp, fish, zucchini sticks, potatoes, onion rings, cheese balls, egg rolls, and even ice cream.

Whenever kitchens have ovens, ranges, broilers, and fryers—whether tabletop or full-size units—the heat, smoke, and grease must be vented properly. A stainless steel hood with adequate exhaust fans is required to meet fire department codes. Consult your local fire department and kitchen equipment supplier for specifications. In addition, a fire suppression system is required. Sensors located above cooking equipment and within exhaust ducts automatically detect fires 24 hours a day. When they are activated manually or automatically, a dry or wet chemical is released, putting out the fire.

In a bar and grill, you will need to serve your entrees on something other than paper plates. Your local restaurant supplier can offer numerous ceramic and china dishware patterns to fit any budget. Match your utensils to your pattern. Avoid cheap looking flatware if you are using nice china plates. Linen napkins can be laundered by companies that specialize in restaurant napkin and tablecloth cleaning. In addition to dishes and flatware, you'll need a separate dishwashing facility away from the bar. Your restaurant supplier can help you choose the right machine.

Pricing your menu is similar to pricing drinks when you figure your costs by the ingredient method. Food costs are much higher than liquor costs, however, usually 33 to 40 percent of the retail price. When figuring prices, account for shrinkage and spoilage. Meat diminishes in weight when stored and cooked. Ten pounds of beef, cooked and trimmed, might yield only 8 pounds of usable meat. Food costs are kept consistent by establishing and maintaining exact portions for each item served. A scale should be used to weigh portions. A kitchen manager or chef should be responsible for ordering all food items and updating menu prices.

If you are using tickets for drink orders, the same tickets can be used for food. Standard abbreviations should be used to speed up servers' recording of the orders. A separate cash register or key on the register should be used, keeping food sales separate from drink sales.

One popular way to serve food is the Sunday Brunch. A limited menu or buffet is offered that includes all of the house champagne a customer can drink. Ramos Fizzes and Champagne Mimosas, made with fresh-squeezed orange juice, can become traditional Sunday drink specials.

Windows, a neighborhood bar in San Francisco, California, has a unique Sunday Brunch for its regular customers. Each week, a different customer plans, buys, and cooks the food for Sunday Brunch. Nobody is charged. The kitchen, which is only used on Sundays, is all that remains of the former restaurant that is now a bar.

Serving food is a great way to increase profits. Carefully evaluate what type of food service would be most profitable for the size of your operation. It will increase the size of your staff and add to its responsibilities, change the physical requirements of your space, and lengthen your business hours. The end result of serving any food is a healthy boost in liquor sales, from which your greatest profits are derived.

Sources

Following is a list of manufacturers, suppliers, and consultants. In most cases, the addresses provided are the main office. The majority of equipment is available through restaurant and bar suppliers and distributors nationwide. These listings are provided as a free service, so mention that you saw it in *Start and Run a Money-Making Bar!*

Alcohol awareness training programs

Anheuser-Busch, Inc.
St. Louis, MO 63118
(314) 577-4065
Contact local breweries.

Training for Intervention Procedures by Servers (TIPS) of Alcohol, and an ID checking guide.

The Century Council
1999 Avenue of the Stars, Suite 2050
Los Angeles, CA 90067
(213) 557-9898

Posters and pamphlets on responsible selling guidelines.

National Restaurant Association
The Educational Foundation
250 South Wacker Drive, Suite 1400
Chicago, IL 60606-5834
(800) 765-2122

Alcohol awareness training manuals.

Teller machines

ATM International
6700 East Russell Road, Suite 8
Las Vegas, NV 89122
(702) 434-1121

1st National ATM
4420 Rainier Avenue, Suite 201
San Diego, CA 92120
(800) 747-4123

Beverage accessories

Bar-Master Sales International
940 Venice Boulevard
Los Angeles, CA 90015
(800) 351-4183

Soda, wine, and liquor guns and systems.

Bunn Omatic
16431 Carmenita Road
Cerritos, CA 90701

Coffee brewers and machines.

DABCO
5024 Worth
Dallas, TX 75214

Liquor portion control training device.

Easybar
123 Foothill Road
Lake Oswego, OR 97034
(303) 635-7713

Liquor dispensing equipment and guns.

Hamilton Beach
95 Scovill Street
Waterbury, CT 06706

Blenders and glass washers.

Illycaffee USA
7360 East Acoma Drive
Scottsdale, AZ 85260

Espresso machines.

Lemons Communications
3501 North MacArthur #417
Irving, TX 75062

Frozen drink machines.

Magnuson Industries
3005 Kishwaukee Street
Rockford, IL 61109
(800) 435-2816

Restaurant and bar supplies. Liquor portion control pourers—premeasured, free-pourers, pourers with fly traps.

National Beer Taps, Inc.
11498 Luna Road, Suite 102
Dallas, TX 75234
(214) 556-2597

Computerized draft beer systems.

The Perlick Co., Inc.
P.O. Box 23098
Milwaukee, WI 53223

Bar stations, beverage dispensing, beer taps, and refrigeration systems.

Tru-Measur Inc.
139 Old Province Road
Barrington, NH 03825
(603) 664-2339

Liquor dispensing systems.

Waring
283 Main Street
New Hartford, CT 06057

Blenders.

Coasters

American Coaster Company
527 Wheatfield Street
North Tonawanda, NY 14120
(716) 693-6540

Coin-operated machines

Atari Games Corporation
675 Sycamore Drive
Milpitas, CA 95036-1110
(408) 434-3700

Happ Controls
106 Garlish Drive
Elk Grove Village, IL 60007
(708) 593-6130

Manufacturer of electronic controls for coin-op games.

ParTgolf
Optronics Limited
2820 West Charleston, Bldg. D
Suite 33
Las Vegas, NV 89102
(800) 350-7277

Interactive live-action video golf game.

Protocol, Inc.
1370 Mendota Heights Road
Mendota Heights, MN 55120
(800) 227-5336

Dispensing machines for personal care products: aspirin, tampons, condoms, perfumes, and colognes.

Ram Star
21210 Highway 60
Platteville, CO 80651
(800) 228-0958

Amusement games.

Tornado Table Soccer, Inc.
4949 Rendon Road
Ft. Worth, TX 76140-0626
(817) 483-6646

Accessories

Globe Slicing Machines Co., Inc.
Box 1217
Stamford, CT 06904

Perky's Foodservice Concepts, Inc.
6800 North Florida Avenue
Tampa, FL 33604
(813) 237-6551

Fresh-baked pizza carts—portable and fixed.

Proprocess Corporation
Doughpro
7328 Madison Street
Paramount, CA 90723
(800) 624-6717

Small, personal pizza-baking machine.

Trak-Air Food Systems
7108 S. Alton Way, Suite J
Englewood, CO 80112
(800) 688-TRAK

Forced hot-air cooking requiring no venting.

Wolf-Range Co.
19600 South Alameda Street
Compton, CA 90224

Decorating

Decorating Your Walls!
4839 East Greenway, Suite 360
Scottsdale, AZ 85254
(800) 858-4310

A one-stop theme decorating source—sports, fifties, sixties, Hollywood, rock 'n roll, country, western, etc.

Nightclub and bar design, training, and marketing consultant

Bruce Fier
FIER BAR CONSULTANTS
7450 Beckford Avenue
Reseda, CA 91335
(818) 344-5527
Fax (818) 344-5556

Fire protection

Ansul Fire Protection
1 Stanton Street
Marinette, WI 54143

Automatic Sprinkler Corporation of America
P.O. Box 180
Cleveland, OH 44147

Food preparation

Nemco Inc.
301 Meuse Argonne
Hicksville, OH 43526

Slicers and cubers.

Glassware

Lancaster Colony
P.O. Box 630
Columbus, OH 43216

Libbey Glass
One Seagate
Toledo, OH 43666

MTC Inc.
4908 West 35th Street
Minneapolis, MN 55416
(800) 328-4009

Plastic cups, mugs, and sports bottles.

Nightwing Enterprises
P.O. Box 3280
Binghamton, NY 13902-3280
(607) 723-5886

Hand-blown glass yards, half yards, and foot of ale with stands.

Tooters Promotions
25 S. Atlantic Avenue
Cocoa Beach, FL 32931
(800) 552-0564

Test tube shooters and shot glasses.

Glass-washing equipment

Moyer Diebel
P.O. Box 4183
Winston-Salem, NC 27115
(919) 661-1992

Frozen drink dispensing machines and glass-washing equipment.

Stero
3200 Lakevill Highway
Petaluma, CA 94952
(800) 762-7600

Webber Glass Washer Manufacturing Co.
440 Colton Street
Winston-Salem, NC 27101

Inventory controls

Accardis Systems, Inc.
20061 Doolittle Street
Gaithersburg, MD 20879
(800) 852-1992

Hand-held computer with bar code scanner for inventory tracking, which attaches to a scale for weighing liquor bottles. (Includes software.)

Lighting/sound/video systems

Lightworks
144 Spring Street
Portland, ME 04101

DKKaraoke
635 Hawaii Avenue
Torrance, CA 90503
(800) USA-SONG

Karaoke sing-along systems.

Pioneer Laser Entertainment, Inc.
P.O. Box 93131
2265 East 220th Street
Long Beach, CA 90810
(310) 952-2113

Laser disc, video and audio equipment, compact disc jukeboxes, and karaoke video sing-along systems.

Runco Video Corporation
1163 Chess Drive, Suite J
Foster City, CA 94404

Sound Chamber
5400 North Cahuenga Blvd.
North Hollywood, CA 91601
(818) 985-1376

Sound Systems Unlimited
6315 Laurel Canyon Boulevard
North Hollywood, CA 91606
(818) 506-8216

Wavelength, Inc.
316 Washington Street
El Segundo, CA 90245

Miscellaneous equipment

Rockeffects International
P.O. Box 13597
Las Vegas, NV 89112
(702) 456-2442

Streamer and confetti projectile systems.

Ship 'n Out
8 Charles Street
Pawling, NY 12564

Brass and chrome railings, sneeze guards for food bars, foot rails, and guard rails.

SICO, Inc.
7525 Cahill Road
P.O. Box 1169
Minneapolis, MN 55440

Portable dance floors.

Upkeeper
P.O. Box 23480
Charlotte, NC 28212
(704) 545-7040

Portable, powerful vacuum cleaners that will pick up cans, cups, swizzle sticks, napkins, and straws with no jamming.

Plastic cards

Yoli Plastic Card Company
18 Shearwater Way
Centereach, NY 11720
(516) 585-5163

Membership, VIP, guest passes, and charge cards.

Point-of-sale systems and cash registers

NCR Corporation
Dayton, OH 45479

Sable Technologies Inc.
101 Lincoln Centre Drive
Foster City, CA 94404
(415) 358-9041

Sharp Electronics Corporation
Sharp Plaza
Mahwah, NJ 07430-2135
(201) 529-8200

Promotional items

Arlen Advertising
1516 South Bundy Drive
Los Angeles, CA 90025-2663
(310) 820-3433

Prize and giveaway items imprinted with your logo: caps, shirts, mugs, wine pulls, sunglasses, and golf and tennis balls.

Harco Enterprises Limited
675 The Parkway
Peterborough, Ontario, Canada K9J 7K2
(705) 743-5361

Standard and custom cocktail stirrers and picks.

Recycling programs

California Restaurant Association
3435 Wilshire Blvd., Suite 2606
Los Angeles, CA 90010
(213) 384-1200

Pamphlet on beginning a recycling program.

Refrigeration

Beverage-Air
P.O. Box 5932
Spartanburg, SC 29304

Creative Environments
2000 Valley Forge Plaza
King of Prussia, PA 19406

Wine storage units.

Crystal Tips Ice Products
655 Glenwood Avenue West
Smyrna, DE 19977
(302) 653-3015

Ice machines.

Kold-Draft
1525 East Lake Road
Erie, PA 16514

The Perlick Co., Inc.
P.O. Box 23098
Milwaukee, WI 53223

Wine Chillers of California
1104 East 17th Street, Suite F
Santa Ana, CA 92701
(800) 331-4274

Wine wells: fast chilling of wines and wine dispensing and storage systems.

Satellite broadcast services

NTN Communications, Inc.
2121 Palomar Airport Road, Suite 305
Carlsbad, CA 92009
(619) 438-7400

Interactive television, satellite broadcasts, and promotional games.

Silent Radio
21 Tamal Vista Blvd., Suite 211
Corte Madera, CA 94925
(415) 924-6408

Satellite-fed electronic moving message boards with games, news, weather, sports, and trivia.

Tavern Television (North American Bar Network)
8580 Cinderbed Road
Newington, VA 22122
(800) 487-7968

Pay per view sporting and concert events, news, promotional games.

Security

Drivers' License Guide Company
1492 Oddstad Drive
Redwood City, CA 94063
(800) 227-8827

ID checking guide for United States and Canada, government, and military issues.

Korden, Inc.
P.O. Box 2193
Costa Mesa, CA 92628

Meshel
957 15th Street
Santa Monica, CA 90403
(800) 729-3094

Laser pointers for security and door personnel.

Secur-Ticket
M-C Industries, Inc.
P.O. Box 5502
Topeka, KS 66605
(800) 255-1865

Wristbands for underage control.

Strayer Coin Bag Co., Inc.
New Brighton, PA 15066

Underbar and backbar
equipment and refrigerators

Gates Manufacturing Company
3189 Jamieson Avenue
St. Louis, MO 63139
(800) 237-9226

The Perlick Company
P.O. Box 23098
Milwaukee, WI 53223

Uniforms

Class Act Uniforms
1401 South Dixie Highway
Pompano Beach, FL 33060
(305) 946-1176

Index